A Modern History of Russian Childhood

The Bloomsbury History of Modern Russia Series

Series Editors: Jonathan D. Smele (Queen Mary, University of London, UK) and Michael Melancon (Auburn University, USA)

This ambitious and unique series offers readers the latest views on aspects of the modern history of what has been and remains one of the most powerful and important countries in the world. In a series of books aimed at students, leading academics and experts from across the world portray, in a thematic manner, a broad variety of aspects of the Russian experience, over extended periods of time, from the reign of Peter the Great in the early eighteenth century to the Putin era at the beginning of the twenty-first.

Published:

Peasants in Russia from Serfdom to Stalin: Accommodation, Survival, Resistance, Boris B. Gorshkov (2018)
Crime and Punishment in Russia: A Comparative History from Peter the Great to Vladimir Putin, Jonathan Daly (2018)
Marx and Russia: The Fate of a Doctrine, James D. White (2018)
A Modern History of Russian Childhood: From the Late Imperial Period to the Collapse of the Soviet Union, Elizabeth White (2020)

Forthcoming:

The History of the Russian Worker: Life and Change from Peter the Great to Vladimir Putin, Alice Pate (2020)
Dissidents, Émigrés and Revolutionaries in Russia: Anti-State Activism in International Perspective, 1848–2015, Charlotte Alston (2021)

A Modern History of Russian Childhood

From the Late Imperial Period to the Collapse of the Soviet Union

ELIZABETH WHITE

BLOOMSBURY ACADEMIC

LONDON • NEW YORK • OXFORD • NEW DELHI • SYDNEY

BLOOMSBURY ACADEMIC
Bloomsbury Publishing Plc
50 Bedford Square, London, WC1B 3DP, UK
1385 Broadway, New York, NY 10018, USA

BLOOMSBURY, BLOOMSBURY ACADEMIC and the Diana logo are trademarks of
Bloomsbury Publishing Plc

First published in Great Britain 2020

Cover design: Tjaša Krivec
Cover image: Three Young Musicians, Rear View, Moscow, 1965. (© Glasshouse
Images/Alamy Stock Photo)

A catalogue record for this book is available from the British Library.

A catalog record for this book is available from the Library of Congress.

ISBN: PB: 978-1-4742-4021-5
HB: 978-1-4742-4022-2
ePDF: 978-1-4742-4023-9
eBook: 978-1-4742-4024-6

Typeset by Deanta Global Publishing Services, Chennai, India
Printed and bound in Great Britain

To find out more about our authors and books visit www.bloomsbury.com and
sign up for our newsletters.

Contents

1

Introduction: The history of modern childhood

In the sixteenth century *Domostroi*, a late-medieval Russian text on household advice for Muscovite elites, children as a social group were not differentiated from servants and lower relatives. In common with the rest of Europe, parental authority had been absolute in medieval Russia; parents could even sell their children into slavery. Secular law did not recognize the murder of a child by its parents. While canon law did view infanticide as a crime, the Orthodox Church's main concern was with the regulation of female sexuality rather than the intrinsic value of a child or its integral being.[1] The 1649 Muscovite Law Code, the *Ulozhenie*, declared the infanticide of illegitimate children murder and punishable by death; yet the murder of a legitimate child by its parents incurred a year's imprisonment followed by a public confession:

> 3. If a father or mother kills a son or daughter: imprison them for a year. After having sat in prison for a year, they shall go to God's church, and in God's church they shall declare aloud that sin of theirs to all the people. Do not punish a father or mother with death for [killing] a son or daughter.[2]

Yet by the second half of the eighteenth century, children and childhood had begun to be seen as the preserve of the state. When Catherine the Great sought to transform the Russian Empire, childhood was key: 'Assisted by Lockean psychology, the field of education proper came to occupy the center of attention and hope.'[3] This book maps out the process of why that came to be, as well as examining childhood in the following centuries.

Childhood is intertwined with so many aspects of the organization of modern states and societies that its study embraces a wide range of topics. A history of childhood can include the everyday life of children, their material culture and their leisure activities (organized and unorganized), schooling and education, juvenile crime, children's rights and the legal system, philanthropy and the development of welfare states, the family and the home, and children's culture and literature. A history of childhood can be structured around cultural representations of children, beliefs about children, or emotions considered appropriate for children or towards children. It can also include children's participation in social movements and historical processes and events as well as the norms and expectations for childhood. Vouching for the importance of the history of childhood, the American historian Stephen Mintz writes, 'Childhood ... is the true "missing link": connecting the personal and the public, the psychological and the sociological, the domestic and the state.'[4] Childhood does not only affect children, a category that we now see as both biological and socially constructed. The political, economic, cultural and social institutions and structures of childhood (schools, welfare states, medicine, material cultures and spaces) have extensive influences as well and we are all drawn into their sphere at various points.

The fact that it is hard to know where the study of childhood ends is in part because the dominant model of a modern childhood in the West, with which we are most familiar, is closely connected to the rise and spread of the state and associated processes of modernization. Since the 1960s, beginning with the publication of Philippe Ariès's influential book *Centuries of Childhood*, academics have interpreted childhood as a historically and culturally constructed phenomenon, rather than a universally given common experience of a biological life stage.[5] Following on from his pioneering work, the history of childhood as written in the West has been derived from, and mapped onto, the history of modernization. Ariès claimed that childhood was an invention of early modern Europe and in fact most of his sources came from France. Before then, once children had achieved some biological autonomy and had developed sufficient physical and mental capabilities, usually at the age of around seven, they became immersed in the adult world. He argued that prior to the sixteenth century there had been no separate 'children's world'; children played, worked, slept and shared the same physical spaces as adults. They were also depicted in cultural representations as merely small adults. They were not considered to need special treatment or any specific separation from the world of adults. Paradoxically, despite their ubiquity, 'the child was a marginal figure in the adult world'.[6] Ariès argued that from the early modern period childhood was gradually 'discovered' by European societies as a result of wider changes in family life, religious beliefs and the growth of capitalism and print culture. European societies began to see childhood as a special phase of life, distinct from adulthood and therefore requiring its own spatial and temporal arrangements. The very slow shift to seeing children as amusing and enjoyable, rather than as strange beings, imperfect adults cursed by original sin, began to take hold in societies at this time as well.

Later research focused on how the eighteenth-century Enlightenment produced a radical change in ideas about childhood, if not necessarily in the lived experiences of most children. Philosophers and natural scientists such as John Locke and Jean-Jacques Rousseau pushed forward the ideas that education and upbringing were key to the development of human potentiality and that children should be treated differently to adults, and separated from them. Then the Europe-wide romantic movement of the early nineteenth century valorized childhood as not just different to adulthood but superior, and fundamental to the later adult self. Children were messengers from heaven, close to God, unique, blessed and a source of inspiration. The child was becoming a symbol. All these ideas were extremely influential on elite thought across Europe in the eighteenth and early nineteenth centuries, including in the Russian Empire.

Further layers were added onto views of childhood in the nineteenth century. The uneven processes of industrialization, nationalism, bureaucracy and record keeping, education, globalization and the development of market relations, the privatization of the family and the spread of the franchise all affected how childhood was framed, regularized, valorized and understood. One of the greatest changes for children was the idea, underpinned by compulsory state legislation at an accelerating speed across the nineteenth century, that all children should receive some kind of formal education outside of the family home for a set number of years. For most of human history, children had been essential to the household and general economy as labour forces. Very gradually, in the modern age children were pushed out of the economy through labour legislation and the spread of compulsory state primary education. This shift from labour to education is key to the modern Western model of childhood. Enforcement of primary education remained problematic until the twentieth century and the form and content of primary education a child received varied enormously according to ethnicity, gender, class and location. Compulsory universal primary education gave states potentially enormous power and resources to reach children and organize childhood.

As well as changing relations between the child and the state, Viviana Zelizer, among others, has shown that as children were pushed out of the labour market into schools and became economically 'worthless', they became emotionally 'priceless' to their families.[7] Children were now meant to be cherished and protected, and childhood was considered as a stage in life that should be free of care and pain. This process of valorization was partly caused by a dramatic reduction in infant mortality, due to advances in medicine and public health. Along with the shift from labour to education, the reduction in infant mortality was another key building block in the creation of a modern childhood.

By the late nineteenth century, children and childhood had gained a new social and political significance and both had become a focus of intense concern for states and societies. The Swedish social theorist and educational activist Ellen Key published *The Century of the Child (Barnets århundrade)* in 1900, in which she argued that children's education, well-being and rights should be the central work of the new twentieth century. Translated into English in 1909, her book became an international bestseller. At the same time, children also began to be constituted as objects of international politics.[8] At this point, childhood had moved from the margins to the very centre. Over several centuries and due to many different inputs, modern childhood had become what Paula Fass has described as 'privileged state'.[9] In the Soviet Union, the state indeed described children as the 'privileged class'.

This 'privileged' state of childhood became an ideal of citizenship and a benchmark to judge the backwardness (or not) of modern states. 'The Christianity and the civilization of a people may both be measured by their treatment of childhood,' wrote Benjamin Waugh, the social reformer and founder of the London Society for the Prevention of Cruelty to Children, in 1886.[10] By the twentieth century, childhood as a life stage had become an important signifier of modernity.

By the modern era, states had begun to partly define themselves through their treatment of children and the lives that children lived in them. Both state legislation and state penetration were needed to create this model of modern childhood. In addition to the shift from work to school, lower birth rate and reductions in infant mortality, historians have argued that there was a fourth factor that contributed to the production of a model of modern childhood: the nation state as it formed after the French Revolution.[11] States became interested in children as future military recruits, obedient citizens, taxpayers and cultural reproducers. As the sociologist Nikolas Rose has written:

> Childhood is the most intensively governed sector of personal existence. In different ways, at different times, and by many different routes varying from one section of society to another, the health, welfare and rearing of children have been linked in thought and practice to the destiny of the nation and the responsibilities of the state.[12]

As well as enforcing schooling, modern states developed and spread medical provision for children, although access to this too was greatly differentiated. The ability of the state to register its population correctly led to finer meanings of age gradation, which had an impact on childhood and children's lives. Once education had become synonymous with childhood, measurable intelligence became one of a child's most important attributes and age segregation became even more important. The state wanted to define the 'normal child' and new sciences of measurement of children's development were founded.

This book is an attempt to trace the history of childhood in Russia through a similar period as just outlined. It examines some of the developments in ideas about childhood, as well as children's experiences, from the late seventeenth century to the early twenty-first century in Russia. It looks at these developments within their Russian context, but also to see how, if at all, they differentiated from the developing model of childhood in Western states.

Childhood was 'discovered' in Russia in the late seventeenth century when Russian elites began to take an interest in childhood, at least of noble children.[13] Enlightenment ideas about childhood had a strong impact in Russia, and Catherine the Great inaugurated the state's interest in 'appropriating' childhood and harnessing it to fashion an imperial subject and strengthen the Russian Empire, although these ideas only affected a minority of children. While the first half of the nineteenth century saw little change, except for the slow growth of education, after the Great Reforms of the 1860s, ideas about what childhood should involve changed rapidly, broadly in line with developments elsewhere. These concepts included the exclusion of children from labour (or more specifically, industrial labour); the need for general primary education; a focus on children's health and welfare; and a belief that children should be separated from adults, protected, cherished and celebrated. However, the political, economic and social structure of Russia acted as a block to the realization of these ideas, which is why debates about childhood, particularly concerning children's education and their place in the family, gained greater prominence and fused with demands for radical reform and eventually with the revolutionary movement. By the end of the nineteenth century the Russian intelligentsia's desire to transform the authoritarian state structure by changing everyday life endowed childhood with 'radical implications'.[14]

Imperial Russia had the highest infant mortality rate in Europe in the early twentieth century. Its reduction was a major priority for the new Bolshevik regime, although it did not achieve this for several decades, when a dramatic drop in the birth rate accompanied it. These developments, added to the enforcement of compulsory primary education from the 1930s, put into place in the Soviet Union some of the fundamental building blocks of a modern idea of childhood, although as we shall see there were still significant differences from the standard Western model. In the Soviet state's view, childhood was political, revolutionary, placed in the public sphere, connected with labour and children were taken seriously as a social group. Children were so important to the state because they were the material for the creation of the Soviet 'new person' (novyi chelovek), a form of humanity never seen before in the world. The model of childhood in the early Soviet years was one that was influenced by the peasant model of childhood, however, as much as it was by Marxism. By the late Soviet period, concepts of childhood in Russia did not differ so much from the Western model, though there were specific features of children's daily lives that did. The current political leadership of the Russian Federation has taken us back to Catherine and her version of the Enlightenment; asserting the state's role through controlling childhood through strategies of 'vospitanie', or moral upbringing, in the service of the state.

Age categories are social constructions and what is considered the ages of childhood changes. The boundaries of childhood shifted across the twentieth century, becoming longer as the school-leaving age was raised from twelve to fourteen and then to sixteen. I have taken the approach that childhood begins approximately at age six or seven. Around seven ('the age of reason') was the age that many societies viewed children as developing some biological autonomy. This came then to coincide with the approximate ages of compulsory school attendance, which is fitting because as elsewhere in the modern world, in the Soviet period children became constructed by the state above all as 'pupils'. This book therefore does not examine pregnancy, maternity, birth, babyhood, preschool years or at the other end later adolescence to any great degree.[15] There is now a substantial body of research on marginalized children and children in Soviet institutions: juvenile delinquents, orphans and the bezprizornie (homeless).[16] Despite the Soviet state's claims about how seriously they took child welfare, institutions for children were notorious for being unhygienic, badly housed and undersupplied. The staff running them, or the local government officials responsible for supplying the institutions, were often corrupt as was proved by endless investigations throughout the decades. I have tried here to examine more deeply ideas of childhood and experiences of children who were embedded in Russian/Soviet families, which is where the vast majority of children experienced their childhoods, albeit partially and temporarily at times. I have tried to avoid being over-normative while drawing out broader patterns and experiences and continuities. 'Russian' is a flexible category of identity, as is 'Soviet'. I have looked mainly at ideas about childhood coming from ethnic Russian/culturally Russified spheres. In the Soviet period, the state created a standardized 'Soviet childhood', which it tried to roll out across the Union. The book adopts a chronological approach, moving from the eighteenth century to the collapse of the Soviet Union in 1991, with a postscript on some aspects of childhood in the modern Russian Federation today. I would like to thank Robert McNamara, Martin Simpson and Mark Rodgers for their advice, all faults and omissions being mine. I dedicate this book to my own child, Gianluca. I hope you had a happy childhood, while not feeling overwhelmed by the expectation to do so.

2

Education, the state and the Russian child in the eighteenth century

In keeping with the influential tradition started by the French historian Philippe Ariès, historians have claimed that childhood in Russia was also 'discovered' in the early modern period. Evidence for this has been sought in changing approaches to education. There was no formal system of primary education in Russia before the early eighteenth century, offered either privately or by the church. Noble boys and girls did receive some education, but this was informal, usually at home or with a single 'master' and its aim, function and content was in the main religious. Max Okenfuss has written that in Russia before the mid-seventeenth century, 'neither child nor education existed independently'.[1] By the late seventeenth century though, reading primers were being produced that revealed an awareness that children had different perceptions than adults and needed special and distinct methods to help them learn to read. European works on children's education and upbringing circulated in seventeenth-century Muscovy, including those by Jan Amos Comenius and Erasmus's *De civilitate morum puerilium*, which was translated into Russian in 1675.[2]

In 1679 the poet Simeon Polotskii (1629–80), who was tutor to the Tsarevich Alexei, produced what has been described as Russia's 'first reader for a youthful audience which cannot yet read'.[3] Around 1680, the monk Prokhor Kolomnyatin began composing a *School Decorum* (*Shkol'nyi Azbukhovniki*), a miscellany of teaching materials which, once printed, began with the words:

> Today children are educated about learning in school and want to learn about letters and how to write well. Those who come to school with full

comprehension are peacefully joined with all their classmates. It is good to teach everyone.[4]

The purpose of the *School Decorum* was practical; to teach specifically *children* to read and write. At this transitional time, though, the main aim of education remained religious. Prokhor recommended that pupils answer the question as to why they study in the following way: 'I study the tiniest part of scripture for the benefit of my soul, for the consolation of my body, for the wonder and salvation of me and all my family.'[5]

In 1694 the poet and scribe Karion Istomin, who has been described as Russia's first children's writer, produced a Primer that joined words with explanatory pictures.[6] Istomin's Primer, which was used up until the nineteenth century, was distinguished by the use of playfulness and humour to appeal to children, showing a change in understanding of their nature. In the second half of the 1690s, Istomin also produced a *Domostroi* for children, which consisted of fourteen stanzas on desired daily behaviours for children inside and outside the home, a 'codification of good manners as an essential part of the new dominating courtly society'.[7] Late-seventeenth-century texts for children started moving away from an emphasis purely on devout learning to teaching secular rules of behaviour for children and giving advice on how to communicate with people of differing social ranks; 'for the first time a teacher's work was devoted not only to saving a pupil's soul, but also to his socialisation'.[8] The content of primers supported the idea of useful (secular) learning, a process Okenfuss categorizes as 'westernization'.[9] This heralded a new approach to the child and its needs and mental capacities.

In 1685 two Greek brothers, the monks Ionnicius and Sofronius Likhudes, established the Slavo-Greco-Latin Academy (*Slavyano-Greko-Latinskaya Akademiya*), the first formal school in Russia. Based in Kitai Gorod, near the Kremlin, it taught the sons of boyars and state officials in Latin using Jesuit textbooks.[10] It was still a transitional educational institution, without strict age segregation. The ages of the pupils ranged from eight to the early twenties, and progression through the grades was predicated on ability, rather than age.

Peter the Great (1682/89–1725) encouraged the development of new attitudes to children and childhood in Russian society. Instrumentalist and populationist concerns typical of the era motivated Peter, who viewed children as future human capital for the state and important to his plans for the transformation of the Russian state in its competition with Europe. In 1712, concerned by the potential waste of human material entailed by the widespread practice of infanticide, Peter ordered that hospitals be established in which illegitimate children – 'children of shame' – could be abandoned anonymously to be raised by the state. Once old enough, the male children were to be enlisted in the navy or trained as artisans, while girls were to become domestic servants. In 1716, Peter made the punishment for the killing of a legitimate child equal to that of the murder of an illegitimate one. He also asserted the right of illegitimate children to get support from their fathers.[11] Abandoned children were viewed by state and society with pity, as a waste of human potential, but were also considered a threat to order. This dual view continued into the early Soviet period, when there were unprecedented numbers of homeless and destitute children due to the years of war and famine and the impact of state policies.

Wishing to catch up technologically with Europe and as part of his 'modernizing' revolution in Russian life, Peter also introduced the first state initiatives in education for children and young people in order to create military and civilian experts to strengthen the Russian state. In 1700, he told Patriarch Adrian of Moscow that Russia needed schools 'from which people could go forth into church service, civilian service, and ready to wage war, to practice engineering and art'.[12] He envisaged a utilitarian, technologically focused and state-controlled education system for Russia. In 1701, Peter founded the Moscow School of Mathematics and Navigational Sciences. This taught fortification, architecture, arithmetic, geometry, drawing and trigonometry and had two primary classes. It was open to all the 'free' classes, but not to serfs. He also founded the Moscow Artillery School in 1701 'to teach the children of artillerymen and other extraneous ranks to read, write, engineering sciences'.[13] The ages of pupils at the schools were mixed, ranging from eight to twenty-three, and progression was still by ability, not age. Other engineering and artillery schools were founded in Moscow and St Petersburg during Peter's reign. Peter also turned the Slavo-Greco-Latin Academy (*Slavyano-Greko-Latinskaya Akademiya*) into a state school.

In 1714, Peter decreed that the male children of noblemen, officials, clerks and scribes who wished to enter government service had to have received some formal education.[14] He launched a campaign to identify and register all young male nobles who were eligible for state service and created the Heraldry to maintain these records. Noble boys were to have learnt 'numbers and geometry' by the age of fifteen and were forbidden to marry if they had not done so.[15] At the same time, Peter ordered the establishment of cipher or mathematical schools in provincial towns, which would teach literacy and mathematics to boys between the ages of ten and fourteen. There were some forty-two in existence at their peak, although the system was abandoned in 1744.[16] Peter's reign also saw the beginning of a network of army garrison schools, which by the 1760s had about 9,000 soldiers' children registered as attending.[17] The Orthodox Church also began founding diocesan schools, which started a 'system of general education, directed, operated, and maintained by the ecclesiastical establishment, as was the case throughout Europe'.[18]

Educational practices in schools at this time were based on Jesuit and German *Ritter Schule* models, with a rigid curriculum and harsh discipline. Learning was through memorization and pupils were whipped and lashed; this would change in the later eighteenth century under the influence of Enlightenment thinking. Peter's favourite theologian and church reformer Feofan Prokopovich's 1720 Primer was required reading in all church schools and was also recommended (apparently successfully) to all 'pious parents, teachers, guardians and masters, and all others who exercise parental authority over children'.[19] The Primer combined basic religious instruction with exhortations on obedience to a clear hierarchy of authorities, its chief purpose being to 'instil a respect for all forms of authority, especially that of the Tsar (or state)'.[20]

Peter's heirs in the mid-eighteenth century continued embedding in Russian society the idea of formal education for elite children, although mainly in the service of the state. In 1731 Peter's niece, the Empress Anna Ivanovna (1730–40), founded the first Noble Cadet Corps (*Kadetskii Korpus*). This was a school for noble boys or the sons of commissioned officers, from which they graduated as officers in the Imperial Army. This was a project of the 'Germans', Field-Marshal Burkhard Christoph von Münnich and Count Heinrich Johann Friedrich Ostermann, both of whom were the *de facto* heads of Anna's government. It was modelled on Berlin's Royal Prussian Cadet Corps, which had opened in 1717. Boys entered the Cadet Corps usually around the age of eight. The curriculum included arithmetic, geometry, drawing, fortification, artillery, fencing and riding as well as foreign languages, history, geography, law, dancing, music and social skills. The vision of knowledge, culture and behaviour underpinning the ethos of the Corps was based on West European models. Von Münnich and Ostermann had Pietist connections and were also influenced by François Fénelon's pedagogical theories on the inner transformation of the individual through education.[21] They were concerned not only with the correct curriculum as a body of knowledge, but also with techniques to achieve the interiorization of approved behaviour and thinking; monitoring, observation, assessment and spatial and temporal regulation.[22] The Charter of the Corps envisaged that pupils would be secluded from the outside world and that there would be continual observation over the pupils, with practices 'designed to create a certain way of life, which emphasised discipline and order, cleanliness, and self-control over one's mind and body'.[23] Reporting systems, books of observation, and formal examinations were used to attempt to shape the students' subjectivity and ensure that they lead 'well-ordered lives'.[24]

In 1736–7, Anna's 'German' ministers created a regulatory framework for the education of noble boys, as Peter had done earlier. Noble boys were to register with the Master of Heraldry or their Provincial Governor at the age of seven and present themselves for academic examinations at ages twelve, sixteen and twenty. They were expected to make efforts in their studies, for which they would be rewarded by the state with service positions. According to Igor Fedyukin, the sons of poorer nobles tended to ignore these educational requirements and rules; the state usually pardoned them when they reached service age anyway and they entered the army as privates.[25] Noblemen with over 100 male serfs or those whose sons could demonstrate learning at the age of twelve were allowed to educate their children at home; others were meant to enrol in state schools.

In 1755 a classical *gymnazia* was opened attached to Moscow University, while in 1758 another one was established by the St. Petersburg Academy of Sciences. These schools educated the children of the elites as well as children from the families of soldiers, priests, artisans and some freed peasants who had noble patrons.[26] By the middle of the eighteenth century, education for boys was becoming a social norm for most sections of the Russian nobility.[27] The very highest level of the Russian nobility still had some resistance to the idea of formal state education for their children and often preferred to have their children educated at home by foreign tutors. Before 1789, Germans predominated among private tutors and teachers until French exiles displaced them. The Russian state tried to exercise some control over the choice of tutor; in 1758, it decreed that the Academy of Sciences and Moscow University should examine potential tutors.[28]

New approaches to childhood arising in the early modern period sharply accelerated as the Enlightenment spread its influence among Russian elites in the second half of the eighteenth century. The English philosopher John Locke (1632–1704) had challenged the predominant Christian theory that humans are born in a state of sin and that even babies and small children need harsh discipline to keep them from their urge to do evil. In works such as *An Essay Concerning Human Understanding* (1689) and *Some Thoughts Concerning Education* (1693), he argued that infants were born as 'blank slates' (*tabula rasa*). As human beings are born with the capacity to reason, their minds and characters develop through experience and instruction. This influential new way of understanding children placed a much greater emphasis on the potentials (and pitfalls) of formal education. It encouraged special ways of treating children and the beginning of their increased scrutiny and control. Locke also put forward the idea that children's difference to adults – their 'childishness' – was something to value and enjoy, rather than a sign of their imperfection. Locke's ideas were enormously influential in the eighteenth century and he is a key figure in changing views of childhood. *Some Thoughts Concerning Education* was translated into Russian in 1759 and influenced the educational policies of Catherine the Great, most obviously in her preference for boarding schools.

After Locke, the other most significant figure in popularizing new attitudes to childhood was the Genevan philosopher Jean-Jacques Rousseau (1712–78). Rousseau went much further than Locke had done in re-evaluations of childhood. He believed that childhood was a special period of life, which should be valued for itself, rather than viewed as a brief, precarious and strange prelude to adulthood. Children's individuality and their nature should be praised. In European thought, the child was becoming a person. Rousseau claimed that children were born in a state of natural innocence and their education and upbringing should reflect this. They should grow up in as 'natural' a state as possible, developing as individuals at their own pace through gradual staged and controlled interactions with the wider world and in an environment protected from adult corruption. His most influential work on childhood was *Émile, or On Education*, published in 1762, a novel about a young boy being educated according to Rousseau's principles.[29]

In addition to Locke and Rousseau, French and German educational writers and thinkers were widely read by Russian elites in the eighteenth century; François Fénelon (1651–1715), Joachim Heinrich Campe (1746–1818) and the French writer the Marquise de Lambert (1647–1818).[30] Books on 'morals and pedagogy', such as Fénelon's *De l'éducation des filles* and de Lambert's *Avis d'une mère à sa fille et à son fils*, were among the most popular genres sold in the bookshop of the Academy of Sciences.[31]

The reign of Catherine the Great (1762–96) at the height of the Enlightenment in the later eighteenth century saw the true beginning of a new concept of childhood in Russia, matching developments in other parts of Europe. Catherine was born in Pomerania in 1729, as Sophie von Anhalt-Zerbst-Dornburg, a minor German princess. In 1745, she was married to Peter, the heir to the Russian throne, who became Peter III on his accession in 1762. He was unpopular among the court nobility, and Catherine participated in his overthrow shortly after he became Tsar. She became Empress of Russia and ruled until her death in 1796. Before he was overthrown, Peter had enacted the Manifesto on the Freedom of the Nobility (*Manifest o vol'nosti dvorianstva*) which expanded the privileges of the nobility and freed them from obligatory state service. Young noble boys were still meant, however, to be examined academically at the age of twelve and arrangements were made for their further education:

However, so that nobody should dare to bring up their children without teaching them the subjects fitting for the noble *dvorianstvo* under pain of Our wrath, for this We order all those *dvoriane* who have not more than a thousand peasants to report their children directly to Our Noble Military Academy, where they will be educated with the most enthusiastic care and each will leave with a reward of ranks appropriate to his educational achievement and later enter and continue service according to the above prescription.[32]

The Manifesto created a privileged private sphere for the noble family, while seeking to increase control of the education of young noble boys. This paradox would continue throughout imperial Russian history.

Catherine viewed herself as an actor in the European Enlightenment and, like Peter the Great, plunged Russia into an era of reform and modernization. Her aim was to mobilize Russian elites to transform and empower the Russian Empire. Childhood would be central to her vision. Catherine and her chief collaborator and adviser on education Ivan Betskoi (1704–95) shared the Enlightenment belief in the power of formal education to develop and mould the human mind.[33] Betskoi was the illegitimate son of Prince Ivan Trubetskoi. He was raised and educated in Northern Europe and Paris. He had served in the Russian army and participated in diplomatic missions abroad. Under Catherine, he was also president of the Imperial Academy of Arts. For Catherine and other Russian enlighteners, education was to be the key to *'la fabrication de l'homme ideal et du citoyen parfait'*.[34] This educational transformation was for elites. Catherine's many plans and reports concerning national education never considered state education for peasant children, the vast majority of Russia's children.

In 1764, Betskoi drew up a *General Statute for the Education of the Youth of Both Sexes* (*General'noe uchrezhdenie o vospitanii oboego pola iunoshestva*). This work, affirmed by Catherine in March 1764, called for the creation of a new kind of citizen, useful to the state, through the education of Russian noble children in special boarding schools. Russian families were meant to send their children to these institutions at the age of around five or six and they would be kept there until they reached maturity. This would isolate them from the potentially dangerous influence of their families and servants, as well as from the perceived backwardness of wider Russian society. Betskoi and Catherine were influenced by Locke's argument that the child's mind was a blank slate at birth and therefore environment and experience are key to the development of the human mind and character. Betskoi was also influenced by Rousseau's belief in children's natural goodness and the need to protect them from the corruption of worldly society. His reform of the Cadet Corps was centred on the notion of 'innate emulation' (*vrozhdennoe svoistvo podrazhaniia*). Tutors at the Corps had to be of the highest moral standard; the younger pupils were not allowed to mix with servants and the older pupils were only allowed to mix with specially selected servants.[35]

Catherine was less impressed with Rousseau's proposals for a natural child-centred education and also with his disdain for the education of girls.[36] In 1763, she banned foreign editions of *Émile* from sale or import, only allowing a censored Russian version; the text was published in full in translation in 1813.[37] For both Catherine and Betskoi, the envisaged outcome of the educational process was to produce active and productive citizens for the Russian Empire and a Westernized nobility. From 1783, pupils in all Catherine's schools were issued with a reader, *The Duties of Man and Citizen*, which emphasized obedience, industry and acceptance of the social order. It opened with the sentence: 'A true Son of the Fatherland should be attached to the state, to the image of governance, and to the laws.'[38]

The educational content in Catherine's schools was based on West European ideals of a body of knowledge as well as the Western behavioural codes for a noble society. This break with Muscovite culture struck contemporaries:

> Our *forefathers* called it *education* when they taught their children the Psalms and how to count on the abacus; after this they would give their enlightened son a book of hours printed in Kiev. ... This *education* can hardly be called education, for the duties of the citizen and the Natural Law were unknown to the youngsters.[39]

Catherine and Betskoi focused not only on devising a curriculum of general formal education, but also equally on embedding in the schools the key Russian concept of *vospitanie*. *Vospitanie* can be translated as 'upbringing' or 'raising' – rather than formal education as the transmission of a body of knowledge. It carries within it the idea of the moral development of character. Guidance published for teachers in Catherine's schools emphasized that their role was not just to impart knowledge but to *vospitat'* (to raise, to bring up morally).[40] The strong Russian emphasis on *vospitanie* in their models of childhood, taken in part from Enlightenment ideals, continued throughout the nineteenth century. It would even gain in importance in the Soviet period, when good moral upbringing in the communist spirit was as vital as the acquisition of a systematic body of knowledge. *Vospitanie* became one of the main tasks of the Pioneer movement. Corporal punishment was forbidden in Catherine's schools; this was another strong continuing element across Tsarist and Soviet educational principles. Betskoi's *General Statute* was distributed to all government offices and to the Holy Synod. In 1766 Betskoi also compiled a guide to childcare, with materials he considered appropriate for raising new generations of educated and disciplined citizens, showing the importance of childhood for the Russian state.[41]

Catherine established a whole range of educational establishments along the principles laid out by herself and Betskoi. The famous School for Daughters of the Nobility (*Institut blagorodnykh devits*), known as the Smolny Institute, was opened in St Petersburg in 1764. Girls boarded there between the ages of six and eighteen, educated in isolation from their families and wider society. The aim was to produce virtuous and accomplished young noble women, capable of raising in turn their own children in the spirit of Enlightenment ideals. In 1765, the *Novodevichii Institut* was opened for the daughters of townspeople, run along similar lines. The syllabus for the Smolny Institute combined academic subjects, including mathematics, languages, history and geography, with the teaching of social accomplishments (music, art, dancing) and instruction in moral virtue. So began the tradition of a formal education outside the home for noble girls in Russia, as well as perhaps the beginnings of the idea of a more prolonged childhood shading into adolescence.[42]

Catherine and Betskoi reformed the Cadet Corps by making them take younger boys and broadening out their curriculum so that they too were more of a 'citizen-factory'. Schools for noble boys also had a closed character. Marc Raeff writes that the removal from their families and from the everyday life on their estates into the closed and disciplined world of the Russian boarding school disoriented and bewildered noble boys, but it also produced a strong horizontal generational bond. He suggests that this generational bond, in addition to their isolation from Russian reality and their reception of a Westernized education in the Enlightenment spirit of transformation, may account for the rationalistic and universalistic characteristics of the thought of the Russian intelligentsia from the early nineteenth century.[43]

As well as education for elite children in St Petersburg and Moscow, Catherine wanted to expand the limited educational opportunities for the children of the nobility and the townspeople in the vast Russian provinces. In 1768, she set up a Sub-Commission on Education to study a variety of European educational models. In 1775, Boards of Social Welfare (*prikazy obshchestvennogo prizreniia*), which were to be financed by the local nobility, were created and ordered to set up schools in towns and large villages across provincial Russia. However, this order had little detail and little impact. In 1782, Catherine invited the Serbian educational reformer Fyodor Yankovich de Mirievo to Russia to help design a new national school system and she established a National Commission on Education. De Mirievo had been an adviser to Joseph II, the Habsburg and Holy Roman emperor, and had been responsible for introducing educational reforms into the Serbian areas of the Habsburg lands. As a result of de Mirievo's work in Russia, a Statute for Popular Schools (*Ustav narodnykh uchilishchakh*) was published in 1786 that called for a national network of schools to be established in provincial towns and large villages for all the free classes. In these four year schools, pupils were to learn reading and writing, Christian teachings, mathematics, drawing, history, geography and the natural sciences, as well as reading *The Duties of Man and Citizen*. Again, the Boards of Social Welfare were to finance these schools. Catherine's school plan was the third national school system devised in Europe, following behind the introduction of compulsory primary schooling in Prussia in 1763 by Frederick the Great and in the Habsburg lands in 1774 by Maria Theresa. There remained resistance to the novel idea of state education, as there would be later to the introduction of compulsory primary schooling in nineteenth-century Europe. In 1790, a town council sent a petition to their Provincial Governor, the head of the Board of Social Welfare, stating,

> Schools are not necessary for the children of merchants and craftsmen. Therefore, we do not intend to send our children to school. We have no desire to support the schools and we see no value in them.[44]

The quality of the urban schools varied according to the enthusiasm of the local nobility, on whose support they depended.

Catherine and Betskoi also established two foundling houses in Moscow (1763) and St. Petersburg (1770) for abandoned or unwanted infants, visibly declaring the state's role in the protection of childhood. These were to have similar functions to their boarding schools. They hoped to raise and educate a new urban class of loyal and useful citizens (a 'third estate') out of the babies abandoned there. These children, regardless of their parents' social origins, were to receive useful vocational training and would become free subjects on leaving the homes. This particular 'citizen-factory' experiment never came to fruition as few of the infants in them ever reached childhood, let alone adulthood. Although great publicity was devoted to these homes both inside the Russian Empire and abroad, the mortality rate within the homes and in the rural fostering system attached to them was as high as ninety per cent. It was not until the 1890s that this rate started declining. The foundling homes, and other similar private ones, only took in a minute fraction of infants whose families could not or would not care for them. In the second half of the nineteenth century, the Moscow home took in 17,000 foundlings a year, while the St Petersburg home took in about 9,000.[45] One of the main functions of the foundling homes was to support the image of a caring paternalistic Romanov dynasty.

Many other Russian Enlightenment figures concerned themselves with childhood and education, including Vasily Nikolaevich Tatishchev (1686–1750), Mikhail Lomonosov (1711–65) and Nikolai Novikov (1744–1818). They established schools, founded societies for the promotion of education and upbringing and wrote books for and about children and aiding the development of a secular publishing industry. The Imperial family and wealthy nobles donated significant sums of money to the Boards of Social Welfare to support individual national schools, although the local citizens residing around these schools seem to have been rather more begrudging.[46] The nobility also liked to be seen donating money to the growing network of foundling homes and orphanages.

By 1800, the educational network in the Russian Empire consisted of around 315 state and private schools, teaching 19,915 children. The Holy Synod taught around 24,000 children at that time. Together this accounted for around 0.5 per cent of the 'school age' population.[47] The numbers of children that Catherine's educational reforms impacted were limited. The Russian state did not try to educate the majority of children – those of the peasants. Some peasant children did get some education offered by village priests, literate rural inhabitants (ex-soldiers) or local landowners. Anyway, pure literacy alone is not equivalent to a concept of childhood.

As well as the very gradual spread of the ideal of education, other aspects of the Enlightenment model of childhood were developing in the Russian Empire. Russian physicians who had studied in Europe took up common Enlightenment crusades, promoting maternal breastfeeding, attacking the widespread practice of swaddling babies, and calling in general for greater focus on maternal and infant health.[48] In 1768, the English doctor Thomas Dinsdale came to Russia to inoculate Catherine and her son against smallpox. Leading doctors Karl Martens and Johann Heinrich Jänish, who worked the hospital of the Moscow foundling home, made important contributions to the development of paediatrics in the 1770s.

Conclusion

In the eighteenth century, the Russian state and elites began to show greater interest in the formal education of noble boys. The state tried to isolate them from wider society (adults), who were seen as potentially corrupting, and to teach them correct behaviour. Children had gained new importance as future citizens of the state. The spatial confinement and segregation of children would be used throughout the Imperial period to enforce estate differences. Eighteenth-century educational developments show the beginning of the sense that several years of formal education outside the home was the appropriate temporal and spatial life experience for elite children and a necessary part of a childhood. By the 1760s, 45 per cent of retiring nobles had attended a Cadet Corps or some other kind of school external to the home.[49]

There was a dramatic shift across the eighteenth century in understandings of children's education. Peter the Great was interested in shaping new 'civilized' individuals, able to operate in polite society, and he also wanted to create state servitors to increase the power of the Russian Empire. This led to a focus on childhood and education. However, Peter retained a pre-Enlightenment conception of human nature as sinful and in need of forceful correction and used violence within the Muscovite tradition of enforced compliance ('progress through coercion').[50] Education was viewed as training to be useful to the state, rather than as inner transformation for the use of the state. It was only under Catherine that the education system was allocated the role of creating new citizens who interiorized self-restraint.[51] The school and education have been very important in the history of Russian childhood, as they were at the centre of discourses on how to shape a new Imperial (and later Soviet) subject. Marc Raeff argues that Russian Enlightenment thinkers such as Ivan Betskoi and Nikolai Novikov fused Locke's emphasis on the power of education with Rousseau's concern for the spiritual and moral development of the child to create a specifically 'emotional, moral and spiritually passionate' tone to Russian ideas about education.[52] This tone lasted throughout the Imperial and Soviet periods.

The Enlightenment, and in particular the influence of Rousseau and Locke, left a powerful legacy of seeing children as 'natural' and 'innocent' but with the coda that their innocence needed to be under constant adult surveillance and control. Catherine – who removed her grandchildren from their parents' care to hers – went further and 'appropriated' or 'manipulated' childhood, enacted a 'strategic exploitation and repossession of childhood' for the state's end and thus set a pattern that has persisted in Russia until today.[53] Social elites who propagated the new Enlightenment ideas about childhood also closely identified with the power of the Russian state and wanted to use childhood to promote a growing sense of Russian national identity. As elsewhere in Europe at the time, childhood was being professionalized, medicalized and commercialized. Children were becoming the concern of the state and childhood was increasingly recognized as a special period of life; at least for higher social groups. These developments would be intensified in the later nineteenth century.

3

Childhood in late Imperial Russia

Throughout the Imperial period, Russian children were born into a legal social category, an estate (*sosloviia*), which defined their place in society. If they were legitimate, they inherited their estate categorization from their father. The four estate categories were the nobility (*dvoryanstvo*); townspeople, including merchants and artisans (*gorodskie obyvateli*); the peasantry; and the clergy. By the mid-nineteenth century other social categories were forming, for example the *raznochinsty* (mixed estate), as well as a nascent 'middle class'. Many historians see a merging of merchants, the urban bourgeoisie, industrialists and the non-aristocratic gentry to form a single cultural and social group in the second half of the nineteenth century. After the Emancipation of the Serfs in 1861, there was greater flux and fluidity in the status and residency of peasants. However, for the majority of the period, the estate a child was born into determined to a great degree what kind of childhood they were expected to have and what kind of childhood they experienced.

Until the twentieth century, childhood as everywhere was a shorter period of life than it is today. Peasant children began contributing to the family economy at the age of around seven or eight. During the eighteenth century and early nineteenth century, noble boys usually entered state service at the age of around twelve. The children of townspeople also entered the civil service or joined the army at aged twelve to fourteen.[1] State decrees from the early nineteenth century distinguished between three categories of children: under eight; between eight and twelve years (*maloletki*); between twelve and eighteen years (*podrostki*). Until 1830, the legal marriage age was thirteen for females and fifteen for males, although in reality few married that young.[2] In 1830, the marriage age was raised to sixteen and eighteen, respectively. By the 1850s, the average age of marriage had risen for both peasant girls and boys: between sixteen and eighteen and between eighteen and nineteen, respectively.[3] As the century progressed, the idea of the ages of childhood was expanded most of all for elite groups, but also for children from non-elite backgrounds through labour legislation restricting industrial work and with the extension of primary schooling into rural areas.

Elite childhoods in imperial Russia

Russian noble families before the era of the Great Reforms of the 1860s, and even afterwards, have often been presented as distinguished by extremely formal, cold, hierarchical and authoritarian relations between children and their parents.[4] The father, as head of the classic 'Russian patriarchal family', stood at the height of power and could be a distant and forbidding figure, frequently absent for long periods on state service. Provincial noble mothers occupied themselves with running their estates and households, while those of the urban elite were more concerned with court life in St Petersburg than in child rearing. Noble children rarely spent time with their parents and certainly had little spontaneous daily contact with them. A child's mother did oversee their daily care from birth, but the actual caring was handed over to what would become a succession of peasant wet nurses, nursemaids and nannies. The child usually had the power in these relationships with intimate social 'inferiors'. As the children grew older, the wet nurses and nannies were replaced with a series of tutors, governesses, companions and chaperones, usually, but not always, foreign. Many boys, and often girls, would be sent away to boarding schools at the age of around ten or eleven. Historians have differed over whether this pattern of childhood experience made gentry children deprived or spoilt or both. Marc Raeff suggests that childhood for noble boys in the eighteenth century was 'an alternation of almost anarchical freedom and shorter periods of very strict discipline and control'.[5] It has been suggested that one of the causes of the growth of the revolutionary movement in the second half of the nineteenth century was a generational reaction against the noble family and its suppression of personal autonomy.[6]

There are however other models and patterns of relations between children and parents in noble families. After 1762, when Peter III abolished compulsory state service for the nobility, many nobles retired to their estates and embraced a vision of paternal enlightened domesticity. Successive Tsars promoted an ideology of a sentimental domesticity which included close and harmonious family relations, a construct which was then disseminated through the Russian periodical press and advice literature throughout the nineteenth century. The Russian gentry family in the provinces remained a productive unit until the second half of the nineteenth century, yet it was simultaneously a sentimental and emotional unit. Memoirs accumulating an image of the pre-reform Russian gentry home as a dark, authoritarian, patriarchal hell may have had their own agenda: an attack on the source of the home's stability – serfdom. Steven Grant points out that the most well-known sources for the stifling misery of the patriarchal gentry Russian family are those of revolutionaries such as Aleksandr Herzen and Vera Figner.[7] Meanwhile, memoirs and ego-documents from other sources reveal a more informal and intimate side to family life. Evenings were often spent together as a family, playing cards, reading, listening to music and dancing, and in the summer months, playing games outside. Estates had swings and equipment for children's outside games. Grant's extensive study of 200 autobiographical writings of nobles born in the eighteenth and early nineteenth centuries shows that many of them describe at least one loving and emotionally involved parent.

From the late eighteenth century, there were 'pedagogical mothers' in the Russian elite who took serious and sustained interest in the raising of their children.[8] In 1837, Natalia Chikhacheva, the mother in a gentry family in Vladimir province, was devastated when the time came for her twelve-year-old son Aleksei to leave the family estate to go to boarding school in Moscow. She wrote in her diary that 'Andrei Ivanovich thinks to send Alesha to a *pansion* in Moscow; I spent all day crying and feel very bad'. As the time for her son's departure approached, she wrote that 'we were all very miserable to be sending Alesha away' and 'I sobbed all day and was miserable; very sick about Andrei and Alesha leaving'. After her son left, she revealed, 'I can't overcome myself and am suffering terribly from sadness.'[9] Some noble fathers saw the education and upbringing of their children as an important task. As noted earlier, the influence of the Enlightenment in Russia meant that *vospitanie* (upbringing, rather than daily childcare) remained a topic of vital social interest throughout the nineteenth century.

Vospitanie was considered an appropriate subject for males to concern themselves with, as it was closely linked to Russia's future development; after all, it was usually elite males who chose how to define the nation. Andrei Chikhachev (b. 1798), Natalia's husband, viewed educating and raising his two children as one of his chief roles, and one compatible with masculinity. Judging by his diaries, both parents were intimately involved with their young children. They physically comforted their children when they were ill, lying next to them for hours and often co-sleeping with them. Yet he was clearly the main parent in terms of daily involvement in their lives. In this, he was influenced by Betskoi's Enlightenment ideals of the formation of character and reason through training and supervision. His son described himself through the prism of these ideas, calling himself a *vospitannik*. The boy's diary entries show his life in a gentry family in the 1830s:

> Learned from *Papinka* how to make envelopes. *Papinka* praised me for my good handwriting. … *Papinka* examined me on the [catechism] and French, and was quite pleased with me and after this we inspected the stables and threshing barn. … *Papinka* and I were occupied with French reading, and he was very much satisfied. After dinner *Papinka* took me with him on a visit to the village of Zimenki to the misters Kultashev, where they praised me very much.[10]

As Pickering Antonova points out in her study, Andrei is teaching his son not only academic subjects but also how to run the estate, as well as introducing him into local social networks. Many years later in the early 1860s, after his grandchild's early death, Andrei Chikhachev also recorded deeply intimate and affectionate memories of him:

> 2. In the [illeg.] around the rooms; – asked me to pick him up in my arms and walk with him all around the rooms … 4. On the windowsill of the billiard room, looking at the model mill. 5. In the hall on the carpet with lots of toys. 6. Loved to imitate the priests. Burned incense. Drew the Zimenki church from a picture. Bowed to the ground when he prayed. Kissed the icon. 7. In the little red jacket and little white hat in the garden, with a flower in his little hand. 8. Loved to look at the [illeg.] – at the steam coming from the samovar. 9. In his walker quickly got around all the rooms. 10. Showed [off] the new little shirts made by his grandma. – Loved to sort out the tiny candies. 11. Came to watch while I broke up sugar. 12. Not long before his passing, held in his hands [by himself] the little book about monasteries. 13. Riding about the rooms, and sitting on my bed, let us know that by this he would be remembered.[11]

Unsurprisingly, gentry childhoods were structured by gender. At around age seven, boys were transferred from the care of female servants to be raised and educated by males in the household. Following on from the pattern established in the late eighteenth century, gentry boys were either home-schooled or sent to boarding schools in towns and cities between ten and twelve years of age. At the highest social level, attendance at elite institutions such as the Noble Institute in Moscow, the various Cadet Corps, the Tsarskoe Selo Lyceum (founded by Alexander I in 1811) and the Imperial School of Jurisprudence (founded in 1835) was considered essential for future careers in state service. These elite schools were meant to instil in noble boys appropriate conduct and emotional behaviour. A study of the characteristics expected of young boys at the prestigious Tsarskoe Selo Lyceum shows that the confusing ideal in the first half of the nineteenth century was that a noble boy should be obedient, respectful and obliging, yet also sociable, open and imaginative.[12] Building on earlier traditions, Tsarskoe Selo was a closed and highly regulated environment.

Despite Catherine's wishes, corporal punishment for boys was common both in the home and in educational institutions; there was no expectation that childhood for noble boys should be free from pain or fear. As boys got older, they spent increasingly more time with their fathers in pursuits considered masculine such as playing billiards and hunting and riding. Girls, who had remained in the female sphere, shadowed their mothers in the running of the estate and household, preparing for a time when they would do this in their own married lives. In general, they were prepared for '*le monde*' and marriage by their mothers. At around age sixteen, a girl became a *nevesta*, or a young woman of marriageable age and entered the adult female world.[13] The elder sisters of the revolutionary Mikhail Bakunin, born in the early nineteenth century into a noble family, received a good education at home. Their future role though was meant to be in the domestic sphere, to marry well and 'enlighten and enliven domestic society' on their own noble estates.[14] In the second half of the nineteenth century, it became more common for girls to go to boarding school.

By the turn of the nineteenth century, there were 315 state schools in the Russian Empire, with around 20,000 pupils.[15] Alexander I (1801–25) established a new Ministry of Education in 1802. Initiated by Count Mikhail Speransky, the Tsar's close associate and advisor, new educational statutes regularized and increased district urban schools for the children of provincial elites and classical *gymnazia* for the children of elites. A bifurcated education system was in embryo, which would last until the end of the Tsarist period, despite increasing demands from educated society (*obshchestvennost'*) for a unified and democratized school system outside of centralized state control.

Aleksandr Nikitenko began attending the district urban school in the provincial capital of Voronezh in 1815 at the age of eleven.[16] He looked back on his school years with gratitude, although the main pedagogical technique was memorization. The pupils studied religion, history, Russian grammar, maths, physics, natural history, Latin and German as well as Catherine's *The Duties of Man and Citizen*. He was appointed class auditor, responsible for compiling daily notes on the behaviour and achievements of his fellow pupils, based on which beatings with a ruler would be carried out.[17] Although these schools were meant for the children of the urban estate, his own experience was that the school was socially mixed. Nikitenko himself was the son of a serf:

> Often, on the same bench you would find the son of a secretary, the son of
> a high official and the son of a serf; a boy from a wealthy merchant's home,
> who rode to school in an elegant *droshky* pulled by a well-fed horse, could

be found by the side of a poor child with an ill-fitting frock coat, full of holes, barely covering his threadbare linen breeches.[18]

Such a socially mixed picture was not welcome and throughout the nineteenth century, it was the priority of the Tsarist regimes to try to segregate children's education along estate lines. It was extremely hard for a serf or peasant child to get formal schooling beyond primary level, or even at primary level. Those that did had to be fortunate in the support they received from those of a higher estate. Nikitenko, who later became a professor and a member of the Academy of Sciences, could not carry on attending school beyond the age of thirteen. He later gained his freedom and attended university as a young man only through the patronage of noble elites. By the end of Alexander I's reign in 1825, Russia had three 3 lyceum, 57 *gymnazia*, 3 major schools, 370 district schools, 600 parochial schools and 360 private schools.[19] Large provincial capitals had *gymnazia*, but many smaller Russian towns had no school at all.

In 1825 young men from some of Russia's most privileged families carried out the Decembrist Revolt, a failed uprising against the accession of Nicholas I to the throne. The new Tsar was determined to strengthen the role of the government in the social direction of elite society, including greater control over the education of boys.[20] This furthered the interest in providing boarding schools attached to the classical *gymnazia*. A Committee on Education set up in 1826 reported that 'children of different social origins should not be educated together. ... The education of the gentry should be completely different and kept apart from the education of other groups.'[21] An 1827 edict forbade the *gymnazia* from accepting serf children. A new Law on Education in 1828 entrenched a highly segregated system, encouraging the establishment of parish or estate schools for serf children, while strengthening the network of district urban schools for the sons of merchants and urban residents and the classical *gymnazia* for the children of the gentry and service class. This attempt to restrict children to the social estate into which they were born was to ensure each estate only got 'that part which it needs from the general treasury of enlightenment'. In the 1880s, the Tsarist government would again try to restrict access to secondary education for non-elite children. It had no interest in encouraging ideas of social mobility or producing a frustrated educated class with no outlet. The most notorious example of this was the so-called 'Cooks' Circular' of June 1887, when Ivan Delyanov, the Minister of Education, directed the provinces to 'free the *gymnaziums* and *progymnaziums* from children of coachmen, menials, cooks, washerwomen, small shopkeepers and the like. For, excepting occasionally gifted children, it is completely unwarranted for the children of such people to leave their position in life.'[22] This reveals a strong resistance by the state to a unified idea of childhood. As part of the Russification drive of the 1880s, Delyanov also imposed quotas on the number of Jewish children who could attend *gymnazia* in the western borderlands of the Russian Empire.

During the rule of Nicholas I (1825–55) children's education, as with everything else in public life, was meant to be based on the ideological trinity of 'Orthodoxy, Autocracy and Nationality' (*narodnost'*), as put forward by Sergei Uvarov, the Minister of Education between 1833 and 1849. As well as trying to control as tightly as possible the official school curriculum, in the mid-1830s laws were also passed to control what took place in private institutions and home education. Russian tutors were given the status of state employees and regulations on the employment of foreign tutors were increased. Education opportunities nevertheless expanded and there were almost half a million children in education by the time of Nicholas's death in 1855.[23]

The 'Great Reforms' and childhood

Russia's failures in the Crimean War (1853–56) ushered in a period of legal, administrative and educational reforms, which brought far-reaching changes into every sphere of public life. The 1860s, the period of the 'Great Reforms', inaugurated a period of change in conceptions about childhood. The Emancipation of the Serfs in 1861 has been linked with the diminution of the power of both noble and peasant patriarch. Reformers and radicals attacked the authoritarian patriarchal family and promoted greater emotional investment in family life and interest in how children should be raised. The romantic genre of the childhood biography reached Russia in the 1850s, exemplified by Tolstoy's autobiographical work *Childhood, Boyhood, Youth*, which created an idealized myth of a Russian gentry childhood.[24] Social ideals of freedom and progress influenced how children were seen within the family. The journalist Nikolai Shelgunov wrote that it was at that time that 'children became the first members of the household and they were given the best, the brightest, and the most spacious rooms'.[25] As noted earlier, Steven Grant and others argue that many emotionally affective families existed in Russia in the late eighteenth and nineteenth centuries and so the 1860s were not quite the watershed they are often presented as being. However, it is clear in the decades after the 1860s that there was a rapid development of concepts of childhood in Russia that were roughly in line with those evolving elsewhere.

The Russian Empire also saw enormous demographic changes in the second half of the nineteenth century. Between 1860 and 1914, the population rose from 74 million to 175 million.[26] The urban population tripled from 6 million to 18 million. However, the majority of Russians still lived in the countryside and most of them were peasants.[27] Most Russian children were peasant children and it is to their childhood that we can now turn, to look at the question as to what model of childhood structured the dominant experience in late imperial Russia.

Peasant childhoods in imperial Russia

The modern model of childhood taking root among Russian elites in the late nineteenth century was founded on a belief in the separation of the world of the adult and that of the child. Yet how distant was the world of the adult and the world of the child in peasant Russia? Was a peasant childhood in Russia in the nineteenth century still as it had been in medieval Europe, not so much a 'childhood' as 'an apprenticeship in the conduct of a caste'?[28] Throughout the Imperial period and even well into the Soviet period, the majority of Russia's children were peasants and they experienced their lives in the basic framework of an agricultural childhood. Settled agriculture, developed around 8000 BC, eventually came to replace hunting and gathering. This transition created basic conditions of childhood common to all agricultural societies. Agriculture brought with it enormous work demands. Children could now do useful work so their early physical independence was encouraged. At the same time, they became economically important to their families and communities and therefore their own economic independence was often delayed. A greater emphasis was placed on the concept of obedience to parents and elders. Larger settled communities with high birth rates and low life expectancy meant that children became a significant social group. Social status became more differentiated between children themselves and between adults and children and this began to be codified in law. Distinctions began in kinds of childhood; a small minority would not do 'useful work' but would be trained and educated. Greater importance was placed on extended families and on the role of grandparents in caring for children while younger able-bodied adults worked. Obedience and early physical independence, as well as age-appropriate contributions to the household, continued to be important for children in the Soviet period, continuing the model of an agricultural childhood well into the twentieth century. European and Marxist ideas about productive work and children's active engagement with the social world would merge with this agricultural model in Russia in the twentieth century.

In the Russian case, rural life was structured around individual peasant family households, farming land which legally belonged to the peasant commune after 1861.[29] Both the peasants' farms and the people who lived and worked on it (who were usually but not always biologically related) were called the '*dvor*', the household.[30] Although there were important regional variations in a country the size of Russia, from the middle of the fifteenth century until the middle of the nineteenth century, extended and multiple families (a married couple with children and unmarried relatives, or two or more conjugal units) predominated among the peasantry.[31] The average peasant household consisted of six to nine persons. Peasant family structure was extremely patriarchal, with both adults and children in the household dominated by the oldest male head of the household, the *bol'shak*. Due to labour needs removing able-bodied adults from caregiving responsibilities, young children were brought up by grandparents, aunts, uncles and older siblings, as much as their own parents. This feature, together with the power of the patriarch, 'raises questions about the importance of the conjugal dyad as the primary social and emotional unit in Russian peasant society'.[32] The important role of the extended family in children's lives continued into the Soviet period. The Russian peasant family model of universal early marriage and extended families differed from the West European one, which was characterized instead by delayed marriage and nuclear families.

After the Emancipation Reform of 1861, the multigenerational, patriarchal peasant family began breaking up due to the impacts of industrialization and labour migration, land shortages and increased household divisions in the lifetime of the *bol'shak*. Possibly the growth of a sense of individualism made younger generations prefer to form their own families. By the time of the 1897 Empire-wide Census, the simple family (a married couple and children) dominated, accounting for just over half of family types.[33] By 1917, the average size of a peasant family had declined from 8.4 persons just before the Emancipation to 6.2 persons.[34] However, many peasant children were still growing up in extended families, partly due to the cyclical nature of peasant family development.

In agricultural societies, children were important and valued contributors to family survival. Russian peasant proverbs reflect this: 'One son is not a son, two sons equals half a son, three sons equal one son.'[35] Peasant children contributed to the family as a productive unit from early on. Peasant children were indulged and admired in their very early years but were expected to start helping by around age five or six. Peasant families may have seen this as education and apprenticeship, rather than labour, as children were learning their future roles and responsibilities through practice. Children were often called according to the labour that they did; boys who ploughed were called *pakholki* (plowboys) and girls who looked after younger children were called *nianki* (nannies).[36] Boys learnt from older male relatives to work in the fields – sewing, threshing, fertilizing soil – and to look after animals. Between the ages of eight and fourteen boys were considered 'half workers', and between fourteen and sixteen, 'half workers of greater strength'.[37] By the age of thirteen or fourteen, peasant boys worked with scythes, sickles, threshers, oxen and ploughs, and were admitted to the village assembly, the *skhod*. At fifteen years, they were considered 'full assistants' to their fathers.[38] Peasants were usually legally considered full workers (*tiaglo*) at eighteen.[39]

Peasant girls began to look after younger siblings or other village children at around the ages of six or seven, partly accounting for the very high infant mortality in Russian villages. In an 1883 survey, a *zemstvo* doctor found that around a third of the seventy-one families with young children that he studied in one Russian village left their children in the care of girls aged six to eight.[40] In some ways, Russian peasant girls had less of a 'childhood' than their brothers did; they had less chance of going to school for example. Starting from the 1930s peasant girls would finally be going to school at the same rate as their brothers and they were gradually removed as a childcare option, one element in the reduction of infant mortality in Russia, as well as the eventual lowering of the birth rate.

At the same age of around six or seven, young girls also began to learn how to spin and sew, perform household labour, cook and clean. In Smolensk province, at the age of five or six years, a girl would be given a thread, which was then burned. She would eat the ashes with bread and water, being told, 'Eat and you will become a good spinner.'[41] Peasant girls usually also performed heavy agricultural work, particularly at harvest time. Along with their mothers and other female relatives, they worked in the fields raking, strewing, reaping, binding sheaves and gleaning. In more industrialized regions of Russia, peasant boys could be apprenticed to artisans or sent to work in mills and factories. Both boys and girls helped with craft and artisan work at home. There is some debate over whether the labour of children in the Russian countryside involved direct economic exploitation or was mainly used for socialization and training. Children's productivity was low and lagged behind their consumption until they reached their teenage years.[42] Peasant children did play as well as work. Peasant children played in groups outdoors, swimming in lakes, rivers and ponds. Their games often mimicked adult economic activities. They wore simple homemade clothes and often went barefoot. Violence was regularly used against peasant boys, and as for gentry boys there was no expectation that childhood should be free from pain.

Universal primary education for peasant children was long an aim of Russian reformers and revolutionaries. In the nineteenth century, and in twentieth century too in many ways, the dream of universal primary education across Russia became seen as 'a solution to the core problems associated with the transitional phases of modernization' and seeped into debates about Russia's place in the world, particularly vis-a-vis the West.[43] Before the expansion in primary education at the end of the nineteenth century, literacy among children was rising. Former soldiers or other literate peasants, the local priest or itinerant teachers taught peasant children in unofficial or 'wild' (*vol'nye*) schools. There were parish and estate schools as well, many run by progressive or well-meaning nobles. The most famous example are the schools at Yasnaya Polyana, run by Lev Tolstoy. After the defeat in the Crimean War in 1856, the Tsarist state recognized that formal education had to be prioritized at all levels in order to keep up with or overtake its European competitors. In 1864 as part of the Great Reforms local elected district and provincial councils, the *zemstva*, were established in European Russia. The *zemstva* were responsible for local needs, including welfare, health, infrastructure and public education. The *zemstva* would play a historically important role in changing peasant children's lives by expanding primary schooling into the villages.

In July 1864, the first proper programme in imperial Russia for a primary education system for peasant children was announced. The *zemstvo* created district school boards, which financed and organized village schools. The syllabus and teacher training was kept in the hands of the Ministry of Education. The last decades of the nineteenth century saw the development across European Russia of the *zemstvo* primary school, based on a three-year programme for children aged between eight and eleven. By 1903 there were 18,871 *zemstvo* primary schools with 1,324,608 pupils.[44] The growth in *zemstvo* schools provoked a response from the Orthodox Church, which with government encouragement increased the number of its schools. The number of church schools increased from 4,540 schools with 112,114 pupils in 1884 to 31,835 schools with 981,076 pupils in 1894, although the numbers began to decline after 1902.[45]

The physical, temporal and organizational model of the village school was worked out and publicized by the educationalist and *zemstvo* activist Nikolai Aleksandrovich Korf, based on his own experiences of teaching peasant children in southern Ukraine in the late 1860s.[46] The model was a one- or two-classroom village school, where a single teacher taught six academic subjects – religion, reading, writing, mathematics, visual methods of teaching (which prepared students to teach the subjects to others or to persist in self-learning) and *mirovedenie* ('world studies', geography and the natural sciences) – to all three years simultaneously. A teaching assistant from the oldest class and a religious instructor, usually the village priest, helped. Religious instruction was compulsory and supervised by the Holy Synod. The school ran six hours a day, six days a week during a six-month school year (autumn to spring). As far as the Tsarist regime was concerned, the purpose of primary education for peasant children was to help stabilize and reproduce the social order. Education was meant to strengthen loyalty to the Tsar and the Russian state and develop obedience and gratitude in children. An early-twentieth-century primary school reading book told children:

> On the Sixth of May the whole of Russia celebrates the birthday of His Imperial Majesty Tsar Nikolai Aleksandrovich; on this royal day the pupils are permitted to not attend lessons. In all the churches the people pray for the Tsar and His Family. The inhabitants of cities and villages decorate their homes with flags. In the evening of the same day, illuminations take place on the streets of cities.[47]

Zemstvo activists, liberal reformers and Russian progressive educational theorists on the other hand hoped that if peasant children were educated, they would not simply reproduce the existing social order but change it. From the 1850s, Russian radicals such as Nikolai Dobrolyubov and Nikolai Chernyshevsky had called for a 'free education' in schools to produce a new generation capable of transforming Russia, in keeping with Russian intelligentsia beliefs that critically thinking individuals can change society and be an active force in historical development. Moderate Russian reformers felt that peasant children were likely to be better off in schools than at home, where it was believed they were denied a proper childhood, showing the shift in the conception of childhood among late Imperial elites. The educationalist S. A. Rachinskii wrote that 'here [in the school] awaits a luxury which really is a necessity of childhood, a luxury for which there is no time in his own family life: constant attention and concern for him by his elders'.[48]

Just as primary education as a hallmark of childhood for peasant children was slowly coming into being, a progressive tradition of pedagogy was beginning from the 1860s. Russian mainstream educational theory was remarkably 'child-centred' from the middle of the nineteenth century, 'focused on non-coercive motivation, fostering self-esteem and initiative'.[49] In 1865, the academic and surgeon Nikolai Pirogov published an influential essay, *Questions of Life* (*Voprosy zhizni*), which called for a unified humanistic education for children regardless of estate. Pirogov argued that the aim of education was to produce a fully developed human being, rather than a servitor as envisaged by the Tsarist state since the time of Peter the Great.[50] He supported the education of girls, although mainly to enable them to be educators for their own children. Konstantin Ushinsky was another important Russian educational theorist in the 1860s whose legacy, like that of Pirogov, was picked up and adopted in the Soviet period. Ushinksy was a graduate of the Department of Law at Moscow University and worked afterwards as a schoolteacher and a journalist. Between 1859 and 1862 he was the Inspector of the Smolny Institute, where he introduced a progressive modern curriculum. He was also the chief editor of the *Journal of the Ministry of Education*. Due to conflicts with the Ministry, he spent much of the 1860s studying school systems in Europe. On his return to Russia, he worked to publicize his pedagogical theories, which he put forward in a two-part volume, *Man as the Object of Education: Educational Anthropology,* in 1867–69. Ushinsky believed in the democratization of education, both in terms of gender and estate, and that the aim of the education of the child was the development of the harmonious personality, the full realization of the individual. He also believed that the purpose of education was to inculcate moral values and a love of labour in children. Ushinsky created popular reading books for primary-aged children – *Children's World* (*Detskii mir*), published in 1860, and *The Native Word* (*Rodnoe Slovo*) in 1864. The latter went through 146 editions prior to the Revolution.[51] Ushinsky, promoting a democratic idea of *narodnost',* put the teaching of the Russian language at the heart of children's education. This marked an shift away from the Enlightenment focus on Westernization in education. As will be seen, many of his approaches to education continued into the Soviet period. From 1946 the Ushinksy Silver Medal was the most prestigious Soviet educational award. Russian progressive educationalists had started a dialogue about children's rights, which would be paradoxically further developed in the Soviet Union in the 1920s. Konstantin Ventsel, the chair of the Pedagogical Society at Moscow State University, believed in the power of education to liberate the human personality and was an advocate of free upbringing (*svobodnoe vospitanie*).[52] Believing that children should be taught in self-regulating communes, in 1906 he founded the House of the Free Child (*Dom svobodnogo rebenka*) and issued a Declaration of the Rights of the Child in 1917.

Harsh discipline and an attitude to children very far from that of the Russian progressive educators continued in some schools, despite the efforts of reformers to stamp it out. Children were frequently humiliated, forced to kneel or confined in small spaces as punishment. Inspectors' reports from the late 1890s show that many forms of physical violence may have been eliminated.[53] Teachers' memoirs show that many newly trained primary school teachers consciously avoided corporal punishment (which was forbidden anyway in law), making the school an oasis of non-violence in a violent peasant world.[54] Some peasant families resisted this and encouraged teachers to use physical punishment. One teacher wrote in his diary about a meeting with a father who had stopped his daughter from attending school. The father informed him:

Ever since she began going to school, our girl has been completely spoiled. They don't give her homework, as they do in other schools. She races off to class as if to play on the streets. This is all because in our school they don't beat anybody, there is no punishment, nothing but fun and games … let her stay at home instead and learn how to spin.[55]

Ben Eklof suggests that most Russian peasants placed a value on literacy and numeracy for their children (or more usually, their sons) but rejected the idea of extended formal education as an important childhood stage. Peasants did not view social mobility as possible: in their world view education was 'the key that opens no doors'.[56] Nor perhaps did they see extended education as particularly desirable. There was a strong culture of hierarchical generational control within peasant society, partly due to the socio-economic structure of Russian agriculture and the needs of the *dvor*. Typical comments from peasants about extended schooling for children include such statements as, 'We've studied our fill, so let's be done with it – after all, we are not going to the royal court!', 'Why literacy – you don't need it to make cabbage soup!' and 'Matryona became neither a beauty nor a cow'. Parents frequently took their children out of school to do agricultural work. This may have been a socially dictated choice, as a form of socialization and control; there was a surplus of adult labour in late imperial Russia and child labour was not particularly efficient.[57] Peasants also may have rejected the *zemstvo* school as an example of the much-resented outside interference in peasant life. There is other evidence though that there was a spontaneous growth in educational aspirations among the peasantry, who wished for more than just literacy for their children. They hoped education could be the key to changing the social system.[58]

Regardless of family attitudes, it seems schooling was welcomed by many peasant children. A former Justice of the Peace wrote:

There is a stunning desire to learn among peasant children. I don't have the faintest idea how to explain it, for it would seem that every imaginable obstacle has been put in the way of the peasant child: the daily trek over snow covered roads for long distances in the winter frost and in flimsy clothing; lessons the entire day and then (spending) their evenings crowded together, under low ceilings in rooms short of oxygen, with a meagre diet largely composed of bread and water. A few of them manage to bring along potatoes and cabbage to supplement their dinner … but none of these discomforts dampens their enthusiasm for study.[59]

Primary school places were over-subscribed; the 1911 School Census showed that a million children were denied admission to school in that year, mainly due to insufficient school places.[60] There was a very high dropout rate in the *zemstvo* schools, with less than one in ten children actually completing the full three-year programme.[61] The average amount of time an individual child spent in school was two and half years.[62] Many children were unable to get to village schools during the winter months due to a lack of proper winter shoes and clothes. Even as late as the 1950s, some children in rural areas were unable to attend schools in the winter because of a lack of winter footwear, that is, because of poverty.

Developments in education for elite children after the Great Reforms

Despite the other progressive developments of the 1860s, in the early 1870s the 'counter-reformer' and Minister of Education Count Dmitrii Tolstoy strengthened the bifurcated secondary school system across the Russian Empire. He proposed a network of vocationally oriented *Realschule* (*real'noe uchilishche*) which would focus on teaching natural sciences and modern languages. These would prepare children of the provincial gentry for future careers in, for example, engineering, mining, veterinary studies and agronomy.[63] For other gentry children, the main form of secondary education would continue to be the state *gymnazium*, in which classical languages dominated the curriculum. The *gymnazia* was the only route to higher education and a career in state service. This system again attempted to ensure state control over the future generations of elite males. Tolstoy also added a preparatory class to the *gymnazium*, the *pro-gymnazium*, for children aged between eight and ten, with the usual aim of taking boys out of the hands of private tutors as quickly as possible.[64]

In 1872, the state issued uniform lesson plans, rules for entrance and progression and graduating examinations for state *gymnazia*.[65] Inspired by a fear of a new revolutionary generation, and also in the tradition of *vospitanie*, each class in the *gymnazia* was to have a class assistant – the *klassnyi nastavnik* for boys and the *klassnaya dama* for girls, who would stay with them throughout their schooling. These class assistants were to establish close relations with their pupils and monitor their behaviour. They contributed an evaluation of each pupil's moral and political attitudes to the final graduation exam.[66] In 1874, Rules of Behaviour for *gymnazia* and *pro-gymnazia* pupils were issued. These stipulated routines of acceptable church attendance imposed curfew hours, listed approved lodgings for pupils, regulated and proscribed public places that pupils could visit outside school hours and outlined permissible behaviour in public. Although corporal punishment was banned, discipline was strict and there were severe restrictions placed on pupils' movements and behaviour both in and outside the school. The emphasis on *vospitanie* and manners was to inscribe markers of status in a highly stratified and unequal society, although the emphasis on discipline and moral character returned in the Soviet period from the 1930s onwards. State *gymnazia* were often housed in impressive and prominent neo-classical buildings in Russia's towns and cities, to underline the 'relationship between education and social power'.[67]

Girls' *gymnazia*, like that of their brothers, usually had boarding houses (*pansiony*) attached. There was an expansion of girls' *gymnazia* from the 1860s. Alexander II approved this proposal to provide 'religious, moral and mental education, which is required of every woman, and especially of future mothers'.[68] This was similar to France, where it was also common in the nineteenth century for middle-class girls to be sent away to board at school.[69] In England on the other hand, girls were usually educated at home, although paradoxically *gymnazia* for girls in Russia were run on harsh 'English' lines.[70] The pupils rose around 7.00 am, washed and dressed, and had breakfast, and this was followed by hours of lessons, with short breaks for lunch and dinner. After dinner, they studied in groups or did needlework, reading or drawing, under observation. Church services took up Sundays, along with the occasional visit from family members.

Being sent away from the family home to a boarding school was often a deeply traumatic experience. Elizaveta Fen (b. 1899) recalled how her mother sent her to a girl's boarding school in Mogilev, the nearest town to the family estate, as she believed her daughter would receive a better moral education in a closed environment. The boarding school felt like a prison to her when she first arrived. The spaces, practices and dress code all served to isolate and discipline. A series of austere buildings fenced in from the outside town formed the school complex. The lower windowpanes had been painted white, and blinds were pulled down on the upper half to block out the outside world. 'Nowhere was there a look-out onto a wider world, an open space, comforting to the eye', she recalled.[71] Inside the school, the pupils were subjected to a regime of almost continual surveillance and their movements were carefully controlled around the spaces. In the French case, control of movement and memorialization in girls' boarding schools were a dulling technique deliberately employed to 'reign in over-active imaginations'.[72]

Gymnazia for boys were run on similarly strict lines. Tolstoy's reforms gave birth to the so-called Tsarist 'bureaucratic police school', the focus of much parental and child discontent in the late Imperial period and the stuff of later Soviet literary nightmares. In his autobiographical novel of the 1890s, *Tema's Childhood*, the writer Nikolai Garin-Mikhailovsky wrote: 'In its current form, the *gymnazia* reminds me of a courtroom with a judge, a prosecutor, and a perpetual defendant. All that's missing is a lawyer to defend this little defendant, who, precisely because he is little, is in particular need of defense.'[73] Opponents of Tsarism claimed these oppressive state *gymnazia* had the opposite effect to that intended, producing young revolutionaries rather than loyal subjects. Progressive educators described state *gymnazia* as the 'dearly beloved daughter of the Russian bureaucracy'.[74] By the beginning of the twentieth century, the government was alarmed that some *gymnazia* pupils were forming discussion groups, intending to oppose the 'detestable school regime' and there were growing concerns about discipline.[75] From 1902, a complete record of a pupil's conduct in their last three years at the *gymnazia* was to be submitted as part of their university application and priority in admissions was to be given to those who had showed political loyalty, or, presumably, apathy. 'Educated society' (*obshchestvennost'*) had a negative and even hostile attitude towards the school. The two most hated features of school life were the constant surveillance and the obligatory religious attendance. Demands for changes in the education system came out in 1905, when public petitions asked for a unified secondary school system run by local authorities, rather than dominated by the centre.

During the 1905 Revolution, *gymnazia* pupils joined in strikes and demonstrations and they were also victims of Black Hundreds' attacks and police brutality. Pupils protested against the war with Japan and passed petitions to school authorities. In February 1905, six *gymnazia* pupils were killed and forty injured by police during a demonstration in Kursk, while other pupils rioted in Minsk.[76] Parents in Kharkov explained their children's political activism as being due to the 'existing pedagogical regime, which is simply an extension of the universal police-bureaucratic structure of the state'.[77] Parents did not want their children punished, under surveillance or forced to attend church services. By the turn of the century, many Russian parents agreed that the purpose of children's education was individual self-development, rather than loyalty to the state.

By the end of the late Imperial period, the *gymnazia* were losing their closed character and more children were going as day pupils. Life for most gentry children from better-off families was bifocal, with the summer entirely free from school and often spent away from the city on family estates in the Russian countryside. The writer Vladimir Nabokov described the long summer months for gentry children as 'schoolless untownishness'.[78]

Childhood culture in late imperial Russia

As I crawl over those rocks, I keep repeating, in a kind of zestful, copious, and deeply gratifying incantation, the English word 'childhood', which sounds mysterious and new, and becomes stranger and stranger as it gets mixed up in my small, overstocked, hectic mind, with Robin Hood and Little Red Riding Hood, and the brown hoods of old hunchback fairies.[79]

Post-revolutionary memoirs of gentry childhoods are one of the most well-known genres of tales about Russian childhood. In emigration, Vladimir Nabokov evoked pre-revolutionary life on his family estate in northwestern Russia and in their residence in St Petersburg. The Nabokov children had an English governess and Swiss and German tutors. English was his first language. The material culture of his and his siblings' childhood was English – Pears Soap, Golden Syrup, tennis balls, English puzzles and English books.[80] Possibly the Anglomania of the Russian upper classes in early-twentieth-century Russia, as exemplified by the Nabokov family and the Romanovs, influenced the spread at that time of a Western model of childhood among elites. Wealthy Russian children spent their holidays in the Crimea and on their country estates or travelled with their families and servants to European holiday resorts and spa towns. They participated in the growing transnational culture of Western childhood. The Scout movement, founded in 1907 in England by Robert Baden-Powell, spread to Russia. Children's literature was a popular genre for Russian writers, and translations of European and American children's books were widely available.[81] Russian writers considered suitable for children included Ivan Krylov, Alexander Pushkin, Nikolai Gogol and Nikolai Nekrasov. Russian children also read versions of transnational 'children's literature', including the American adventure stories of Thomas Mayne Reid and James Fenimore Cooper as well as works by Jules Verne, Daniel Defoe, Mark Twain, Arthur Conan Doyle and Alexandre Dumas, all of which would eventually be published and widely read in the Soviet period as well from the 1930s. Transnational children's literature was not necessarily limited to elites. A survey of village children carried out in 1916 showed that their favourite fictional characters included Jonathan Swift's Gulliver and Harriet Beecher Stowe's Uncle Tom.[82] There was a well-developed consumer culture for children in the late nineteenth century for those who could afford it. The Children's World department store opened in St Petersburg. Children were taken to the opera, ballet and theatre. There was a thriving print culture, with a wide number of children's magazines and book series.

The Europeanized elites of St Petersburg and other major cities continued to employ foreign women – German, British, French, Swiss or Belgian – to look after their children. Compared to Russian women, the governesses from Western Europe followed a more 'Spartan' regime – plenty of long walks and cold baths, which were then thought to be healthy for children.[83] There could be frequent changes of carers, as well as deep attachment to individual women. The writer Irène Némirovsky (1903–42), who grew up as an only child in a wealthy family in Kiev and St Petersburg, had an extremely difficult and complex relationship with her mother. She transferred all her love to her governess Zézelle, hired by her mother from the French House in Kiev. As she became an adolescent, she lived in fear that her mother would deliberately separate her from her beloved governess. Before her mother had the opportunity to do this, Zézelle committed suicide in St Petersburg in 1917.[84] The difficult fate of the figure of the loyal governess or Russian nanny after the Russian Revolution is presented in Némirovsky's fiction, such as in *Snow in Autumn* (1931) and *The Wine of Solitude* (1935). For gentry girls, the transition to adulthood was marked by a move away from women who had cared for them. Elizaveta Fen was struck when her Russian nanny Anyuta began to refer to her as '*baryshnia*' (young lady), after she returned to the family estate from her first term at boarding school aged twelve: 'The days were over when, as my nursemaid, she presumed to teach me manners by making use of some of her peasant lore.'[85] At about the same age, she was allowed to attend all-night church services during Easter and Christmas with the adults of the family.[86]

Dmitri Obolensky (1882–1964), who came from one of Russia's oldest and wealthiest families, recalled how the children of the family occupied two enormous nurseries in their St Petersburg palace. One of the nurseries was large enough to contain an aviary and an aquarium. Even so, their English governess organized their daily lives according to the fashionable 'English' style of ice-cold baths and plain food. As was common with the children of the highest levels of the Russian aristocracy, the Obolensky children did not attend outside schools but were taught at home. Unusually, Vladimir Nabokov attended as a day pupil the progressive Tenishev School from the age of eleven. After a morning of lessons, the Obolensky children would be driven around St Petersburg in an open carriage and go for a stroll through the Summer Gardens.[87] In winter, these strolls were replaced by tobogganing and skating in the Tauride Gardens. As with the Nabokov family, groups of servants were constantly on hand to facilitate all their pleasures. The wealthy Nabokov family had around fifty servants looking after them in their city and country estates.[88] Even children of the minor gentry had servants. Elizaveta Fen's brother was astonished when their new servant Ivan spontaneously sat down on his bed while they were chatting. She also recalled a similar sense of astonishment when the same Ivan leant forward to taste an egg for her after she wondered aloud if it was bad.[89] Despite being alert to the visible signs of social inequality in Tsarist Russia, Fen recalls that her political awakening was actually through literature. An older sibling gave her *The Gadfly* (1897), a novel about the struggle of revolutionaries in the Italian *Risorgimento* by the Irish revolutionary Edith Voynich, and Leonid Andreyev's *The Seven Who Were*

Hanged (1908), a short story about a group of revolutionaries waiting to be executed.[90]

The spatial and temporal separation between parents and children were dissolving for many gentry families, but often remained in place for the upper aristocracy. Obolensky recalled that in his family, the children ate separately and in the evenings would be tidied up and taken into the dining room to greet their parents and be given a lump of sugar.[91] The older practice of large extended kinship groups and open-ended families remained common here as well. The main carer for the Obolensky boys had been their father's valet, who was married to their nanny. He had been left in Russia as a child by his Hungarian father and had been taken in to be raised by the family. When Dmitri Obolensky was six, a tutor appeared in his life, a student from St Petersburg University. This student moved in with the family and stayed with them until they left Russia during the Civil War.

The school year ran from the middle of September to May. After this, gentry children who went to school in Russia's cities would depart for their country estates for the summer, accompanied by a group of servants. A traditional trope in memoirs of privileged pre-revolutionary childhoods is the reunion with Russian nature on the country estate after the months in the city – the pine trees, lilies, forests, ponds and lakes. 'Barefoot in the forest all day long. Fishing in brooks for gudgeon, helping with the horses in the stable yard, the harvest, in short the freedom of which you dream all winter.'[92] Here we see clearly the Enlightenment and romantic link between the child and nature. This is echoed by a Don Cossack boy who remembered his final years of boyhood in Russia before the Revolution in the form of a timeless annual rhythm structured by religious holidays, the school year and the agricultural cycle:

> Every morning you'd cheerfully get up, drink some tea, grab a supply of pies and bread rolls and set off for school. It was just wonderful there. Three months go by, and then it's Christmas. You practice your *tropar'*, chanting to your father, mother, sisters and even your little brother who is too young to understand anything. You ask your mother to wake you up early for matins three days in a row. You stand there peacefully in church, crossing yourself and chanting the *tropar'*. The service finishes. You do not return home yet, but run around crying 'Glory to Christ'. Your pockets are stuffed with sweets, biscuits, coins. ... The Christmas holidays pass and it's back to school. All the boys are excited, sharing their adventures, counting up their pocket money, sometimes scrapping with each other if they won't share. It all quickly calms down again. Lent begins and you fast for five weeks. Then, its Easter, a simply indescribable holiday. The bells ring all day

long, we all roll eggs, Easter salutations and greetings, presents and gifts. Lessons are over by the end of April and on the last day of school there are performances, a play, poetry readings, certificates handed out. ... Then work in the fields. Simply wonderful.[93]

Children, public health and welfare in late imperial Russia

As well as the spread and enforcement of primary education, another major element in the modern Western model of childhood is the reduction in infant and child mortality and a focus on children's health. This medicalization of the child was accompanied by a growing interest in children's welfare. New 'child experts' began developing sciences based around the measurement of children's development and abilities in an attempt to identify the 'normal child'. All these developments took place in imperial Russia in the pre-revolutionary decades.

The Russian Empire had an extremely high infant mortality rate, the highest recorded in Europe. Around 280 out of 1,000 infants died in the first year of life. In Moscow province, this figure was 366 and in St Petersburg in 1869, it was recorded as 748 per 1,000. In the 1880s and 1890s, an estimated 1.2 million babies died annually before reaching their first year.[94]

Mortality rates were extremely high among peasant children. Russian reformers viewed the traditional Russian peasant home (izba) as a place of 'darkness', unhygienic and unsafe for babies and children. They noted that other ethnicities in the Empire – Armenians, Tatars, Jews, Bashkirs and Balts – had lower rates of infant mortality, supporting their conclusion that there was something specifically harmful in Russian peasant early childcare practices.[95] Traditional features of Russian early child rearing practices regarded as dangerous by medical and social activists included swaddling, the use of hanging cribs and cradles which babies were left in for long periods, and the lack of hygiene in the peasant hut. A high number of infant deaths were attributed to the short period of maternal breastfeeding and premature introduction of solid food, which caused intestinal disorders that left babies vulnerable to disease. All experts' fears and suspicions focused on the soska, a package made up of chewed food tied up in a rag that was placed in a baby's mouth as a comforter while the mother was outside working. This was regarded, and actually was, a fatally unhygienic practice. These very same concerns carried on into the Soviet period and spurred on the sanitary campaigns, in which the state mobilized children to spread new hygienic practices.

Activists disliked peasant women's reliance on local female experience and seeming indifference to experts like themselves. There had been a general historical conception that the high infant and child mortality rates prevalent before the era of modern medicine and public health discouraged parents from forming deep emotional attachments to their infants.[96] The seeming indifference of peasant women to their babies' deaths perturbed Russian reformers of the village. David Ransel paints a more subtle picture, arguing that Russian peasant mothers, overworked and essential to the family economy, were forced to place the survival of the whole family as a unit as their priority. With advice from female relatives and neighbours, they quickly decided which babies were more likely to survive and thus invested more in their care.[97] Babies who were considered unviable from birth were called 'ne-zhilets' and were allowed to die. As well as being responsible for all the domestic household labour, peasant women worked intensively in agriculture during the summer months. The summer was the time most fatal to newborn babies. In one district of Moscow province in the 1870s, 67 out of 100 children born in the summer died within a month.[98] Labour pressure structured how mothers cared for their children in Russia (as elsewhere) well into the twentieth century.[99]

As well as trying to reduce infant mortality in the countryside, a new generation of 'child savers' wanted to rescue children from the supposed moral and physical dangers produced by urbanization and industrialization, processes by now well underway in many parts of the Russian Empire. The term bezprizornie, used for street or homeless children, first came into usage in the 1880s.[100] The regulation of poor children's health and welfare lagged somewhat behind that in Western Europe and the United States as the Tsarist government disliked and discouraged the sort of philanthropic activity and research that spurred these developments elsewhere.[101] However, an array of private charitable and medical organizations were established in the last decades of Tsarism. The growing socialist movement also provided childcare facilities for working-class women and addressed issues of child poverty.

In the absence of a large middle class, professional employees of the zemstvo (doctors, statisticians, educationalists) often acted as bearers of the child welfare movement outside the major cities. Alexander II's reforms had created a public health system embedded in the zemstvo. Doctors who worked for the zemstvo created a professional identity as social reformers, transforming the living conditions of the Russian peasantry. From the 1890s, zemstvo doctors set up rural summer nurseries to tackle the problem of high seasonal infant mortality. In 1877, scientists and medical professionals founded the Russian Society for the Protection of People's Health (*Russkoe obshchestvo okhraneniia narodnogo zdraviia*). The Society had a section for health education and health considerations in child rearing, which conducted research projects on sanitary conditions in schools and set up summer nurseries for children.[102] In 1867, the Prince Oldenburgskii Children's Hospital had been founded in St Petersburg, followed by the St Vladimir Children's Hospital in Moscow in 1876 and the St Olga's Children's Hospital in Moscow in 1887.[103] In 1889, the first free maternity hospital had been founded in Moscow, run by the obstetrician A. N. Rakhmanov.[104] The first two were the initiative of Professor Karl Raukhfus, the Romanov family's paediatrician, who also founded the Society of Paediatricians. In 1913 he established the All-Russian Guardianship for Maternal and Child Welfare (*Vserossiiskoe popechitel'stvo po okhrane materinstva i mladenchestva*), which was under the patronage of the Empress Alexandra. By 1917, the All-Russian Guardianship was running 500 summer nurseries in villages, catering to around 35,000 children, and 29 urban crèches with 900 children.[105] In the tradition of the work of the *zemstvo* doctors, it sought to reduce infant mortality by educating peasant women on hygienic care for their infants and themselves. Leading obstetricians, gynaecologists and paediatricians founded the Moscow Charitable Society for the Protection of Motherhood (*Blagotvoritel'noe obshchestvo Okhrana materinstva*).[106] With imperial funds and private donations, this was an attempt to 'create a system of maternal and child protection based on the latest discoveries in biomedical science, specifically paediatrics, neonatology and obstetrics'.[107] It provided medical support, shelters, and housing and labour training for destitute single mothers and their babies during pregnancy and afterwards. In 1904 the All-Russian Union to Combat Child Mortality (*Soyuz dlya bor'by s detskoi smertnosti*) was founded by leading physicians and social activists.[108] The First Infirmary for Nurslings in Moscow was opened in 1910.[109]

From the 1820s, Houses of Industry (*dom trudolubia*) had been founded to provide vocational training for orphaned and abandoned children. These eventually became multipurpose institutions aimed at adults but children were still placed in them. This was unacceptable by the later nineteenth century and many new philanthropic organizations tried to separate the child from the adult in welfare institutions. The All-Russian Guardianship encouraged the establishment of separate children's institutions based on the principle of work relief, named Olga's Children's Asylums after Nicholas II's eldest daughter. By 1912, it had 239 day or live-in work relief institutions for minors, in which they were given some form of vocational training, for example as cobblers, carpenters or dressmakers.[110] The Society for the Care of Indigent Children (*Obshchestva popecheniya o neimushchikh detyakh*) was founded in 1883 by two Russian lawyers, M. V. Dukhovskii and P. N. Obninksii. This organization recruited volunteer 'district guardians' to investigate the circumstances of poor children and recommend appropriate and effective relief methods to help them. It also had a Division for the Protection of Children, which looked into the neglect and mistreatment of apprentices and pursued legal cases on their behalf. It published a journal, Children's Aid (*Detskaya Pomoshch*), which was 'filled with projects for improving poor relief, information on the latest Western innovations, and translations of major works such as Henry George's *Progress and Poverty* and Octavia Hill's *Homes of the London Poor*'.[111] A Union of Children's Aid Organisations in St Petersburg was organized in 1902 by the Society for the Care of Poor and Sick Children (*Obshchestvo popechenie o bednykh i bol'nykh det'yakh*) to coordinate the activities of all charities working with children.[112] The Tsarist state also became involved in children's welfare. Around twenty government departments were responsible for overseeing Tsarist charitable institutions. The Office of the Institutions of Empress Maria (*Vedomstvo uchrezhdenii imperatritsii Marii*) was the main government department that oversaw charitable work with children. It ran orphanages, institutions for blind and hearing-impaired children, rural nurseries as well as a number of maternity homes and children's hospitals.[113]

By the turn of the twentieth century, 'the child' was becoming a major subject of scientific interest and observation, transformed by the human sciences into 'an idea and a target'.[114] Child psychology developed rapidly as a discipline in the first decade of the twentieth century in Russia. Russian scientists were influenced by the theories of child development of Sigmund Freud, Alfred Binet, Theodore Simon, G. Stanley Hall and James Sully.[115] The rise of the use of experimental methods in science, combined with a growing interest in the child, led to the establishment of a new scientific discipline, pedology (*pedologiia*). In 1904, the Konstantin Ushinsky section of the Pedagogical Museum conducted the first systematic courses in child psychology, led by General Apollon Makarov and the experimental psychologist Aleksandr Nechaev.[116] In 1906 it held the first All-Russian Congress of Pedagogical Psychology, with the participation of Makarov, Nechaev and Vladimir Bekhterev.[117] Nechaev ran a Laboratory of Experimental Pedagogy under the auspices of the St Petersburg Pedagogical Academy. In 1907, Bekhterev, a professor at the Military Medical Academy in St Petersburg, founded the War Department's Psycho-Neurological Institute, which included a Pedology Institute, in which learning was investigated as a function of the nervous system and the brain.[118] In 1911 an Institute of Child Neurology and Psychology, headed by the neurologist Grigory Rossolimo, was established at Moscow State University.[119] In 1912 Georgii Chelpanov, professor of philosophy at Moscow University, opened an Institute of Psychology, which studied the psychological foundations of education. Ivan Sikorsky, professor of psychology at Kiev University, set up a clinic to study childhood there.

Child and industrial work in late imperial Russia

The picture of working-class childhood in Tsarist Russia drawn during the Soviet period was one of endless exploitation in factories or mistreatment as apprentices. As well as factory labour, children worked for wages, or sometimes just food and shelter, in agriculture, craft industries and domestic service and were possibly even more exploited than those in industrial settings. While this picture undoubtedly remained true in many ways, by the late nineteenth century legislation limiting industrial child labour was passed approximately in line with other European states. This was in spite of the slow expansion of the usual alternative to child labour, primary education. The first workers the state showed any concern for were children as a social group.

The working-class family needed all its members, including children, to contribute to the household budget. Children worked in industry often alongside older family members or were recruited from the countryside or orphanages and other childcare institutions. This was a long-standing tradition. A 1722 Senate Decree stated that children in the towns of Moscow and Ryazan who 'wander about on the streets begging' were to be placed in apprenticeships in city factories. A 1744 Senate Decree ordered the apprenticeship of soldiers' orphans.[120] Imperial orphanages had long provided labour for state-owned and private mills, mines and factories. In 1804, the Imperial Senate issued a Decree to send orphans and poor children between twelve and fifteen years of age out of St Petersburg to the Aleksandrov Textile Mill 'to learn the textile craft'.[121] Child labour played an important role in factory textile production from the beginning; at a state woollen factory in 1797, about 40 per cent of the workers were children or adolescents.[122]

Industrialization intensified in Russia from the middle of the nineteenth century, with the necessary increase in factories and industrial enterprises using child labour. Prior to this, child industrial labour seemed unremarkable and acceptable. However, by the 1850s and 1860s, state officials, provincial governors, the *zemstva,* industrialists, academicians, doctors, medical officers and social activists initiated a broad public discussion about the ills of child industrial labour. As elsewhere, the arguments made in favour of child labour by industrialists were that children were better off in factories than staying at homes or working in cottage industries and that their labour was essential to both their family's well-being and to Russia's industrial development. The Tsarist government commissioned reports and studies into factory working conditions for children. In 1845, it prohibited work between midnight and 6.00 am in Moscow factories for under-twelves. This was after an 1843 textile strike had revealed that many children were working eleven- or twelve-hour days at a time, both day and night.[123] In 1847, it was forbidden for children under fifteen to work more than an eight-hour day in state mines and metallurgical works. In 1859, a government review of working conditions in St Petersburg factories discovered that children were still working night shifts in some cotton mills, and were working fourteen-hour days in others. Violence against children in the workplace was normalized to a disturbing degree.

From the 1860s onwards, both public debate and legislative attempts to place limits on child labour in industry escalated. Reformers, as elsewhere, were concerned about the impact of work on children's health and morality. Medical studies of the impact of factory work played an important role. One report read:

> In cotton-spinning factories, children suffer from anaemia. The hands of children who clean machinery are irritated with a rash because of mineral oil. Children who work in preparatory shops suffer from soreness of the breathing canals and throat … [and are] dirty in the extreme, covered with some kind of odd lesions, and looked very exhausted.[124]

Campaigners were concerned about children's exposure to machinery, toxic chemicals, the heat and the noise, as well as their exposure to the adult working milieu, considered corrupting on many levels. Children, mainly boys, were working twelve-hour days, five and a half days a week. The state became concerned about the health of its future soldiers. State officials felt they had a paternal obligation to protect children, showing a shift in understandings of childhood and the state's relationship to the child. The belief that childhood, even for the poorest, did not belong in the world of work and that the child must be separated from the adult was starting to take hold of Russia's elites.

In 1874, the Commission for Technical Education of the Russian Technical Society carried out an inquiry into child labour. It found that 17.8 per cent of workers in enterprises surveyed were under eighteen years of age.[125] As in England and France, the highest concentration of child labour was in textile production, particularly in the cotton industry. Twenty-two per cent of the cotton industry labour force was aged between six and eighteen, helping with auxiliary work such as setting up bobbins, sorting, cleaning and working on carding and scotching machines.[126] The numbers may have been higher in the provinces.

A State Committee chaired by Count Pyotr Valuev, the Finance Minister, examined the Commission's recommendations; a maximum shift of six hours a day and three hours at night for children aged between twelve and fourteen years; limits of eight hours a day and four hours a night for fourteen- to seventeen-year-olds. Children under twelve should not work in factories and those under ten should not be apprenticed. Although special interests in the Committee watered down these proposals, the 1870s saw a further significant transformation in public attitudes towards child industrial labour. This was due to the activities of the growing broad social welfare reform movement in Russia, which devoted attention to the child in a myriad of settings.[127] Journals covered child industrial labour, denouncing its existence and abuses against children. After the Great Reforms independent professions and a print media had developed, which allowed a 'public opinion' to emerge, which united with paternalistic state employees to limit child industrial employment.

From the 1880s, proper restrictions were put on industrial child labour. In 1882, the Finance Ministry issued the first decisive act restricting the industrial employment of children, 'Regulations concerning the Hours and School Instruction of Young Persons Employed in Factories and Mills'. The regulations prohibited the employment of children under twelve in factories, plants and manufacturing establishments. The Ministry issued a list of thirty-six types of industry and work in which the employment of children under fifteen was also prohibited as injurious to health: certain textiles, oil refineries, mills that processed minerals, chemical plants that produced acids, paints and varnishes, spirit distilleries and slaughterhouses.[128] An eight-hour day (excluding rest periods) was fixed for twelve- to fifteen-year-olds, with no more than four hours to be worked without a break. Night work was prohibited, as well as work on Sundays and holidays. Further legislation in 1885 and 1886 prohibited night work for children under seventeen. This legislation was applied to all factories, private businesses equipped with steam colanders, steam or mechanical engines, machines and lathes and all establishments that had more than sixteen employees in European Russia. This covered 25,913 enterprises, with approximately 870,969 workers.[129] The regulations did not affect child labour in agriculture, domestic service or artisan or cottage industries. Another aspect to the legislation was that twelve- to fifteen-year-old workers who had not received any primary schooling were to be offered the chance to attend school for three hours a day, for up to eighteen hours a week. Factories were advised (though not compelled) to open schools on their premises. In 1884, Finance Minister Nikolai Bunge introduced a bill, 'Regulations concerning the School Instruction of Young Persons Employed in Factories or Mills, The Duration of their Labour and the Factory Inspectorate', which made education compulsory for young workers and tightened up the inspection regime. By 1899, there were 446 factory schools with 44,400 pupils.[130]

It has been argued that one of the motivations for legislation restricting child industrial labour was the economic slump of the late 1870s and early 1880s, which led to workers being laid off, rather than to a new sense of 'childhood'. There were also some later reversals. In 1890, under pressure from industrialists the government allowed twelve- to fifteen-year-olds to work on Sundays and increased shifts to six hours or sometimes nine, depending on the industry.[131] Yet on the other hand, in 1897 all legislation restricting child labour was extended to rural handicraft workshops.

Official statistics seemed to show a genuine and rapid drop in the number of children employed. Before 1884, 24 per cent of textile workers were children, but the figure was only 5.5 per cent a year later.[132] This shift was possibly connected to lay-offs due to the industrial recession as well as evasions and subterfuge but some of the reduction must have been genuine. In 1883, *maloletki* (those aged between twelve and fifteen years) had made up 10 per cent of the workforce, but this dropped to only 1.2 per cent by 1905.[133] By 1908, the most common age of entrance into factory work in Moscow province was between fifteen and seventeen years.[134] In 1913, only 1.6 per cent of industrial workers were children between the ages of twelve and fifteen and 8.9 per cent were adolescents between fifteen and seventeen years.[135] Working children were involved in the labour movement and participated in demonstrations and strikes. There were 'children's strikes' in St Petersburg's Novaya Cotton-Spinning Mill in 1878 and in the Kening Textile Mill and the Nevskii Cotton Mill in 1903.[136]

Family law in late imperial Russia

The Tsarist state upheld the patriarchal authority of males, both father and husband. Civil law placed both women and children as their dependents. Children inherited their legal status from their father and took their father's surname and patronymic.

Patriarchy was entwined with the estate society and Tsarism; challenges to patriarchy were seen as seditious attempts to limit the power of the autocracy. The hierarchical structure of imperial Russian society allowed for 'broad personal authority, unquestioning obedience, filial duty, paternalistic obligations and male preference'.[137] Children were subordinated to parental power. Parental power could only be terminated by the death of the parent, or by the deprivation of all rights of status, if children did not follow their parents into exile. The child was officially under the father's authority, and in his absence the mother's (or some other guardian). In reality in divorce cases towards the end of the Imperial period, judges increasingly gave mothers custody of children.

Some small steps were taken towards improving children's rights at the turn of the twentieth century. Attempts were made to enhance the rights of illegitimate children, who under the *Svod Zakonov*, had no legal recognition. In 1902, a law was passed that children of Christian denominations could be legitimized by their parents' subsequent marriage.[138] From 1909, minors (under seventeen) were supposed to be sent to special 'corrective and educational institutions'. The first juvenile court opened in Moscow in 1910.[139]

Conclusion: Childhoods at the end of imperial Russia

When a group of Russian university students in Moscow were recently asked to list terms they associated with Russia before the Revolution, the words that came up most frequently were 'ignorance', 'darkness' and 'illiteracy', 'giving a vivid idea of the semantic matrix that imposes the stereotypical image of Russia in the minds of the masses'.[140] In the final years of Tsarist Russia, educational opportunities for children were myriad, legion and yet restricted. The hierarchy of opportunity that shaped Russian children's lives was a strong conditioning factor on access to education. The chances of attending primary school as a child varied according to social estate, family economics, gender, ethnicity and location within the Russian Empire. In 1911, less than 21 per cent of eligible children attended primary school in half of the European Russian *guberniya*; only in Moscow, St Petersburg and Yaroslavl *guberniya* was there over 40 per cent attendance.[141]

In his opening address to the State Duma in 1906, Nicholas II included the expansion of public education as one of the state's priorities and responsibilities. That year the Ministry of Public Education drew up a plan for the implementation of universal primary education within a ten-year period. In 1908, the Third Duma (1907–12) passed an educational law on extending primary education. There was considerable progress in educational provision between 1900 and 1917: the number of schools rose seventeenfold and the number of pupils more than doubled.[142] Expenditure on education as a proportion of the regular state budget also doubled between 1900 and 1914.[143] In 1915 there were 80,801 state primary schools with 5,942,000 pupils, while the Russian Orthodox Church operated 34,000 parochial schools, with

1,900,000 pupils.[144] It seems that around 8 million children aged between eight and eleven years were receiving some form of official schooling. This was about half of the primary school–age cohort.[145] Around a third of pupils were girls.[146] In 1885 factory inspectors had reported that only 35 per cent of young workers were literate or semi-literate, but in 1918, 93.6 per cent of young workers aged between fifteen and nineteen years were reported to be literate.[147] Plans for a unified secondary school system, ending the system of the classical state *gymnazia*, remained unrealized until after the Revolution, although various vocational, craft, commercial and industrial schools had been added into the mix. There were only half a million pupils in secondary schools in Russia in 1914, although elsewhere in Europe secondary education was also reserved for the reproduction of elites.[148] School was a feature of more and more children's lives, but most schooling was irregular and incomplete and not the predominant experience required of childhood as a 'privileged state'; this would have to wait until the 1930s under Stalin. While the Tsarist regime hoped to use what education there was for children in Russia to produce loyal subjects in all estates, the Russian intelligentsia saw the education of children as vital to the political and social transformation of Russia. Criticisms of Russian authoritarianism were framed in the 'language of education'.[149]

The complex economic, social and cultural changes in Russia after the 1860s, which have been summarized as 'bourgeois modernization', transformed gentry childhoods, particularly those of girls.[150] The economic difficulties facing the gentry class after the abolition of serfdom meant that young gentry women needed to work outside the home when they reached maturity. Their education became a more important consideration. As there was less money for servants, gentry mothers took more of a direct role in child care and their children's education. Towards the end of the period, conscious (*ideinie*) gentry parents emerged, who embraced a self-reflective role and kept pregnancy and parenting diaries.[151] More equal relations, emotional closeness and shared daily life between generations replaced the earlier pattern of ritualistic daily meetings with parents. For gentry children in the last decades of Tsarism, early childhood at home was becoming about preparing for school. Mothers often taught their younger children until they were ready to go to the *pro-gymnaziam* at the age of ten or eleven. By the turn of the twentieth century, 60 per cent of gentry children attended schools outside the home.[152]

Childhood for elites is 'a period of preparation for an aspirational adulthood'. Gentry parents had been previously concerned with establishing their children's status in life.[153] Now more were concerned with the child's personality, as well as with the more traditional Russian concern with *vospitanie*. There was a new understanding of childhood as a special, unique and creative period of life, strengthened by developments in culture, science and welfare. The welfare of poor children in both town and countryside in Russia became an object of philanthropic and medical attention in the second half of the nineteenth century. A child-centred tradition in pedagogy, psychology, medicine and culture had taken hold. A wide array of philanthropic organizations focused on childcare education, summer nurseries, children's hospitals, milk stations and children's clinics, day shelters (*priuty*) and urban playgrounds. All of this was widely covered in the flourishing press, where Russian public opinion was formed.

This idea of childhood was still not universally applied to the majority of Russian children in the villages. At the beginning of the twentieth century, the Russian Empire had the highest infant mortality rate in Europe. As late as the 1890s, less than 50 per cent of children born in European Russia reached their fifth birthday.[154] In Moscow in 1912, 28 out of every 100 children died within the first year of life.[155] The causes of infant mortality were tightly woven with the entire social, political, economic and political structures of late imperial Russia. In 1904, the 9th Congress of the Pirogov Society adopted a resolution that 'since the principle reason for the abnormally high rate of children's mortality in Russia is the material insecurity and inadequate mental development of the population, this Congress expresses its deep conviction that the successful struggle against this evil is possible only on the basis of broad social reforms'.[156] Social reforms were not enough and instead a revolution would take place, which was intended to and eventually did change children's lives entirely.

4

Childhoods in Revolution, Civil War and austerity, 1917–29

The Soviet state claimed for itself the distinction of being the first state in the world that had made care for the lives and health of children its own legal obligation. *Sovnarkom*, the newly formed Council of People's Commissars, declared that 'concern for the child is the direct responsibility of the state'.[1] In the immediate post-revolutionary period, a panoply of institutions for and about children were established, often with the support and involvement of non-Bolshevik education and welfare specialists. These included experimental institutions and research stations on pedagogy, child psychology and physiology, as well as children's homes and other forms of welfare institutions for some of the millions of children who found themselves outside of family and kinship support networks.[2] Under the 'Palaces for the Children' policy, the new government turned estates and residences of the former nobility as well as monasteries into children's institutions.

The Bolshevik view was that modernity required the medicalization of childhood, involving not only a reduction in infant mortality and the elimination of diseases such as scarlet fever, diphtheria and cholera, but also the extension of state power over children's bodies. The state took responsibility for the health of the population and promised free healthcare, with special attention to children. Adult and child healthcare were separated from the beginning and by the late 1920s, the training of paediatricians had begun in medical universities.[3] Although the welfare state operated unevenly and took several decades to spread, public health initiatives radically altered Soviet childhood. The instillation of modern hygienic daily practices among children (hand-washing, individual towels, the use of separate beds and individual bedding) was seen as one of the first steps on the path to socialism. These kinds of practices were pushed heavily in preschool institutions, schools and through the Young Pioneer and Octobrist movements.

The 1920s saw attempts to promote an ideal of 'rational upbringing', with a model of an active, politically engaged and liberated child.[4] The new Soviet government wanted to destroy traditional rural beliefs and practices, including those of child rearing. They harnessed the energy of children themselves in campaigns against corporal punishment, superstition and religion and campaigns to promote hygiene and literacy. While some historians have noted that very little changed for Russia's children in everyday life during the 1920s, others have pointed to the creation of a generational group conscious of its own power and enthusiastically committed to the transition to the Bolshevik model of modernity.

Radical and progressive trends in pedagogy and child science begun in late imperial Russia continued into the 1920s. The Soviet state continued to support the discipline of pedology, through a multitude of research centres including Moscow's Central Pedological Institute (*Tsentral'nyi pedologicheskii institut*), the Moscow Experimental Institute of the Defective Child (*Eksperimental'nyi defektologicheskii institut*) and the Pedological Institute of the Bekhterev Psycho-Neurological Institute (*Psikho-Nevrologicheskii institut*) in Petrograd. The First All-Russian Congress of Pedology in December 1927 attracted almost 2,000 delegates.[5] This period of experimentation was brought to an end when Stalin consolidated his power in the 1930s.

Women's full emancipation from patriarchy required them to be freed from the private domestic sphere, including from responsibility for childcare. After the revolution, many Bolsheviks questioned how children could be liberated as well. It was assumed that the 'bourgeois' family was a *perezhitka*, a survival or vestige of an outmoded superstructure and would eventually wither away under communism. But what would its fate be now in the 'transitional' phase between capitalism and socialism?

Children as symbols were highly valued by the new Bolshevik state from the beginning. They were to take the Soviet state along the 'bright path' to the future and become the new person of the communist future. However, the first years of Bolshevik rule were ones of demographic, economic, social and personal catastrophe. The Civil War and its consequences of disease, displacement and famine proved devastating to Russia's children. Millions died prematurely, became orphaned or separated from their families, missed out on education, suffered from illness and poor health, bore the emotional and financial burden of supporting families in the absence of adults, became displaced as refugees inside Russia and in Europe, witnessed atrocities and fought as child soldiers. Around half a million children had been placed in various children's institutions by 1921, while millions more were homeless or left outside family groups. Alongside its transformative visions, the Bolshevik regime spent most of the 1920s dealing with the consequences of the Civil

War for children, their 'flowers of the future': homelessness and vagrancy, state poverty and family breakdown. At the same time, it used children to both enter and create modernity.

Marxism, Bolshevism and the family

Marx and Engels saw the family as part of the superstructure, a reflection of the current dominant economic and social relations, rather than an ahistorical entity.[6] They had attacked the bourgeois family in *The Communist Manifesto* (1848) – 'Abolition of the family! Even the most radical flare up at this infamous proposal of the Communists.'[7] In *The Communist Manifesto*, they wrote that children were exploited by their parents and that social education should replace home education. In *The Origins of the Family, Private Property and the State, in the light of the Researches of Lewis H. Morgan* (1884), Engels argued that the family had evolved into different forms through history and was a 'series in historic development'.[8] Under capitalism, both women and children were the property of adult males and private property supported the structure of masculine dominance. Marx and Engels were critical of the family life of the bourgeoisie, which they saw as characterized by hypocrisy, avarice and oppression. Despite bourgeois hypocrisy about the sanctity of the family, in capitalist societies proletarian children had been 'transformed into simple articles of commerce and instruments of labour'.[9]

Marx and Engels believed that there was the potential for genuine family love based on equality, once intimate relations were no longer corrupted by property ownership and poverty and exploitation had been eliminated. Marx saw the potential for a new kind of family being capable of effecting social and economic transformation, fostering sociability and a revolutionary consciousness.[10] This is the attitude that the Soviet leaders would adopt from the 1930s.

As far as children and childhood are concerned, in 1847 Engels wrote in *The Principles of Communism*, a draft programme for the Communist League, that after a proletarian revolution there would be 'education of all children, from the moment they can leave their mother's care, in national establishments at national cost. Children should be educated collectively by the nation and there should be social responsibility for all children.' He also wrote that there would be 'equal inheritance rights for children born in and out of wedlock'.[11] After the abolition of private property, illegitimacy would cease to carry any stigma. These measures would free children from dependence on their parents. The Bolsheviks fully embraced these socialist principles in the early years after the revolution, building also on the legacy of progressive legal thought in the last decades of Tsarism, outlined earlier.

In the early Soviet period, parents were targets of hostility by the new government and parent-child relationships were portrayed as exploitative. The *Komsomol*, the new youth organization founded in 1918, had the task of bringing generational struggle into Russia's towns and villages. In reality, the Bolsheviks did not have one coherent policy towards the family. More radical Bolsheviks such as Zlata Lilina, Alexandra Kollantai and Anatoly Lunacharsky called for the immediate destruction of the bourgeois family and the total monopoly of the state over childcare and education.[12] The 'nationalization' of children was promoted as a policy option, while Alexandra Kollantai suggested founding a state fund for raising children. Following Marx and Engels, Bolshevik theorists Nikolai Bukharin and Yevgeny Preobrazhenskii wrote in their *ABC of Communism* (1920) that while under capitalism children had been considered the property of their parents, under socialism they belonged to all of society and society had the right to educate them.[13] Zlata Lilina, a long-standing member of the Bolshevik Party who was in charge of school administration in the 1920s, notoriously said at a conference on education in 1918 that the Bolsheviks should 'rescue these children from the nefarious influence of family life. ... In other words, we must nationalise them. They will be taught the ABCs of Communism and later become true communists. Our task is now to oblige the mother to give her children to us – the Soviet state.'[14] Lunacharsky, who headed *Narkompros* (the Commissariat of Enlightenment) in the 1920s, was another to argue that Soviet children should be raised collectively. He wrote that 'there is no doubt that the terms "my parents", "our children" will gradually fall out of usage, being replaced by such conceptions as "old people", "adults", "children", and "infants"'.[15] Bolsheviks such as Aleksandr Goikhbarg suggested the founding of children's towns and settlements where children would be bought up collectively by experts away from the corrupting influences of their parents, in the best tradition of Catherine and Betskoi.[16] As we will see, this preference for collective upbringing diminished in the Stalinist period but resurfaced briefly and in more muted forms under Khrushchev in the late 1950s and early 1960s. It was always only a preference, delayed until the future communist state would have the resources to offer rational collective upbringing. The Soviet state was always too poor.

The Russian intelligentsia joined in this clamour for children's liberation. In 1918, the educational theorist Konstantin Ventsel published a draft Declaration of the Rights of the Child, a prototype of later UN Conventions, in which he proposed ideas on a child's right to material support and free development, as well as its right to be heard and have freedom from punishment.[17] In 1921, the physician Fedor Orlov-Skoromovsky wrote in his childhood memoir that 'the hour of the children's rebellion against their parents in every family has come. And this is not a frightful time: it is a wonderful long-awaited time.'[18] The older generation may not have found this as threatening as it was meant to be. Lev Kopelev's father regularly shouted at him for reading and believing in Bolshevik 'rubbish'. When Elena Bonner's little brother warned their grandmother that she could not tell him off as she was not a Party member, her grandmother merely replied to him: 'It looks as if now you'll not only stand in the corner, but get a spanking for those words.'[19]

Some revolutionary activists felt that the collapse of the family during the crisis years of 1917–21 was a positive development on the path to socialism. Others though saw that children are vulnerable in times of social and economic collapse. In the absence of a stable and wealthy state, they needed the protection of a family. The Bolshevik commitment to the collective upbringing of children was also challenged by contemporary medical experts who argued for the importance of the mother-child bond for survival in infancy and early childhood.[20] These debates would feed into developments in children's rights and family law during the 1920s and early 1930s. All Bolsheviks agreed that there would eventually be full state childcare, although much of the interest in childcare was about liberating women from responsibility for childcare so that they could fully enter the social and economic arena as equals to males, rather than a concern for children themselves.

There was general distrust of the family even among those who accepted it had a place in the transitional period, as exemplified by the statement from Alexander Slepkov, the editor of *Komsomol'skaya Pravda*:

The coordination of the family with the general organisation of Soviet life is the task of every Communist. … One must not shut oneself off in the family, but rather, grow out of the family shell into the new Socialist Society. The contemporary Soviet family is the springboard from which we leap into the future. Always seeking to carry the entire family over into the public organisations, always a more decisive overcoming of the elements of bourgeois family living – that is the difficult but important task which stands before us.[21]

The Russian Civil War

'A fiery mass moved across all Russia.'[22]

The revolutionary year of 1917 passed off without much direct violence in many parts of the Russian Empire, certainly in comparison to the years of Civil War that followed. This was not always the case, for example, in naval ports such as Kronstadt, Sevastopol and Stavropol. In the countryside, peasants began clearing out 'gentry nests' to start the long-awaited land distribution. A long period of intimate violence had begun for children from elite backgrounds. For many this only ended when they left Russia as refugees in 1920–1. Thousands of Russian children left at the end of the Civil War with the mass evacuations across the Black Sea to the Eastern Mediterranean region. Others left with family groups across the borders into neighbouring European states. In the 1920s, Russian émigré activists established a network of Russian national boarding schools across Europe for these children to be educated in. As well as providing an education, the aim was to preserve a cohesive generation loyal to Russia, who would one day return when the Bolsheviks had been overthrown and aid Russia's transformation into a modern democracy.[23] In 1924, the pupils in these schools were asked to write essays on what they had experienced in Russia between 1917 and 1921.[24] These writings were elicited by adults in a closed school setting in which the children occupied a very vulnerable position; many were orphaned or separated from their families, while others had families who could not care for them properly due to poverty. The context in which the work was produced (writing to 'please' the adult) is important; however, the essays provide a composite picture of elite children's lives during Civil War. They show the events and atmosphere of the revolution and Civil War in often unfamiliar ways, as perceived by a specific generational and social group.[25] Often rather than any particular political developments, these testimonies recall vividly for example the intense – and tense – emotional responses of the adults around them. Many liberal families shared in the general enthusiasm for the February Revolution, the abdication of Nicholas II and the promises of a new future for Russia; refugee pupils from these families recalled the joyful expressions, excited voices and high spirits of parents or older siblings in the early months of 1917. Cossack families and the families of Imperial Army Officers did not share the celebrations of the overthrow of the Romanov dynasty and the declaration of a Republic. Children from these families recalled a sudden mood of gloom and despair and their parents weeping in church when the Abdication Manifesto was read out. Other pupils, particularly from military families, were struck by the tension and anxiety in their homes caused by the shocking news of the collapse of the front and the desertion of soldiers from the Imperial Army.

Other shared recollections of the early stages of the revolution include meeting with the 'arrogance' of previously loyal servants or soldiers or the sudden display of hatred and resentment on the faces of local peasants in their estates or villages. Their testimonies bring the revolution into domestic and local spaces. These essays privilege the visual, spatial and performative aspects of the revolution; *gymnazia* teachers in red ribbons, the portraits of the Tsar being removed from the classrooms, posters and manifestos on city walls and fences, the sudden appearance of Kerensky's portrait in private and public spaces, and large crowds of working people taking over the streets. One particular vivid shared memory was that of soldiers hanging the medals or epaulettes that they had ripped from their officers onto the ears of dogs and horses and parading the animals around town.[26] Common aural memories were the public reading of the Tsar's Abdication Manifesto of 2 March 1917 in schools and churches across the Empire, the singing of revolutionary songs and then the beginnings of street battles, shooting and shouting on the streets outside as the year went on. Some older children joined in the celebrations over the February Revolution. One girl remembered how she and her friends made 'red flags' out of the pink pages of their school books.[27] Others wore red ribbons and sung revolutionary songs at public meetings. Many though were indifferent to events or unaware of what was happening, particularly in more remote areas.

The October Revolution, when the Bolshevik Party took over power from the Provisional Government in the name of the Soviets, was not such a public event as the February Revolution. Only children in Moscow and Petrograd experienced it in real time. Some recalled feeling intense curiosity, watching street fighting from city apartments in Moscow and Petrograd. One wrote candidly that 'as soon as the Bolsheviks came on the scene, I hated them intensely mainly because everything became very expensive and so I wasn't bought so many toys'.[28]

The Russian Civil War which broke out in early 1918 had a devastating impact. By the summer of 1917, there were already peasant attacks on country estates and the Imperial Army was collapsing, with deserters roaming the countryside. After the Bolshevik Revolution in October 1917, life became more precarious and the violence escalated into a full Civil War, which went on until early 1921. For many children and adolescents, particularly in areas such as Ukraine and Southern Russia, where the majority of the battles, atrocities and occupations took place, the war period 1918–21 was one of terror, hunger and loss. Food was rationed in the cities from summer 1918 and in short supply elsewhere. One boy, twelve years old in 1918, remembered the shock of being told for the first time by his mother that that was 'all there was'. He began an apprenticeship in a boot-making workshop in the hope of getting higher rations as a worker.[29] In January 1919, the Soviet government reintroduced the Tsarist wartime policy of *prodrazvyorstka*, the compulsory seizure of grain and later other agricultural produce from peasants to supply the Red Army and urban workers. Not only did this impact the health and well-being of children in rural areas, but it made little difference to the severe food shortages in the cities. Gentry families across provincial Russia were thrown off their estates by local peasants and Bolsheviks, while Decrees in April and August 1918 confiscated the property of urban private residences and real estate. One boy, who had been 12 in 1918, later wrote how 'we had to leave our own dear nest, in which all my early childhood had been lived. My heart was so full of sadness and bitterness. From that day began our family misfortune.'[30] Many elite families, particularly army families, fled to avoid repression and tried to move to non-Bolshevik areas in Ukraine and Southern Russia. At this point, families often split up. Adult males went into hiding or joined anti-Bolshevik military groups, while women, children and the elderly tried to either survive where they were or get to White-held areas. At other times, the marital relationship was prioritized and children were left in the care of other relatives while their parents tried to stay together. These family wanderings all around Russia in increasingly poor health and poverty were one of the most common memories of the Civil War period among this particular group; 'from that moment on [the confiscation of the estate] we began our wanderings', one girl wrote, 'and were never again to find shelter for ourselves'.[31]

Another of the most common experiences of the Civil War for those social groups in areas controlled by the Red Army – and therefore experienced mainly by women and girls – was the repeated searches of their homes by the new Soviet political police, the Cheka, revolutionary sailors and soldiers or local Bolsheviks (or simply thieves posing as such, as depicted in Mikhail Bulgakov's Civil War novel set in Kiev, *White Guard*). They were looking for hidden Imperial Army Officers, 'counter-revolutionaries', weapons and, more often than not, cash and valuables to take away. Children were interrogated about the whereabouts of their parents. In one family, all the children were trained to tell the local Bolsheviks that their father was a shoemaker.[32] At other times, their peasant nannies passed them off as their own children. The emotional dimension to this 'world turned upside down' is made emblematic by the girl who remembered above all the shock of seeing her father disguised as a peasant so he could escape incognito.

The vast majority of Russia's children had always worked to contribute to the family economy. They were now joined by children from previously well-off backgrounds. In the absence of adult males and in a situation of economic collapse and displacement many adolescents and even relatively young children worked for their family survival. They worked selling sunflower seeds or newspapers, in factories and workshops and in agriculture and trade.[33] Some later expressed pride in this expression of their own agency, as well as their ability to support their families at such a time. One boy remembered:

My father had to leave our home when the battles began in our small town and so a difficult task fell to me as the oldest son. My first duty was to protect my mother and my younger siblings who were in grave danger. Our house burned down and our whole family stood on the brink of disaster left on the streets in the freezing cold. Although I was still a minor and physically weak, in that difficult time I worked and worked and saved from destruction my beloved brothers and sisters and my old mother.[34]

One of the main historical debates within the history of childhood is how much agency children have. While some of the essays can be read as narratives of survival, in others there is little sense of agency. Many found it hard to express what had happened. In their writings, the metaphors and phrases used to describe the period 1917–21 portray a sense of powerlessness and helplessness; it was a noise, a wave, a storm, a fiery mass, a hurricane, a fire, a red serpent, a threatening storm cloud, Satan's red laughter.[35] However, many adults found the revolution ('the Catastrophe') impossible to work into a coherent narrative.

Older boys and adolescent males joined the various anti-Bolshevik armies, sometimes with older male relatives, at other times on their own initiative. As one wrote, 'I was torn from my school bench and without any military training was sent to the front.'[36] This became an increasingly demoralizing experience. Meanwhile in areas controlled by the Bolsheviks, current and potential Red Army soldiers were assured that their families would be looked after in the rear.[37] The call-up age was eighteen for the Red Army, but younger adolescents signed up. Workers were urged to fight to defend their children and protect them from a White victory.[38] Class war was evoked with young men being urged to sign up to destroy the 'landlords' sons' (*synky pomeshchikov*).[39]

During the Civil War, individuals were treated as part of a family collective and pursued and killed for their family links. The Red Terror was aimed at the 'bourgeoisie as a class'. As a response to peasant uprisings in the summer of 1921 in Tambov, the Bolsheviks established rudimentary concentration camps where family members of so-called 'bandits' were kept as hostages, including hundreds of infants and children.[40]

Even in the difficult early years of the Civil War, the Soviet state established an array of structures and institutions to protect children, at least on paper. Once the war was in full swing by the summer of 1918, nearly all resources were put into the rapidly growing Red Army. An Office for the Protection of Maternal and Infant Care (*Okhrana materinstva i mladenchestva, OMM*) was set up at the beginning of 1918. There was a strong continuity in personnel and approach with the maternal and infant welfare organizations of the late Imperial period and it focused on the health of mothers and babies and the provision of crèches for working women. In 1918 and 1919, the government issued several decrees that increased food rations for children and certain food products were prioritized for them.[41] Baby clinics in Moscow and St Petersburg distributed free milk from foreign aid organizations.

In January 1919, *Sovnarkom* created the Council for the Defence of Children (*Sovet zashchity detei*). This was staffed by representatives from the Commissariats of Enlightenment, Social Welfare, Health, Food Supply and Labour. This state body had the power to veto orders from other Commissariats, if those orders were considered to pose harm to children. Its main responsibility was to organize the supply of basic essentials to children as well as their evacuation from the starving cities into grain growing regions. In 1921, it was acknowledged that the Council had achieved very little. It was replaced by another body attached to the Central Committee of the Bolshevik Party; the Union-wide inter-agency Extraordinary Commission on the Improvement of Children's Life (*Chrezvychainaya kommissiya po uluchsheniyu zhizni detei pri VTsIK*). This body, which lasted until 1935, was known as the *Detkomissiya*, the Children's Commission. The *Detkomissiya* was instigated by Feliks Dzerzhinsky, then Head of the Cheka, the first Soviet state security organization tasked with fighting counter-revolution. This inaugurated the strong connection between the political police and children in the Soviet Union, which would be strengthened under Stalin in the 1930s.

The Board of the *Detkomissiya* consisted of representatives from the Commissariats of Food Supply, Enlightenment and Health; Trade Unions; and the Workers and Peasants Inspectorate.[42] Its remit was to take responsibility for children's material well-being and defend their interests. Its priority for a long time was the millions of homeless and abandoned children – products of the economic and social crises and the famine. It was also responsible for monitoring the growing number of children's institutions needed to cope with these crises. Widespread starvation in urban areas during the Civil War meant that even those families that had survived together often had to give up their children to state institutions. These institutions were plagued with issues that would persist over the next few decades; lack of food, fuel, basic inventory, clothing, medical supplies and experienced (or even caring) personnel. Children frequently ran away from them due to the atrocious conditions and ended up back on the street. At the beginning of its existence, the *Detkomissiya* admitted that as far as Russia's children were concerned, 'we are not discussing here any kind of "improvement", or the granting of particular benefits, but of saving lives'.[43]

The Bolsheviks attacked private philanthropy as bourgeois and gradually closed down Tsarist charitable organizations, many of whose patrons and staff had left Russia anyway during the Civil War. They did try, though, to harness social energy themselves and from the early 1920s began to carry out campaigns to mobilize support for children's well-being. The *Komsomol*, the *Zhenotdel*, the trade unions, workplaces and Red Army units were all supposed to help children; raising funds, helping with campaigns, organizing food kitchens and playgrounds and 'adopting' (*shefstvo*) and supplying children's institutions. The 'stimulation of public initiative had become an essential part of children's welfare policy'.[44] Week-long campaigns – 'Week of the Child', 'Sick and Homeless Children's Week', and 'Mother and Infant Protection Week' – were launched. For 'Week of the Child' for example, households were expected to donate bed frames, mattresses, bedding and clothes to families with children. The Children's Friend Society (*Obshchestvo Drug detei*), founded at the urging of the *Detkomissiya* at the end of 1923, had around one million members by 1926 and almost two million by 1931.[45] Its members across the Soviet Union raised funds for children's institutions, publicized issues of child welfare and tried to help homeless children and young people into education and work. Much 'public initiative' came from the top down. In the early 1930s the Soviet state ordered that military units, plants, factories and collective farms should formally attach themselves to schools and children's institutions in a system of patronage (*shefstvo*), guaranteeing to provide them with material support.

The 1921 famine and the *bezprizorniki*

In the summer of 1921, a severe drought affected the Volga region, the Northern Caucasus, Southern Ukraine and the Crimea resulting in a terrible famine, which eventually caused around 5 million deaths.[46] Estimated numbers of children living in the famine-affected areas range from 7.5 million to just under 10 million.[47] Now instead of sending children out of Russia's starving cities to the countryside, the state had to evacuate children out of rural areas. The 1921 famine became an international event. Herbert Hoover's American Relief Administration (ARA), the Save the Children Fund, Red Cross societies, Mennonite and Quaker organizations, among others, were allowed in to help with famine relief. Ten million children met the criteria for support from the American Relief Agency.[48] The state fed 1,500,000 children. The efforts of international organizations, who were also involved in helping Russian refugee children in Europe, formed a major contribution to the growing internationalization of child suffering and construction of children as 'deserving victims' at the beginning of the twentieth century.[49]

In October 1921, the representative of the *Detkomissiya* in the Tatar Republic, which was in the famine region, informed Moscow that of 1,304,425 children only 254,157 were getting any help with food from either the state or the ARA. He notified them that

the children's situation in the cantons is very difficult. Many children are nothing but skeletons, with yellow skin stretched over their stomachs which are swollen with dung, with sorrowful eyes and slumped shoulders, gathered around their exhausted mothers, who are barely alive. Everywhere emaciation has provided fertile ground for dangerous fevers, typhus is spreading, some terrible things are happening to the children. The little children are perishing – the flowers of life are perishing.[50]

By October 1921 only 307 primary schools out of 2, 256 were still functioning in the famine-affected Volga region provinces and districts of Simbirsk, Saratov, Serdobsk, Vyatka, Malmyzh and Iransk.[51] Not only did children die of hunger-related diseases in their villages due to the famine, but they were orphaned, abandoned by their families, given up to institutions or decided to strike out on their own in the hope of survival. Hundreds of thousands made their way to Russia's towns and cities. A Soviet journalist reported on the children he saw in the railway station at Ufa, a city in the Urals:

Their bodies are filthy; their faces deathly pale, skin and bones. In the rain and slush they sit and silently watch passers-by and travellers. The fortunate among them receive alms on rare occasions. On every street, wherever one turns, there are children starving, homeless, and even dying in the dirt and dampness.[52]

Urban areas such as markets and transport networks – railways and their stations, rivers and their harbours and wharves – became these children's habitus. Those who survived did so generally by banding together and forming criminal gangs, causing a major social problem for the new state. The largely urban phenomenon of masses of homeless and vagrant children, the famous *bezprizorniki* (also known as *bezprizornye*) has long been considered emblematic of children's fates after the revolution. They were very visible both to the Soviet authorities and to foreign observers throughout the 1920s. Most were boys from peasant families between the ages of ten and fourteen. At the end of 1923, 70 per cent of them in Moscow were from the Volga region, which had been at the heart of the famine.[53] Others came from urban families who would not, or could not, support them. Some had families, but preferred life on the streets.

In order to save lives the state had organized the evacuation of around 150,000 children out of rural areas, generally placing them with peasant families in non-famine regions.[54] Most peasant families resented having another mouth to feed and official reports detailed the physical and emotional abuse suffered by these children.[55] Many of these ran away, adding to the number of *bezprizorniki* on city streets. At their height, it was estimated that there were anything from 4 million to 7 million homeless children. The numbers dropped sharply in the second half of the 1920s, but rose again at the end of the decade as a result of the collectivization and dekulakization campaigns. Russian poverty, the appalling state of children's institutions and family breakdowns in the 1920s regularly provided new additions.

Narkompros set up reception centres (*priemniki*) for homeless children across the Soviet Union.[56] After being registered and assessed, children were placed in children's institutions if they could not be reunited with their families. The state wanted to rescue and rehabilitate these children. In the early Soviet period, children who had committed crimes were seen as victims of the capitalist past or the current economic and social collapse and offered the chance of rehabilitation. *Bezprizornost'* and crime were linked. Juvenile crime rates soared in the early 1920s. The most common crime committed was theft. Girls often resorted to prostitution; a survey in 1920 of 5,300 street girls up to the age of fifteen showed that 88 per cent had engaged in prostitution.[57] Studies of juvenile crime in the 1920s show that 60 to 70 per cent of apprehended children had lost one or both parents; the figure was highest among recidivists.[58]

The state security police, now called the OGPU, also set up communes and colonies for juvenile delinquents, many of who were *bezprizorniki*. There was a strong commitment to their transformation which was seen as emblematic of the Soviet revolutionary project of transformation. One well-known example of this was the Dzerzhinsky Labour Colony near Kharkov, established in 1928 and run by a teacher, Anton Makarenko (1868–1939). Earlier in 1920, Makarenko had been put in charge of a colony for juvenile delinquents in Ukraine, the Maxim Gorky Labour Colony, where he created what later became the 'dominant model for the Soviet pedagogical establishment'.[59] Makarenko later described the arrival of new colonists to the Dzerzhinsky Colony in his novel *Learning to Live*: *Flags on the Battlement*, highlighting this transformation:

> The boys' heads were shaved, they were bathed and put into uniforms. All their old clothes were burned, and an older colonist came to clear away the ashes. '"There go all your biographies!" he said to the nearest boy with a sly wink.'[60]

Makarenko rejected the progressive pedagogical theories about the 'liberated child' as well as the current sciences of child development propagated at the time. He believed that social environment was the major determinant of behaviour, external conditions are formative and personalities could be 'designed'.[61] Children's institutions should be run along disciplined lines with a strong collectivist ethos. Children's engagement and self-organization was encouraged, but they would be guided by adult role models. Makarenko would go on to become the leading

Soviet pedagogical expert under Stalin and in fact until the end of the Soviet Union, and he produced some of the classic texts of Stalinism.

While some Russians tried to see positive qualities of resilience and resourcefulness in the homeless children and praised their disdain for bourgeois morality, most saw them as a threat and had little sympathy for them. As Nick Baron writes, 'unchildish' children outside the family disrupt spatial and temporal notions of childhood.[62] The *bezprizorniki* were unchildish even in their appearance, wearing 'jackets obtained from some grown-up man or woman… reaching below the knee, with dangling sleeves'.[63] Although the numbers dropped in the second half of the 1920s, the *Detkomissiya* estimated that there were still around half a million *bezprizorniki* in children's homes and on the street in 1926.[64] There were still almost two and a half thousand children's homes at this time with around a quarter of a million children in them.[65] By the second half of the 1920s, a different approach both to juvenile crime and family breakdown was developing, one that sought to strengthen the role and responsibilities of the family. This would come to full fruition in the middle of the 1930s.

Children's lives in the 1920s

In 1921 after the final victory in the Civil War, the Soviet government introduced a series of liberalizing economic measures designed to help rebuild the Soviet economy and usher in a period of relative social peace between the Bolshevik state and the peasantry. The New Economic Policy (NEP) has been presented as a 'golden age' for Soviet Russia, but it was not necessarily so for children. The state dramatically reduced spending on social programmes and welfare, including on children's institutions. Budgeting was devolved to local authorities who often to Moscow's fury did not prioritize children's services, despite the child-centred rhetoric from the centre. Local authorities tended to abolish the 'open institutions' such as clinics and crèches, while preserving the children's homes and orphanages.[66] In 1923, local budgets were described by *OMM* officials as 'sliding towards the eighteenth century, the time of Peter the Great'.[67] Child poverty was one of the most serious issues to face the Soviet government in the 1920s.

The demobilization of 4 million Red Army soldiers, combined with the move to cost accounting in enterprises created high levels of female unemployment. Even though women formed a slightly smaller share of the waged labour force than men, they made up around 60 per cent of those registered as unemployed.[68] The government realized that this had a particularly negative impact on the children of single mothers, who were considered vulnerable to being enticed into crime. According to the 1926 Census, 11 to 12 per cent of children in urban areas lived in female-led households.[69] Cutbacks to state childcare made the position of working mothers harder. Due to lack of resources to tackle this challenge, the state focused on health education (*sanitarnoe proveshchenie*) to reduce infant and child mortality through organizations such as the *OMM*.[70]

In rural areas, where the majority of children lived, childhood may have continued much as before the revolution. The Soviet state tried to penetrate the Russian village through the local school. The village school made some progress in the spread of some of the basic habits and practices of modernity among children, especially in terms of hygiene and sanitation.[71] This may have given children a sense of power over their environment, a modern sense of self-awareness and agency. Children joined in the militant Bolshevik struggle with the old village world, but traditional ways and political literacy merged as well. A pupil's essay from 1926 revealed this as they wrote that 'I go to church just on Easter and on big holidays. We go together with our comrades, and we never go by ourselves.'[72] Children joined in local election campaigns, organized anti-religious exhibitions and literally and metaphorically forced windows open to let sunlight into the 'dark' huts. They were encouraged to set up 'children's corners' in their homes to oppose the 'red corner', where icons were usually placed in Russian homes. Partlett argues that they developed a sense of generational group identity (a 'new childhood identity') based on allegiance to the Soviet cause, castigating their opponents as 'dark'.[73] This generational solidarity was strengthened by participation in group activities in the village such as the anti-religious campaigns. It was this kind of outreach, rather than school itself, that could create a new modern identity based on a belief and mastery of the natural sciences and new daily practices.

Despite all the talk of sunlight in peasant huts and propaganda and enlightenment work by the Commissariat of Health and the *OMM*, infant and child mortality remained very high. The *OMM* reported that the infant mortality rate in the second half of the 1920s fell from approximately 280 deaths per 1,000 live births in 1913 to 129 in 1925 but this was in urban areas and the central regions.[74] A doctor who visited northeast Leningrad *oblast'* in 1925 reported to the *OMM* that only three out of twenty-five children could be classified as healthy in one town he had visited. In another area, only three out of nineteen babies born over the previous year had survived.[75] The campaigns for summer nurseries, which had started in the late Imperial period to look after peasant babies while their mothers worked in the fields, had to continue; in 1925 there were 1,853 summer nurseries, rising to 2,924 in 1926.[76] These must have taken in a small amount of the babies who needed care. Young girls were still spending their days looking after babies and spent more time with them than their own mothers, who worked too hard to look after their infants.

These young girls picked up childcare practices from their grandmothers as their mothers worked, and so the traditional three-generational pattern of childcare culture persisted. Apart from care from older siblings, children were largely left to their own devices. A woman born in 1925 remembered:

> In every home there were five or six children. In general, here in the village no one paid much mind … or gave the kind of attention to children as they do today. … Mother left for work and said, 'You need to sweep the floor, put some water there, look after the chicks.' That was it. Then she'd come home and feed us a meal and [returning to work] tell us not to leave the house.[77]

As far as rural child rearing was concerned there was 'a strong conservative bias that kept alive and powerfully reinforced the beliefs and practices of the past'.[78] It was not until the post–Second World War period that this chain of intergenerational female knowledge could be broken.

Children and education

After taking power, the Bolsheviks saw the creation of new schools with new teachers as a major priority in the transition to socialism and the creation of the 'new person'. The modernization of the education system, at least on paper, began soon after. In October 1918, a Decree on the Unified Labour School was issued. This inaugurated a comprehensive system of free compulsory co-educational, secular schooling for children aged eight to thirteen at primary level and then fourteen to seventeen at secondary level.[79] Under the revolutionary new regime, the role of the school was to transform society and raise an entirely new generation, rather than transmit a fixed body of knowledge and ensure social replication. The hierarchical power relations between teachers and children were to be dismantled through the encouragement of children's participation in school councils. Bolshevik educators and their supporters believed that children learn through experience, so the Soviet school was meant to be an educational commune linked closely with the surrounding world. Work ('socially useful labour') was to be part of a child's life at school as well as at home and in the community. The idea of productive work as an essential part of a child's education was derived from European thinkers such as Rousseau, as well as from Russian radicals and educational theorists such Nikolai Chernyshevsky, Lev Tolstoy, Konstantin Ushinsky and Pyotr Lesgaft. *Narkompros* officials in the 1920s were also influenced by European and American progressive educational theorists including John Dewey, Georg

Kerschensteiner and Maria Montessori. In 1919, *Narkompros* set up a series of Experimental Stations of model schools using these new methodologies. The educational theorist and activist Stanislav Shatskii (1878–1934) ran the First Experimental Station in Kaluga. This consisted of sixteen primary schools, one secondary school, a central school colony and six kindergartens.[80] Shatsky promoted the development of the individual personality through collectives, and adopted the approach favoured by Rousseau, believing that childhood should be valued for itself rather than viewed as a stage in the preparation for adulthood. Creativity, music, exploration, discussions and game playing were encouraged. Children's agency was celebrated and as well as co-running the school, they were to transform village life. 'Socially useful work' outside school could include encouraging literacy and organizing libraries, running fire safety courses as well as carrying out studies of local socio-economic life. Children's institutions were to spread messages of hygiene as part of the medicalization of childhood and establish new practices, which 'emphasized the child's entry into a new space structured by "scientific" norms'.[81] A new consciousness was to be shaped through the prism of science and health and the site of this transformation was to be the school.

There was to be no central curriculum and all homework, assessments and exams were abolished. Punishment, both mental and physical, was banned. The prohibition of all forms of punishment for children was a long-held tradition of the Russian intelligentsia and was embraced in full by the Soviet state. Nadezhda Krupskaya wrote:

> It must be made clear that every person who beats a child is a partisan of the old slave faith, a partisan of the old slave views, a partisan of power of the landlords and capitalists, although they might not even be conscious of it.[82]

Physical aggression towards children by adults continued of course, although it may have become more taboo. Soviet Displaced Persons who spent time in Germany during and after the Second World War expressed surprise at how normal the physical punishment of children was over there.[83] Political education, usually initially through songs, anniversary celebrations and stories, was inserted at all levels of children's education.

The chosen pedagogical approach of *Narkompros* in the schools of the 1920s was the so-called 'Complex method'. Learning was structured around the three themes of nature, labour and society, rather than trapped in individual academic subjects. The Marxist dimension to this approach was the belief that by 'linking abstract knowledge to concrete objects, children would begin to see the power of the active, educated mind in altering the environment'.[84] The implementation of the 'Complex method' was not a success, as most school teachers were either 'holdovers' from the Tsarist period or had received little formal training and found it confusing or simply ignored it. Parents and teachers combined to successfully resist the imposition of radical methods of pedagogy in the 1920s.[85] By the middle of the decade, voices calling for children's education to focus on the acquisition of literacy, numeracy and other basic skills became louder. Lesson plans, approved textbooks, testing and finally a core curriculum were introduced. This was a shift back to the Lockean idea of the child as blank slate or empty vessel, rather than as autonomous co-creator of the world. By the late 1920s a reorientation of educational policy was underway, moving from placing children in the natural and social world to placing them in the political and industrial world. A comparison between themes suggested in primary school textbooks across the decade illustrates this:

1922–1923: winter outside; winter evening; discussions; what we said about the work of a man; collecting mushrooms; in the sun.

1927–28: our river; Lenin; industry of our region; summer work; war; our agricultural soviet.[86]

Shatsky now wrote that there was no 'liberated child, there is just a child, who reflects all the possible educational influences of his environment'.[87]

Alongside the extension and reform of primary education, the 1920s saw the foundation of what would become the key social movement for children and eventually almost the embodiment of Soviet childhood, the All-Union Pioneer Organisation in the name of V. I. Lenin (*Vsesoyuznaya pionerskaya organizatsiya imeni V.I. Lenina*). The Young Pioneers was established in 1922 for children between the ages of ten and fourteen. It was led throughout the Soviet period by the *Komsomol*, the Communist Youth Movement for those between fourteen and twenty-five years of age. At its inception, it was a relatively small organization, with several hundred thousand members. In 1940 it was 14 million strong and embedded within the mass education network.[88] By the late Soviet period, it included in its membership almost the entire age cohort. Although highly politicized from the outset, it also incorporated the activities and approaches from other children's organizations, particularly the Scouts, whose movement in Russia it supplanted. The Pioneer movement placed a strong emphasis on the formation of character (the all-important *vospitanie*) and on outdoor activities, embracing the post-Enlightenment understanding of the bond between the child and nature.

Symbolism and ritual was important from the beginning, with the red kerchief as the ultimate signifier. The Pioneer oaths and commandments changed in emphasis over the Soviet period, reflecting the changing pressures on children and understandings of what childhood involved. The examples from the 1920s foreground the revolutionary child-as-agent:

> I, a Young Pioneer of the USSR, do solemnly swear, in the presence of my comrades, that I will staunchly support the cause of the working class in its battle for the liberation of labouring people all over the world, and for the construction of socialist society, that I will honourably and unwaveringly follow the commands of Il'ich and the laws of the Young Pioneers.[89]

1 The Pioneer is faithful to the cause of the working class.

2 The Pioneer is the youngest brother and helper of the *Komsomoltsy* and communists.

3 The Pioneer is a comrade of Pioneers and workers' children worldwide.

4 The Pioneer loves labour.

5 The Pioneer is honest and truthful (his word is like granite).

6 The Pioneer is healthy, robust and never falls in spirit.

7 The Pioneer strives for knowledge. Knowledge and ability are strength in the struggle for the workers' cause.

8 The Pioneer carries out his duties quickly and accurately.[90]

Desirable Pioneer habits included time-management, self-discipline and resourcefulness, abilities and characteristics that remained constant throughout the Soviet period. The Pioneer movement helped dissolve the binary distinction between work and play. A movement for younger children was founded in 1923, the Octobrist (*Oktyabryata*) movement, when the children born in 1917 began to start school. As the Pioneers were led by the Komsomol, the Octobrists were led by the Pioneers. Their symbol was a red five-pointed badge with a picture of Lenin as a young boy. The role of the Pioneer and Komsomol movements in directing children's 'self-organization' was also strengthened towards the end of the decade.

By 1927, 65 to 70 per cent of children were attending some primary school, which was clearly an improvement on the pre-revolutionary period.[91] However, only about 10 per cent of children went on from primary to secondary school.[92] A school census of 1926 showed that working-class and peasant children still rarely progressed beyond primary level.[93] The secondary school had barely changed; *Narkompros* complained that 'the dead hand of the classical *gymnazium*' still had the Soviet school in its grasp.[94] Peasant girls were still least likely to go to school. There was mass absenteeism on religious holidays and only 15 per cent of primary school–aged children had joined the Pioneers.[95]

Family law in the early Soviet period

Many Bolsheviks and other Russian radicals saw age differences as sources of inequality. They sought the abolition of private parental rights and the equalizing of the rights of all children regardless of the circumstances of their birth. Like Marx and Engels, the Bolsheviks believed that 'the rights of the children had to be proclaimed, because their parents were exploiting them'.[96] A revolutionary new Code of Laws on Acts of Civil Status, Marriage, Family and Guardianship Law was passed in September 1918, building on an earlier Decree issued in December 1917. The new Code's main author, the legal scholar Aleksandr Goikhbarg, was the Head of the Bureau for Law Codification. Goikhbarg was one of those radicals who had expressed the hope that the family would quickly wither away, and had encouraged parents to reject their 'narrow and irrational love for their children'.[97] The Code introduced radical changes in children's legal status as well as for women, on whom the historiographical focus has been.

While Tsarist law had upheld patriarchy, under the new Code men and women had equal rights. Either could be the head of a household, and parental authority was to be exercised conjointly; children no longer belonged legally to their fathers. Children did not have to take their father's name, patronymic or his nationality. In the event of parental separation, children could live with either parent and consensual agreements were encouraged. Where separating parents could not agree on issues of children's upbringing, local courts could decide what was in the best interests of the child. Parents were legally obliged to ensure their children received an education and training and protect their personal rights. Parents could be deprived of their rights by the courts and forbidden to have contact with their children if contact was deemed not in the child's best interests.

One of the most significant clauses of the new Code, as far as children are concerned, was the abolition of the legal distinction between legitimate and illegitimate children, which had been earlier decreed in December 1917. This distinction, along with inheritance, had been seen by socialists as one of the major underpinnings of private property. The Code stated instead that 'actual descent is regarded as the basis of the family, without any difference between relationships established by legal or religious marriage or outside marriage'.[98] This revolutionary step would be reversed in 1944 when illegitimacy was reinstated as a legal category. This was to encourage men and women to have sexual relations, without fear of any financial consequences if a child resulted and so increase the birth rate. The 1944 reinstatement of the distinction between legitimate and illegitimate children was widely unpopular in Soviet society, and was in the main reversed in the 1960s.

In the early decades, the new Soviet legal system was universally supportive of women, married and unmarried, who pursued the fathers of their children for the financial support to which the children were legally entitled. A legal process was established for the ascription of paternity by unmarried women. A man identified as a father under Soviet law became financially responsible for child support. Judges in paternity cases in the 1920s generally took the assumption that the mother was ascribing paternity truthfully, even in the absence of substantial evidence. It was felt that the child's right to paternal protection and financial support was the most important right at stake.[99] A 1925 survey of 300 cases in the Moscow courts showed that awards for child support were granted in 99 per cent of the cases brought.[100] Actually enforcing the award was another matter altogether. Many men evaded the law by moving around or changing jobs, although some non-payments were due to genuine poverty rather than a malicious withholding of child support. That would have made little difference to the child concerned though. The 1918 Code also abolished child labour first for under-fourteens and then for under-sixteens.

Russia's traditional rural socio-economic conditions complicated the establishment of children's rights. In the early Soviet decades, the majority of Russians were peasants engaged in non-waged labour in subsistence agriculture on family farms. All property was held in common by the household. The 1917 revolution had not changed these conditions; in many ways, it strengthened them, as the peasants confiscated and redistributed among themselves land not only from the gentry class but also from peasants who had split off from the commune and bought land privately after the Emancipation in 1861. There were more small peasant family farms than ever. The indivisibility of the peasant household was reaffirmed by the new Soviet Land Code of 1922, which stated that 'the property of the *dvor* cannot be awarded in payment for the share of an individual *dvor* member or given out by them for their personal needs'.[101] How then was a mother to realistically get child support payment from a child's father, if she left the *dvor*? In 1923, the Commissariats of Land and Justice affirmed that a child had the right to support from the *dvor* if the personal means of an individual peasant (usually the father) was not sufficient. If a mother did leave the *dvor* with her children, she could win an entitlement to some share in land, property, livestock and financial support, if she had participated in the *dvor* for six years. However, the enforcement of these awards was even harder than in urban areas and the issue of poverty even greater. Most

Russian peasant families had nothing to share. Sometimes judges awarded payments in kind. Many peasant men asked instead for custody of their child; one wonders if this was to avoid monetary payments and gain another working hand.

The Land Code also undermined the abolition of the distinction between legitimate and illegitimate children, as only children of married parents had claims to common household property. It also seemed to preserve traditional patriarchal values, as children had rights to a share in a *dvor* by birth, but no automatic rights to share in the property of another *dvor* should their mother remarry and enter one with them.[102] This was adjusted in 1925 by the Commissariat of Land who decided that children gained automatic rights when entering a new *dvor*. At the same time, the Supreme Court ruled that a parent who left the *dvor* with children was entitled to take the children's shares with them.

The new 1918 Family Code also abolished adoption. This has been viewed as another revolutionary attempt to destroy the family but it was at least partially motivated by a desire to end the economic exploitation of children that was considered inherent in adoption. Legal adoption was gradually reintroduced later in the 1920s but was never pushed as a serious state policy until the aftermath of the Second World War when there were multitudes of orphaned, abandoned and displaced children. In April 1918, inheritance was abolished in the RFSFR, with the estate of the deceased passing to the state apart from property (farmhouse, furniture, wages) worth under 10,000 roubles: 'Children have no rights to the property of their parents, or parents to that of their children.' There was a retreat from this quite soon. In 1922, direct descendants could inherit up to 10,000 gold roubles and by the middle of the 1930s, personal inheritance had become acceptable again as the state increasingly incentivized society with material rewards.[103]

The Soviet state saw children as both active agents and in need of protection. While measures were taken to assert children's rights to material support, protection and education as well as their legal equality, some commentators considered that the new family laws were making children (along with their mothers) vulnerable in the period of transition to socialism. Article 81 of the 1918 Family Code allowed divorce by mutual consent or by the desire of one party, if a judge approved this. Immediately divorce became affordable, accessible and unopposable. As a result, Russia had the highest divorce rate in Europe in the 1920s, with one divorce for every seven marriages in the European part of the USSR in 1926; in urban areas, it was one divorce for every 3.5 marriages.[104] Some Soviet jurists worried that children were the victims of high rates of marital breakdown, at a time of widespread poverty and unemployment when the state was too weak to step in and protect them.

In 1918, the age of criminal responsibility was raised to eighteen although it was reduced back to sixteen in the RSFSR in 1922. A *Sovnarkom* Decree in January 1918 abolished prison sentences and court trials for minors. Commissions on the Affairs of Minors (*Komissiya dlya nesovershennoletnikh*) were established instead. These bodies consisted of a medical doctor and representatives from *Narkompros* and the Commissariats of Justice and Social Welfare. There were around 275 Commissions operating in the RSFSR by the middle of the 1920s, half of the number that had been envisaged.[105] Rehabilitation – 'medico-pedagogical'– work was prioritized over punishment, although in March 1920 *Sovnarkom* ordered that over-fourteens could be transferred to normal courts if Commissions felt that was more appropriate. Despite high ideals, the Soviet state did not have the resources to offer rehabilitation to all the children who fell into crime, above all the street children. Between 1922 and 1924 the Commissions dealt with 145,052 cases of juvenile crime.[106] The most common action taken was a verbal reprimand. They have been described as 'a great bureaucratic revolving door, taking in thousands of *bezprizorniki*, processing their vital statistics, and spewing them back onto the street'.[107]

Bezprizornost', juvenile crime and family breakdown were viewed as interlinked in the early Soviet period. Goldman argues that it was the problem of homeless children more than any other factor that was responsible for the eventual shift to a more conservative family policy in the 1930s.[108] In the second half of the 1920s, this social issue was viewed as a product of family breakdown or dysfunction, rather than of famine. From this point, the Soviet state began making it clear that 'the family' – and its legal definition was broadening – had also to take responsibility for the child, not only the state. This was partly a matter of resources; the family brings children up for 'free' for the state. State funds should go in support of single mothers to keep their children with them, rather than on mass institutions, child support payments should be enforced, and parents who abandoned their children should be fined or forced to take them back.

Fostering and guardianship now began to be promoted as viable alternatives to mass institutionalization. Stringent conditions were drawn up for rural fostering; the child should be 'psychologically disposed' to agricultural work, be literate and healthy.[109] Peasant families seeking to foster a child had to demonstrate that they were not only looking for an extra worker. As well as other financial and tax advantages, the state gave foster families additional land, which was to become the child's share when it reached maturity. Only a small minority of children in need of care were fostered in this period and despite the detailed regulations little actual monitoring was ever done. A total of 52,000 children in the Russian Republic were transferred to foster families in 1923–24.[110] In 1926, adoption was re-legalized and peasant families were again encouraged with tax breaks, financial benefits and extra land allowances to adopt a child.[111]

The belief that changes since the revolution had benefitted adult males at the expense of women and children influenced the new Code on Marriage, the Family and Guardianship introduced in the RSFSR in 1926.[112] Dmitrii Kursky, the Prosecutor-General of the RSFSR and the Code's author, wanted to strengthen the support given to children and their mothers by recognizing in law de facto marriages and the rights thereby derived from it. Family responsibilities were increased and mutual rights based on consanguinity were strengthened. The new Code made clear that parents were obliged to support their children financially until they came of age and 'prepare them for socially useful activity'.[113] The Code still asserted that 'parental rights are to be enacted exclusively in the interests of children, and if they are not so enacted the courts may deprive parents of their rights'.[114] Guardians were appointed to represent the interests of children under 14 if their parents were unable or unwilling to represent their interests.

Parents deprived of rights for cruel treatment or failing to fulfil their duties still had financial responsibility for their children. Older siblings and grandparents were also made legally responsible for the support of minors, if parents could not or would not care for children. Step-parents also had legal responsibility to provide for minors if they had been doing so before the death of the natural parent or if the natural parents were now unable to do so. As noted above, adoption was re-legalized if it was in the best interests of the child, but the adoptive family had limited rights.[115] Adopted children still had rights to inheritance from their birth family and could keep their patronymic and surname if they wished. The adoption had to take place with the consent of any living parents who had been actively responsible in their children's lives and had not been deprived of parental rights. Children above the age of ten had to give their consent to an adoption. Adoption did not excuse the biological father of the child from paying for maintenance. On the other hand, undermining attempts to protect children, obtaining a divorce was made even easier, becoming essentially an administrative process that could be carried out without the knowledge or consent of the other party.

Under Article 158 of the Criminal Code, malicious or wilful refusal to pay child support entailed criminal responsibility. It was punishable by six months in prison or a fine of 300 roubles.[116] The equivalent value of any property inherited from someone who bore legal responsibility for minors had to go towards the support of the child. The welfare and the interests of the child were meant to be paramount in all decisions. Paternity continued to be forcefully ascribed, with courts willing to formally charge one male, even if the claimant had multiple sexual partners at the time of conception. It was a criminal offence for someone liable for child support to withhold a change of address, employment or earnings from the authorities. In June 1927, the Soviet government came up with a three-year plan to tackle *bezprizornost'*, including giving more support to single mothers, increasing labour training for adolescents and the encouragement of foster care and adoption rather than the development of further children's institutions. In 1928, the NKVD instructed local authorities to tighten up the enforcement of regulations on child support.[117] This was 'an early administrative attempt to emphasize family responsibilities'.[118] All this presaged the shift back to a focus on the family's responsibility for children, an approach that became dominant in the 1930s and beyond.

Children's culture

The 1920s have been seen as a Golden Age for Russian children's literature. In 1924 a Central Committee Resolution announced a commitment to developing children's literature according to the principles of class-consciousness, internationalism and education through labour. These socialist themes though were often applied in a playful way. Many of Russia's most important modernist writers and illustrators worked in children's literature, producing works of great creativity.[119] Writers such as Evgeny Shvartz, Vitali Bianchi, Aleksander Vvedenskii, Daniil Kharms, Vladimir Mayakovsky and Yuri Olesha all wrote imaginative and creative works for children. Many worked for the *Raduga* publishing house with Samuil Marshak and Kornei Chukhovsky, two of the most important Soviet children's writers who would go on to dominate the official Soviet culture for children in the 1930s and beyond. In the relatively relaxed period of NEP, not all works had to be entirely political, although popular themes in children's literature in the 1920s included narratives of the lives of children in Tsarist Russia, the revolution and the Civil War. The Soviet child hero (increasingly identified as a Pioneer) made an appearance at this time in adventure stories set in the revolution and Civil War. Stories about the *bezprizorniki* and their rehabilitation, such as Grigory Belykh and Leonid Panteleev's 1926 novel *Respublika ShKID* and Nikolai Aseev's *Sen'ka bezprizornik* enjoyed massive popularity.[120]

The 1920s also saw attacks from the centre on traditional folk tales and fairy stories, which were considered un-Marxist, with their structuring around magic, fate, miracles and hierarchy. There was an attempt to control children's reading, with libraries viewed as 'pedagogical institutions'.[121] In 1918, *Narkompros* set up a Children's Cinema Section in the Department of Secondary Education. In 1919, the 8th Party Congress announced that cinema was to be a key tool of extracurricular education and propaganda. A survey of

3,000 children (aged between eight and nine years) in 1924 revealed that 41 per cent had visited the cinema four times or more a month.[122] A proper children's cinema did not become a reality until the 1930s, along with much other phenomena of the childhood of 'privilege'. There was an ambiguous attitude to the cinema and children's viewing was monitored and controlled; separating the child and the cinema was one of the Soviet regulatory obsessions. Radio broadcasts for children began in 1925.[123] The Soviet children's press began in the 1920s as well, with the founding of children's journals and magazines, the most important for schoolchildren being *Pionerskaya Pravda*.

Conclusion

Despite the hopes for a revolution in children's lives, in many ways life carried on as it had done for the majority of Russian children, with poverty as the major factor structuring their lives. Infant and child mortality remained high, school attendance was patchy, and there was little separation from the world of adults. In the 1920s, the Soviet state did not have the resources to transform education. Higher education and adult literacy was prioritized during NEP. Many schools barely functioned, while others carried on teaching as they had before the revolution. Experimentation was always marginal. Compulsory, free and comprehensive schooling did not become a reality until the 1930s. In the late 1920s, only 16.2 per cent of urban preschoolers attended any kind of official childcare institution, while only a miniscule 1.25 per cent of rural children did.[124] Most children until the age of seven or eight were looked after by relatives, siblings, or neighbours in the communal apartments, or accompanied their mothers to work or were left to look after themselves.

By 1920, a basic organizational framework had emerged to look after vulnerable children without family care that lasted until the end of the Soviet period. Children aged up to three were the remit of the Commissariat/Ministry of Health, while the leading role for those over three was given to *Narkompros* as the state wanted to provide not just social care for them but also education and *vospitanie*.[125] In the 1930s though the NKVD emerged as a competitor, operating 'a parallel secret social policy'.[126] The 1930s would see many other changes in Soviet children's lives as well as a modification to ideas about childhood, as the Stalinist regime launched the Soviet Union into a period of unprecedented social, economic and cultural change. No social group was unaffected by this, including children, who were an important social group in the state's modernization goals.

5

Stalinism and the making of Soviet childhood

It has been suggested that the changes in attitude towards children in late imperial Russia were more significant than those across the Soviet period, at least after the initial fervour of the early revolutionary years. After Stalin took control of the direction of the Soviet Union in the late 1920s, children were re-imagined as passive, grateful and detached from political engagement, in a way that was more similar to the Western model.[1] The model of childhood shifted from the liberated, powerful and revolutionary child of the 1920s to a model characterized by dependence, obedience and gratitude. This is best exemplified in the famous slogan introduced in the 1930s, 'Thank you Stalin for our Happy Childhood!' After Stalin consolidated power, the paternalistic state expanded and began extending more control over all its subjects; children were no exception. At the same time, Soviet pedagogy retreated from experimentation and the idea of the 'liberated child'. The new approach led to the canonization of Anton Makarenko as the 'All-Union Teacher', who emphasized discipline and hierarchy with adults in the *Komsomol*, school or home given responsibility for organizing the child's world. Official culture for children under Stalin also became more conservative to meet the new conventions of the doctrine of socialist realism, which was decreed from the centre after 1934; the 'Golden Age' of creativity in children's literature was over.

There have been a challenges or modifications to this model of a passive and dependent childhood introduced from the 1930s. Some historians have suggested that the ideal of the revolutionary, active child persisted all through the Stalinist years and beyond. Olga Kucherenko and Lisa Kirschenbaum have argued that the Soviet state sought to empower children and young people to serve in the revolutionary cause. Children and adolescents were still expected to play important roles in social, political, economic and cultural transformation.[2] Julie DeGraffenried has argued that the challenge to the experience of childhood of the Great Patriotic War (1941–5) ruptured a passive, dependent and grateful model of childhood. Children had to be fully mobilized in the war effort, which put an unprecedented strain on all social groups.[3] While dominant Soviet pedagogues like Makarenko emphasized the imposition of discipline and hierarchy in children's everyday lives and practices, they also viewed children as having the potential to be responsible and independent, serious and committed.[4] The balance between power and dependence is a complex one. During the Cultural Revolution in China, Mao and the Chinese Communist Party evoked in the 'liberated' and militarized children emotions of gratitude and deference that they would be expected to feel towards older family members. Children and young people dared rebel against their parents as another even higher authority had given their permission.[5]

Historians have also differed on their interpretation of the role and function of the family unit in Soviet society and children's place from the 1930s. Family structures had been put under enormous pressure as a result of the First World War, the Russian Revolution, the Civil War and famine. In the 1930s and 1940s they were subjected to further pressure due to collectivization and dekulakization, terror, population displacements and the Great Patriotic War. Research on Soviet childhood has often focused on children in institutions, partly because the Bolshevik Party and the Soviet state had an ideological, albeit shifting, commitment to institutions. At certain times, the state claimed that institutions were the best places in which children should grow up, against all the evidence of its own reporting mechanisms. Access to significant archival sources is another reason why there has been a focus on children's institutions. An impression can be gained that a significant percentage of Soviet children therefore spent time in institutions, when in fact it was always only a small minority. Most children grew up in some form of family unit, however shattered and truncated. Soviet childhood in the early decades was usually spent within 'fragile, female-dominated family structures' – fragile but families nonetheless.[6] A leading Russian demographic historian has noted that

> despite all of the tragic events and the demographic catastrophe of the 1930s … the traditional attitude to the family continued to rule in society. The family continued to exist and even to strengthen, taking in the overwhelming majority of the population in family relationships and ties.[7]

After its earlier hostility towards the family in the revolutionary period and the 1920s, the Soviet state began to consider the family as the basic 'cell' at the foundation of Soviet society, an attitude that continued until the end of the Soviet Union. This was in keeping with Marx's theories that a new form of family could act as a promoter of genuine transformation. From the middle of the 1930s, one of the major functions of the family became the correct upbringing of children, something the state had considered it incapable of performing earlier. The Soviet state's shift towards supporting the family was a part of the so-called Great Retreat that began in the mid-1930s, when the regime adopted increasingly conservative social and cultural policies in an attempt to gain support from what was still a largely peasant population. The rationale behind the Great Retreat was seemingly an attempt at mobilizing the Soviet population for what was predicted to be a fast-approaching military confrontation with capitalism.[8] The Party presented it differently, declaring in 1934 at the 17th Party Congress – the 'Congress of Victors' – that the transition period was completed and socialism had now been implemented in the Soviet Union. As a part of this, a new socialist family had developed which could now contribute to the appropriate raising of children, supported by the necessary levels of surveillance, control, reward and punishment.

Was the Soviet family a private refuge from a totalitarian state or a place of generational conflict? Catriona Kelly suggests that parents saw their relationship with their children as part of a private emotional sphere.[9] Others have argued that in this period children's private and domestic lives were different to their highly disciplined public lives in Soviet schools and youth movements. Just like Soviet adults, they had perfected 'the art of dissimulation and hypocrisy'.[10] Donald Raleigh's study of the generation born immediately after the Great Patriotic War suggests that children's attitudes and identities were fundamentally shaped within the family.[11] In one view then, the integrity of the family survived the assault by the state. The totalizing claims of the Soviet state certainly fell short in reality.

Others though have claimed that Soviet socialization institutions or 'disciplinary organizations' such as the Soviet school, the Pioneer movement and the official culture for children had a greater influence on them than their family and were thus more constitutive of a 'Soviet childhood'. Children's culture has frequently been singled out as an especially strong force on children and childhood in the Soviet Union. In the 1930s, as the Soviet state began to monopolize all cultural life and impose strict censorship, an official children's culture was created – books, journals, films, radio broadcasts, supported by 'an elaborate superstructure consisting of writers, illustrators, critics, librarians, psychologists, school methodologists, publishers and other professionals'.[12] This culture was key to identity formation for Soviet children long past the Stalinist period. Many Soviet children lived in family structures in which all adults usually worked long hours outside the home. This suggests that the overall influence of the family on Soviet children can perhaps be described as 'thin'. Olga Kucherenko argues that the first fully 'Soviet' generational cohort – consisting of those who were born after the Revolution and completed all their education in the 1930s – strongly identified with the Soviet project. They had absorbed and internalized the lessons of Soviet patriotism. She cites the regime's ability to mobilize children and adolescents during the Great Patriotic War as evidence of this. This generational cohort had a strong sense of a shared social identity, identifying as 'nashi' (our lot).[13] Is it possible that the family ties broken by the series of upheavals between 1914 and 1932 were replaced by loyalty to the Soviet state?

The state certainly intended that the Soviet school would be a 'second home', backed up by mass participation in the Pioneer movement and official after-school cultural and sporting activities. Many remember it that way. A former pupil at an elite school in 1930s Moscow said, 'We all loved our school, it played a colossal role in our life. We spent our days and evenings [there]. Our parents worked, so the school brought us up.'[14] Despite the state's intentions, though, for many children it was the street – or rather the spaces between urban apartment blocks, where they spent most of their time outside school in the company of their peers – that was the major socializing influence on their lives. A common collective memory of mid-century Soviet childhood is that they grew up in these spaces, not the school and youth organizations – 'Dvor nas vospital' ('We were raised by the yard'). This free play had an element of spontaneity and was outside the control of the state and its values of rational play and cultured behaviour. One woman who grew up in Leningrad in the 1930s recalled,

> The yard did not like children of the intelligentsia; they were noticeable because of their clean clothes, were envied for their 'arabic balls' [rubber balls] and bicycles, but most of all they were disliked for their inability to adapt to life and they were nicknamed 'gogochek' ... . This was the most humiliated clique in the schools of the 1930s.[15]

Soviet authorities tried to regulate and control the dvor, giving house committees of apartment blocks or local Komsomol groups the task of turning it into a space for rational play. Pioneer Palaces and clubs were increasingly organized in which children could attend a range of cultural, educational and sporting activities outside of school. Yet it remained a private space in many ways. In her memoir of growing up in the 1940s, Ludmila Petrushevskaya described the courtyard as 'that little corner of earth where, to the music of streetcars and accordion, every Saturday the mystery of passing from childhood into youth took place'.[16]

The transformation of the Soviet Union: The 'Revolution from Above'

As soon as Stalin consolidated his power at the end of the 1920s, the Politburo launched the entwined processes of forced industrialization and the collectivization of agriculture causing fundamental changes in Russian social, economic and cultural life. This was accompanied by attempts to create a new Soviet elite, as well as renewed attacks on 'vestiges' of the old way of life. This involved further criticism of the supposed traditional Russian 'patriarchal family' in the village as well as efforts to harness children's excitement and enthusiasm for the technological progress of the first Five Year Plan of 1928–32.

The official children's culture focused on the Five Year Plans for the industrialization of the Soviet Union, celebrating the wonders of science and technology. The ambitious plans for an unprecedented pace of economic development were lauded for their romance and excitement and described as more fantastical than a novel by Jules Verne. 'Give to the Five Year Plan!' urged Gleb Krzhizhanovsky, the director of *Gosplan*, the State Planning Committee, at the first All-Union Meeting of Young Pioneers in 1929.[17] Children now played such games as *Dneprostroi*, *Kolkhoz* and *Pyatiletka*.[18] Science and technology were deployed in children's literature to create the image of the USSR as a modernist utopia.[19] Samuil Marshak's 1931 poem War with the Dnieper (*Voina s Dneprom*) is a classic example: 'Man said to the Dnepr/I shall block you with a wall/So that/Falling/From the heights/The conquered/ Water/Will quickly/ Move machines/And push/Trains.'[20]

Probably the most emblematic children's book of the first Five Year Plan period was Mikhail Il'in's *The Story of the Great Plan* (*Rasskaz na velikom plane*) which was published in 1930.[21] This book celebrates man's mastery over nature, the narrative of Soviet industrialization, and presents feats of transformation through the application of science and technology. Children were told that they also had the power of transformation and were important actors in the process. The book suggested ways in which children themselves could contribute to the Plan – for example, by collecting scrap metal and donating them to industries. As Lisa Kirschenbaum notes, 'The joys of childhood were grafted to the aims of a regime bent on rapid industrialisation.'[22]

The Soviet Union was creating a future-oriented society, which held out the promise of dramatic advances for future generations, against a backdrop of chaos and poverty in the present. The rapid nature of Soviet industrialization and the urbanization associated in the 1930s with it created a housing crisis, as well as deterioration in living standards and nutrition. The *komunal'ka* (communal apartment), where several families lived together in the large pre-revolutionary flats previously belonging to the Russian elites, each with some allocated living space but sharing kitchen and bathroom facilities, was becoming the exemplar of Soviet urban living arrangements. Communal apartments could be stressful to live in for adults, particularly for women who were still responsible for domestic labour and were more likely to come into conflict with other residents. Children seem to have enjoyed these living arrangements more, as the communal apartment held the promise of sociability. Until the 1950s, many families lived in makeshift settlements, dormitories or barracks, where the approved dividing line between the child and adult world could not easily be drawn. Bolshevik educator Zlata Lilina condemned the atmosphere in factory barracks, where children were exposed to swearing, domestic violence, alcoholism and sexual behaviour.[23]

The industrialization drive meant an enormous increase in women taking up waged labour outside the home. Between 1928 and 1937 an additional 6.6 million women entered into employment in the industrial and service sector.[24] Despite the rhetoric about women's emancipation from domestic slavery, state funding prioritized capital investment and the promised crèches and childcare facilities did not materialize on anything like the necessary scale. By the end of the first Five Year Plan in 1932, only around 8 or 9 per cent of preschool children were attending a formal Soviet childcare institution.[25] The state now had a new concern alongside *bezprizornost'*: the phenomenon of *beznadornost'*, or the lack of supervision over children, who now usually had both parents working long hours outside the home. It was feared that unsupervised children would visit the 'wrong' places – cinemas, markets or on the street – causing mischief and being vulnerable to exploitation by adults, when they should be in after-school activities. One thirteen-year-old who had been picked up by the authorities had told them, 'My father works as a janitor. Where? I don't know. He is never home and I mostly hang out in the streets or in the bazaar. I don't study or work. I rob apartments.'[26] From 1931, harsher measures were taken to get children off the streets and, as will be discussed below, 'deviant' children were put back under the control of the criminal justice system and taken away from the remit of social welfare or education.

Interviews carried out in the United States in the 1950s with Soviet citizens who had been displaced during the Second World War and had chosen not to return home seemed to reveal a picture of working-class and peasant Soviet family life as chaotic and best characterized by benign neglect. In a continuation of the agricultural model discussed earlier, total physical independence for children from a very young age was expected and encouraged. A young worker from a peasant background was critical of his sister's approach to her children: 'They were as free as the wind, always running around and she sat at home while they were outside. They were barefoot and only clad in a little shirt. In the wintertime they ran about undressed.'[27]

For the minority of children whose parents made up the Soviet elite, living conditions were far less austere and even luxurious in comparison with many of their peers. They had their own bedrooms in large modern apartments in prestigious city centre buildings reserved for Party workers; access to state dachas and vacation houses for holidays and weekends; trips to the Crimea; passes to the theatre, opera and ballet; music and dance lessons; private tutors and a series of nannies and *domrabotnitsy* at home.[28] Soviet elite families also encouraged early physical and emotional independence. Both parents usually worked and additionally spent what free time they had studying or engaged in political and social activism. Most of these families had a live-in 'worker' who ran the household and looked after the children. These women were officially categorized as *domrabotnitsy* (house/domestic worker). *Domrabotnitsy* were typically peasant women from the countryside who had been displaced by collectivization and dekulakization and escaped to the cities. In 1939 there were 372,488 registered *domrabotnitsy* in the RSFSR.[29] These women can be considered as a conduit for peasant culture, bringing village socio-cultural norms, religious beliefs and rural practices into the lives of urban Soviet children. After a complaint from her daughter's school, a woman discovered that their *domrabotnitsa* had been discussing religion with her. After a standard anti-religious lesson, her daughter had apparently stood up, crossed herself, pointed at the teacher and declared, 'Lord forgive her, for she knows not what she does.'[30] Another woman remembered how her urban family was horrified when she greeted assembled guests for a birthday celebration in their apartment with a mangling of a peasant phrase that she had learnt from her *domrabotnitsa* – 'Be as healthy as a cow and happy as a pig!'[31]

Children's culture in the Stalinist period

The 1930s saw the real development of an influential state-controlled Soviet culture for children, which played a determining role in identity formation and childhood experiences for several decades. Soviet cultural products for children constantly asserted the superiority of the Soviet system to the contemporary capitalist one, as well as to the past of Tsarist Russia. Schooling in the Tsarist period was presented as violent and soul-destroying, and *gymanzium* teachers as little more than police spies.[32] Life for the majority of Russia's children before the Revolution was portrayed as one of poverty, exploitation and endless hard work. The children's press was full of stories of the deprived lives of working-class children in capitalist states, and compared them to the privileged life that Soviet children were enjoying. Children's films such as *Torn Shoes* (*Rvanie bashmaki*) (1933) and *Karl Brunner* (1935) presented the miserable lives of workers' children in contemporary Germany. Samuil Marshak's popular *Mister Tvister* (1933) is an inventive children's satirical poem about a racist American capitalist who is horrified to discover socialist ideals of equality when he visits the Soviet Union with his spoilt daughter. A man who had grown up in the 1930s recalled:

There were no doubts. I was proud of my country! I learned from newspapers, films, in Pioneer Camps that the conditions were abysmal abroad ... that the bourgeoisie oppressed the poor there. ... I wouldn't even imagine that they could live better than us, in the Soviet Union.[33]

The state manufactured a branch of the Stalin cult for children. Pioneer songs were written about him:

We heard the name of the leader in our cradles
From the mouths of our loving mothers
From our fathers' shoulders we have seen
The friend of happy children![34]

Public images of Stalin with children had mass circulation. State propaganda depicted Stalin as smiling, paternal and protective, and described him with the words 'kind' or 'affectionate' (laskovo).[35] The photo of Stalin being embraced by seven-year-old Gelya Markisova at a Kremlin reception is one of the visual icons of the Stalin era. First published in Pravda in 1936, it was widely displayed in Soviet spaces for children: kindergartens, schools and Pioneer camps. Like the ubiquitous slogan 'Thank you Stalin for our Happy Childhood!', the image has been used as a counterpoint to present opposing memories and understandings of childhood in the Stalin era. 'For years the portrait of Stalin with the smiling little girl Gelya in his arms was everywhere we looked. It was hung in virtually all kindergartens and symbolised a happy childhood,' wrote one woman in her contribution to a 1991 collection on the Gulag, before going on to describe her own actual childhood of 'sorrow and fear' growing up in a dekulakized family.[36] Children were expected to respond to the cult by writing to Stalin and thanking him for his gift of a 'happy childhood'. This encouraged practice could be subverted. In 1937, a twelve-year-old peasant girl wrote to Stalin to describe how her unhappy childhood of undernourishment and deprivation prevented her attending school as she believed he would wish her to. In her letter, she deployed all the stock Soviet phrases about a 'happy childhood' to persuade him to intervene personally in her circumstances.[37]

It was literature more than any other art form that was at the centre of Soviet children's culture. It outlined and developed a moral code, based on courage, bravery and sacrifice.[38] Soviet children's literature has been described as designed to trap children in a 'network of signs and meanings, from which there is no escape. In this network, they can easily be revealed, identified, and, ultimately, controlled and normalized.'[39] In September 1933, the Central Committee established a central publishing house for children, known as Detgiz in an extension of control over children's culture.[40] In the first six months, it published almost 8 million copies of 168 books. Its first chief editor was Samuil Marshak. The writer Maxim Gorky argued that children's literature should 'promote the development of interest in art and knowledge among children ... familiarize them with the old reality destroyed by their fathers and with the new reality that will be built for them by their parents. ... We also need cheerful, funny books that help to instil a sense of humour in children. Pre-schoolers need simple yet artistically developed poems that serve to provide a foundation for games.'[41] The children's poet Agnia Barto claimed that children's literature should be 'amusing in form, but serious in content'.[42]

Most public libraries contained only approved curriculum literature for children.[43] State-approved reading lists consisted of a mixture of pre-revolutionary Russian, Soviet and foreign classics. The latter were often the same authors – Jules Verne, Thomas Mayne Reid and Fenimore Cooper – who had been popular with children and adolescents before the Revolution, including the young Lenin and Vladimir Nabokov. A 1930 list of books considered suitable for twelve-year-olds recommended a memoir of Lenin by one of his sisters, Panteleev and Belykh's *bezprizornik* classic *The Republic of ShKhid*, and works by the canonical pre-revolutionary writers Alexander Pushkin, Mikhail Lermontov, Anton Chekhov and Lev Tolstoy. In addition to these Russian/Soviet classics were children's editions of *Gulliver's Travels* and *Don Quixote*; slightly older children read Emile Zola and Jack London.[44]

Both Soviet and pre-revolutionary literature was taught in schools through the examination of character, revealing the continued centrality of *vospitanie* to understandings of childhood. In Soviet children's culture, children were encouraged to identify with positive heroes prepared to sacrifice themselves or show extraordinary heroism and bravery. One example of a Soviet positive hero is Sasha Grigoriev, a boy who grows up to be an Arctic pilot. Sasha was the main character in the 1940s adventure novel *The Two Captains* (*Dva kapitana*) by Veniamin Kaverin. Awarded the Stalin Prize in 1946, it was reissued forty-two times over the next twenty-five years and made into a film in 1955 and then again in 1976. Sasha's motto was, 'To strive, to seek, to find and not to yield.' Other examples include Mustafa in the 1931 film *Road to Life* (*Putevka v zhizn'*), Nikolai Ekk's classic, which focused on the attempts to transform the *bezprizorniki*, and the young boy Malchish-Kibalchish in Arkady Gaidar's 1935 *Tale of the Military Secret* (*Skazka o voennoi taine*), who is prepared to die rather than betray the Red Army to the bourgeoisie. Another favourite was the eponymous Misha Korol'kov in Sergei Mikhalkov's 1938 novella about a Pioneer boy from Sakhalin who is caught by Japanese fascists while onboard a Soviet ship in the Pacific. Misha refuses to surrender his red Pioneer scarf or to submit to their interrogations. Elena Krevsky writes that 'the secrets and mysteries of the so-called Bolshevik soul or Bolshevik subjectivity' lie in Soviet children's stories.[45]

The 1930s spy mania permeated official children's culture in books, in books such as Lev Kassil's 1938 book *Uncle Tolya, the Spycatcher* (*Dyadya Kolya, Mukholov*) and Grigory Adamov's *The Mystery of the Two Oceans*

(*Taina dvukh okeanov,*1939) as well as in films made by *Soyuzdet'film* such as *The High Award* (*Vyskoya nagrada*) (1939) and *The Patriot* (*Patriot*) (1939). The children's press was heavily politicized in terms of domestic enemies as well. The state included children into the sphere of political terror. 'We know how to punish our enemies!' was a headline in *Pionerskaya Pravda* during the so-called Shakhty Affair, the 1927 show trial of fifty-three leading mining engineers who were accused of deliberately sabotaging the Soviet economy.[46] During the Great Terror at the end of the 1930s, letters from children were published in *Pionerskaya Pravda* demanding the death sentences for 'vile murderers, traitors and spies'.[47] One man remembered:

> I admired Stalin extremely and when he conducted the trials against the older communists, Bukharin and so on, I was happy about it and even did the following thing. I had an album with portraits of communist leaders. As soon as one leader was tried and shot, I took the photo out of the album, nailed it on the door and shot this photo myself.[48]

Yuri Orlov, the physicist and human rights activist, wrote how as a school pupil he had scratched out or spat on pictures in his textbooks of the leading Bolsheviks accused of treason in the Moscow Show Trials.[49]

This period saw the proper beginning of Soviet children's cinema. In 1936, the first studio in the world dedicated to producing children's films, *Soyuzdetfil'm*, was established in Moscow. Children's film became more important in identity formation in the post-war decades. At the same time, the state rehabilitated fairy stories and folktales as genres appropriate for Soviet children. Meanwhile, the expanding periodical press for children presented a construct of the richness and benefits on offer for this Soviet childhood of privilege. It highlighted the child-centred activities provided by the state, taught children about Russia's history and literature, focused on current Soviet scientific and technological achievements and celebrated the geography and landscapes of the Soviet Union.

Due to the increasingly tense international situation in the 1930s, the Soviet regime shifted emphasis from revolutionary internationalism and the class struggle to patriotism and the 'defence of the Motherland'. As part of this, children were encouraged to interact with the vast physical spaces of the Soviet Union through reading articles in the children's press about the folklore, ethnography and history of all the Republics, pen pals, geography lessons in school and Pioneer trips and tourism. Those who crossed, measured and transformed Soviet space on air, sea and land – pilots, sailors, geologists and explorers – were promoted by the state as children's heroes.

The Soviet children's press re-affirmed the values of what was being taught in schools and in the Pioneer movement, and what was instilled through children's literature and films. It formed part of the closed system in which the state tried to manufacture and capture Soviet childhood. Key children's texts circulated between different media. For example, Valentin Kataev's 1945 book *Son of the Regiment* (*Syn polka*), which describes the fate of an orphan boy who attaches himself to a Russian artillery regiment in the Great Patriotic War, was made into a film by *Soyuzdetfilm* in 1946, before being embedded in the school curriculum. Between 1940 and 1941 the Soviet children's all-time classic *Timur and His Team (Timur i ego komanda)* was first made into a film, the script of which was published in the children's periodical press and also performed on Moscow Radio. Finally, it was published as a standalone book and added to the school curriculum.

The author of *Timur and His Team* was Arkady Gaidar (1904–41). Gadair produced two of the archetypal texts of Soviet children's literature: *The Tale of the Military Secret* (1935) and *Timur and His Team*. Gaidar's real name was Arkady Golikov. He had joined the Bolshevik Party in 1918 and became a Red Army commander at the age of sixteen. In addition to fighting the White forces during the Civil War, he was involved in the suppression of peasant uprisings and was temporarily expelled from the Party for 'harsh treatment of prisoners'.[50] He was discharged in 1924 due to injury and became a journalist and writer. After the German invasion in June 1941, Gaidar went to the front as a journalist for *Komsomol'skaya Pravda* but was killed in October that year fighting alongside Soviet partisans. His own complex and violent biography was in his works; he wrote in his diary, 'I dreamed of people I had killed as a child'.[51] Gaidar's books focused on bravery and sacrifice. In the *Tale of the Military Secret*, the young boy Kibalchish refuses to give away the Red Army's 'military secret' to the Chief Bourgeois even under torture. In *Timur and His Team* (1940–1), the titular character and his friends form a group devoted to secretly doing good deeds in their local communities. The Timur phenomenon had an enormous impact on schoolchildren who began forming similar groups, beginning what became known as the Timurivite movement (*Timurovtsy*). This movement was mobilized during the Great Patriotic War into helping the families of Red Army soldiers in the rear. A follow-up, *Timur's Oath* (*Klyatva Timura*), was published in the press from July 1941 and a film version was released in October 1942.

Childhood within the family

In the Russian family, you had the authority of the father. In the Soviet family, you have the authority of the Party.[52]

Based on interviews with Soviet Displaced Persons who chose not to return to the Soviet Union after the Second World War, the American sociologist Geiger drew a picture of a frequently tense family situation in the pre-war Soviet Union. The parent-child relationship was 'colored, occasionally dominated by their differences'.[53] One of his interviewees recalled:

> I was corrected at home, but I still believed what they told me in school. I believed that my father was old, and did not know about living conditions, that he was bourgeois and did not like the Soviet regime. I believed that everything was good, everything was correct in the regime.[54]

In interviews conducted by the American historian Larry Holmes in the 1990s, former pupils of one of Moscow's elite schools still identified themselves as having been part of an 'exceptional generation' inspired by the Revolution and the Civil War and fully in support of Soviet socialism. One former pupil remembered:

> Propaganda gave meaning to our lives. For us, the tsarist sky was grey; the socialist blue. We believed in communism. We wanted to become warriors for the world revolution. We were all convinced communists.[55]

Another who grew up in the 1930s recalled:

> We believed in Stalin, loved him and thought that the enemies, hidden or obvious, were in reality trying to topple Soviet power, give away factories and plants to the capitalists, return the land to the landlords and the kulaks. We hated our enemies, without really knowing who they were, believed everything that was said about them.[56]

Parents and children argued over the merits of the regime and debated about religious belief. Some families adopted the tactics of accommodation, or outward compliance – agreeing to speak openly only to each other, while presenting a united front to the outside world. Parents sometimes encouraged their children to fit in to Soviet society and take advantage of the opportunities presented to the enthusiastic. There were differences in opinion within generations. Women may have been more religious:

> My mother kept icons in the house and frequently prayed. My father always told her she should not make her children cripples. He said she should let her children be like everybody else, not handicap them by making them religious.[57]
>
> My mother was religious. She had icons. ... Father had pictures – of Stalin, Karl Marx, Engels, Voroshilov, Budenny.[58]

One remembered how as a boy, to tease his religious aunt, he had covered over the family icon with a picture of Stalin.[59]

The portrait of Pavlik Morozov, the Pioneer 'boy hero' supposedly murdered by his family in 1932 for informing on his father's anti-Soviet actions, hung in Soviet schools until the 1980s.[60] How common were cases of children denouncing their parents? In December 1940, *Pionerskaya Pravda* covered the story of a boy from Smolensk who had reported his father to the authorities for 'anti-Soviet' behaviour, in this case drunkenness and theft from state enterprises.[61] Such stories were meant to remind children (and their parents) that the interests of the state and the Motherland were meant to come above all else. Children were also likely inadvertently to get family members into trouble, perhaps more than betraying or denouncing them.

Although a leading role in raising children now belonged to the Soviet school and the Pioneer movement, the family was still seen as the basic 'cell' of Soviet society and responsible for its children. Soviet families were given strict normative guidelines on raising children. Makarenko broadcast *Lectures to Parents* on the radio in 1937 informing listeners how children should be treated in the new Soviet society: no patriarchy, no violence, no ultimatums, but instead firm guidance into the life of Soviet collectives. He also published *The Collective Family: A Handbook for Russian Parents* in 1937. Marxism taught that individuals do not become social beings on their own autonomously, but through support. In the posthumously published *A Book for Parents* (*Lektsia dlya roditelei*), which was based on Makarenko's articles and radio broadcasts, he repeated that the family should act as a collective in which parents prepare their children for Soviet life. Makarenko recommended consistency, discipline, orderliness, and duty and high expectations in parental approaches to children, but also love, care and mutual respect and affection. The Soviet family was not a place for extreme emotions.

Had a child-centred family arrived in the Soviet Union in the 1930s, with the 'priceless child' at its heart? One woman born into a peasant family in the Urals in 1936 recalled about her childhood:

> There were no (close) relationships between any of the fathers and the children. … It wasn't customary for fathers to have warm personal relations. … I had no sense at all my parents were 'bringing me up', whether from my father's side or my mother's. I don't think it was characteristic of that social stratum at all.[62]

Research suggests that changes in child rearing and the spread of the modern model of childhood only reached rural Russia after the Great Patriotic War. In more remote areas, this process did not happen until the 1960s and 1970s.

Traditional practices held out against the advances of Soviet-style modernity, and new mothers continued to learn about child rearing primarily from older women. Infants continued to be raised from birth with the same practices as generations had been raised before them, with the use of the *soska*, swaddling and the hanging crib. One of his interviewees who had been a child in the 1930s told Ransel that, back then, 'I was uneducated. Until aged 10, I was brought up to believe in devils, unclean powers, witches, and such.'[63] Some women did self-consciously change; one of his interviewees recalled how in the late 1930s she chose to give birth in a maternity hospital rather than at home with a village midwife. 'I was already Soviet' she told him.[64]

For some Soviet urban families, family life had become the central focus of concern. Geiger drew on the account of a nurse, married to a university lecturer, 'Because we had a dearly-loved only child, we lived and worked for him. He was the main aim of our life. My husband and I wanted to make him a decent, honest and diligent man.'[65]

The collectivization of agriculture and the destruction of the Soviet 'Kulak'

At the end of the 1920s, the Soviet regime decided to push for the all-out collectivization of agriculture and impose its economic, political and social control on the peasantry, who still formed the majority of the population. Collectivization was accompanied by a ferocious attack on peasants labelled as 'kulaks', or rich peasants. These were supposedly opposed to the Soviet regime and exploiters of the rest of the village. They were not only forbidden to join the new collective farms but were often forcibly exiled from their homes and regions. The whole peasant household was targeted in the dekulakization drive, which bought extreme violence and distress across the Soviet Union and affected the lives of millions.

In January 1930, the Politburo issued the Resolution 'On Measures for the Liquidation of Kulak Households in Districts of Wholesale Collectivisation'. This divided 'kulak' families into three groups, with quotas for numbers in each group. The first group, Category 1, was designated as 'counter-revolutionaries'. The adult male was to be immediately arrested and then imprisoned or executed and their families were to be exiled. Those in Category 2 were to be exiled as a family to Northern Russia, Siberia, the Urals or Kazakhstan. Families placed in Category 3 were allowed to stay in their home regions but were not allowed to join the collective farms. All the property and inventory of these families was to be seized and redistributed to the collective farm – that is, to their previous neighbours. This Resolution was put into immediate effect. Those who suffered through dekulakization as children later recalled how these measures played out in real life. They, indeed, were attacked as a family unit, had their property confiscated and were expelled from their homes – a traumatic process which sometimes took several weeks.

> Mama cried, papa also cried, and we children all cried. Papa said 'What will I feed the children? How will I plough? … They took our last cow. We all cried, we shouted, milk was the only thing we had been living on … Then they drove us from our house.'[66]
>
> In 1932 my family was living in Belorussia. … We had two horses, one cow, two pigs, and our own land for ploughing. We planted rye and everything we needed to eat. My father took care of the whole family, and took the extra produce to the market. We led a peaceful life. Then they summoned my father to the village and asked him to join the collective farm. He refused. So they arrested him. … They took our horses for the collective farm, and when our food ran out my mother took me to Kharkov and left me at a railway station there. After that I was picked up and sent via a child receiver-distributor to the Kalinin Children's Home in Pavlovsk, Voronezh Province.[67]

Between 1930 and 1931, approximately 1.8 million peasants of all ages were forced out of their homes mainly in Ukraine, southern Russia and the North Caucasus and sent into exile under the new category of 'special settlers' (*spetspereselentsy*).[68] Based on demographic data around 40 per cent of *spetspereselentsy* were under the age of sixteen.[69] The representative of the *Detkomissiya* in the Urals estimated that there were around 56, 000 under-sixteens among those exiled to his region.[70] Children and their families spent weeks travelling in unheated cattle cars only to arrive in remote makeshift camps without any infrastructure or supplies. Some of these settlements had to be built from scratch by those exiled themselves. One remembered of her girlhood in such a place, 'You began to wonder if you were cattle or a human being … no-one needed you to be alive.'[71] Another recalled:

> In 1930, they took my father here in Novosibirsk when I was in the second grade. His old mother was with us, that is, with my sister and me. They sent us off alone on a barge. It was very dirty. They were sending me to Narym where my mother was. They gave my sister to someone here in Novosibirsk to be a nanny. It was terribly painful to be separated from everyone and going alone to mama. People died along the way. They threw their corpses off the barge into the woods along the banks. That's what they did to the children's bodies, too.[72]

Veniamin Makarovich Kurchenkov was deported with his family to Narym in Siberia in the spring of 1931 and later described the experience:

> Finding ourselves in the marshy taiga without a roof over our heads, among vast swarms of mosquitoes, people were in hellish conditions (*katorzhnykh usloviiakh*). We ate a sort of gruel with a tiny bit of flour, and grass, green shoots, and on that we had to lug wood, build huts. ... People began dying in droves. Most families had a lot of children, and it was the children who first began suffering terribly. Their mothers were tormented too, as they were not strong enough to save their children. Entire families perished.[73]

Kurchenkov himself lost over half of the members of his family and ended up being placed in a children's institution.

Other victims of dekulakization were housed in appalling conditions in towns in former monasteries or barracks while the adult males with them were sent away for forced labour. Mothers and other concerned onlookers wrote to Moscow pleading for some mitigation of the living conditions of the children with them. To strengthen their appeal they used the language of the regime, with its rhetoric on the importance of children and the special role that the younger generation would eventually play in the building of communism. 'Children should not answer for their parents and perish as a class,' wrote one group of special settlers to the Soviet president Mikhail Kalinin.[74] 'We are fighting for a healthy generation, for the future builders of socialism, yet at the same time we are throwing living children into the grave,' wrote others to him.[75] The letters emphasized the innocence and potential of childhood.

A medical director responsible for *spetspereselentsy* in Omsk, Siberia, wrote to Moscow that 'there is no milk, there is no meat, no sugar, no fats and no cereals whatsoever. There is not enough bread – not enough rye rations, and the children are proceeding to complete extinction'.[76] He wrote again later enquiring whether it was state policy to torture children by starving them to death.[77] Another report in May 1933 to the *Detkomissiya* in Moscow from the Northern Region described how the condition of thousands of children there was worsening and the death rate among them had doubled.[78] The majority were starving and in need of special nutrition. In the absence of this, they were reduced to going out to the local villages to forage for food or steal.

Unknown numbers of children died of hunger and disease or were abandoned or orphaned due to the policies of collectivization and dekulakization. Peasant families were coerced into disintegration as many adult peasants, particularly men, did not wait to be arrested and exiled, but fled in advance and joined the millions being recruited into the new industrial projects of the Five Year Plans. Sometimes family members disappeared forever. Consequently, there was an upsurge in the numbers of children placed in Soviet institutions. Between 1931 and 1933, the number of children in institutions in the RSFSR more than doubled, growing from 105,561 to 241,744.[79] Thousands more were left outside institutions to fend for themselves, and there was the inevitable return of *bezprizornost'*. Some very young children who ended up in state care at this time were assigned new names and dates of birth to cut all links to their previous life and social identities, ostensibly to 're-forge' them. Sometimes they found out their real identities only in the 1990s after the collapse of the Soviet Union. One such man recalled a childhood 'lived in a grey zone between belonging and non-belonging'.[80]

As would happen during the Great Terror in the late 1930s, though, the state soon realized it could not provide enough institutional support for the children of its victims. It began to encourage *spetspereselentsy* parents to give their children to other relatives outside the special settlements who were willing to look after them. It also called families in exile to be reunited in cases where the adult males had been sent off separately for forced labour.[81] In 1930, a special commission with representatives of *Narkompros* and the NKVD was established to examine what should happen to abandoned or orphaned kulak children in the special settlements. It initially considered placing kulak children in the ordinary child welfare system.[82] However, it decided to keep them in the special settlements, although the famine of 1932–3 resulted in the state beginning to encourage their relatives to take them away.

Eventually, an infrastructure was established for the children of special settlers. By 1933 there were 370 nursery schools, 1,105 primary schools, 136 secondary schools, as well as 242 vocational colleges, with around a quarter of a million children across the various regions to which exiles had been sent.[83] From 1938, children could apply for passports to move away from the settlements at the age of sixteen to continue their education outside. This was a way of enforcing a generational divide in 'suspect' families.[84]

In 1932–3, there was another major famine across the major grain producing areas of the Soviet Union, in particular in Kazakhstan, Ukraine and the Volga region. This was in large part caused by the chaos of the collectivization and dekulakization campaigns. Unlike in the earlier famine of 1921 the Soviet state did little to mitigate its impact on the rural populations and did not request any outside help. An estimated 5 to 6 million people died, many of them infants and children. The famine also caused further *bezprizornost'* and child abandonment.

The collectivization drive was simultaneous to the implementation of compulsory universal primary schooling. Schools in rural areas were meant to be part of the collectivization 'front'. Support for collectivization was embedded into the school curriculum and activities. Children were encouraged to help on collective farms, promote the use of new agricultural technology and work to expose the 'backwardness' of the old rural economy. Although children had always worked on family farms, the state repackaged this as 'socially useful labour' to be carried on outside schools. Children were mobilized to participate in attacks on the 'dark' village ways, with renewed campaigns against religion, patriarchy and superstition. While understandably much research has focused on the trauma of both collectivization and dekulakization for children, some research suggests that participating in collectivization and its associated processes weakened the village and may have given children a powerful sense of agency and community which they enjoyed or even 'transferred feelings of loyalty to the state to children'.[85] Meanwhile in the 1930s, children in elite urban schools were encouraged to write poems celebrating collectivization: And one will boldly say/Upon seeing the lengthening shadows/That here One-Horse Family Russia/ Ceased to exist.[86]

There is now a broad conceptual agreement with the modern model that a childhood spent in poverty and work is not a 'childhood'. Certainly, there was no childhood as a state of privilege for many Soviet children in families labelled as kulak, or even for those who grew up on the collective farms in the 1930s and 1940s. As one woman summarized it decades later: 'We had no childhood. We were poor. We did not have anything. We had to work very hard. Everything we owned was taken away from us.'[87]

Terror and repression

When historians question whether the Soviet state deliberately victimized children, they look at the successive waves of state terror between 1917 and 1953, as well as the policies of collectivization and dekulakization. During the Red Terror of the Civil War period, the Soviet regime sought out family members of those it labelled as enemies. The 1926 Criminal Code allowed for the arrest of members of a suspect's family and in 1934 a Politburo Protocol declared that 'socially dangerous' elements could be imprisoned or exiled for up to five years, allowing the arbitrary pursuit of relatives of those already arrested.[88] The focus of much research has been on the so-called Great Terror of 1936–8, known in Russia as the *yezhovshchina*, after Nikolai Yezhov, the chief of the NKVD at the time. One of the most well-known aspects of the Great Terror is the attacks on leading Communist Party members and other Soviet elites, most notably in the series of famous Show Trials. However, alongside these public events were a series of so-called 'mass operations' starting in 1937 with NKVD Operational Order No. 00447. This set targets for the arrest, execution and exile of those who were placed into categories of 'anti-Soviet' elements: former kulaks, members of former political parties, religious activists and those who had fought against the Bolsheviks during the Civil War. Later mass operations targeted entire ethnic and national groups in the Soviet Union such as Poles, Finns, Latvians and Koreans, among many others. The majority of the political prisoners produced by the Great Terror were adult males. In 1940, minors (under the age of eighteen) made up only 1.2 per cent of the Gulag population.[89] The term 'Children of the Gulag', though, is used to refer to not just children in the camps, but those whose parents or carers were incarcerated in them because of the devastating impact this had on their lives. Children were victims of repression when their adult family members were arrested, executed or exiled.

The laws, regulations and practices of the Terror targeted the families of those arrested. Several NKVD personnel usually arrived at the family home without warning, often at night and arrested the victim (sometimes arrests were carried out at work). A long search for incriminating materials was conducted before the arrested was taken away. Sometimes children slept through these events, but for those who did not it was a catastrophic and traumatic event. One woman remembered about her father's arrest:

> The search was at home. We never saw my father again. They arrested him at home. ... Well, I remember very well my feelings that everything had perished, yes, simply everything had perished. Already, never would anything return. ... That was in the morning, in the day time. It was in the morning. Afterwards I got dressed and Nanny took me and walked along the street with me. And we simply walked silently up and down the street. ... Mama wanted to jump off the balcony but she did not jump.[90]

The arrest of the head of the family usually meant the loss of the family home, as remaining family members were soon evicted.[91] The state registered all family members of the arrested, including children, and placed them under observation. In July 1937, the Politburo decided to launch a campaign to arrest the wives of those convicted of being 'traitors' and 'oppositionists' over the previous year. NKVD Operational Order No. 00486 of 15 August 1937 ordered the internment of wives for between five and eight years in special camps.[92] Their children were to be treated as follows: nursing children aged up to a year to eighteen months were to remain with their mothers in the camps; those aged between one and three would be placed in camp orphanages or children's homes nearby; children aged between three and fifteen would be placed in state orphanages unless other relatives could be found to look after them. The state allowed those aged sixteen and older to live independently if they had the resources to do so, to stay with relatives, sign up for labour schemes or stay in an orphanage. Many adolescents were arrested themselves after the family adults and if categorized as 'socially dangerous' could be placed in camps or NKVD Labour Colonies for minors. Further NKVD reception centres were set up to take in the children of arrested wives. By June 1938, there were over 15,000 children of the recently repressed in state orphanages and space was needed for 10,000 more.[93] As usual despite the threat of total institutionalization, relatives were encouraged to take responsibility for the children.[94]

In January 1938, the NKVD reiterated and reissued instructions on how relatives could obtain guardianship for children of the repressed. The local NKVD was to keep such children under regular observation. The NKVD should ascertain their moods, their friendships, their behaviour and what influence they were having on those who had taken them in.[95] Just as adults did, children wrote letters to Stalin begging him to look into their parents' cases and trying to convince him of their parents' particular innocence.

The extended family stepped in to care for children whose parents had been arrested. One family recalled that after the NKVD arrested their mother, their grandmother met Nadezhda Krupskaya at a function in Moscow. When she told Krupskaya what had happened, Krupskaya offered to help arrange for the grandchildren to go to a good orphanage, in response to which their grandmother apparently replied, 'Give up your own children to an orphanage.'[96] Their grandmother looked after Elena Bonner, her younger brother and her cousin after their parents' arrest and exile in 1937. All of her grandmother's efforts were directed at saving them and bringing them up. All three children survived the Terror and the war, but her grandmother died in the Siege of Leningrad. Bonner wrote in her memoir of that period, 'Many years ago I read a book of poetry by Vladimir Kornilov. There was the line: "… and it seemed that in our years there were no mothers. There were only grandmothers…". Grandmothers there were!'[97] She refers to her generational group of children whose parents were taken in the Terror as 'strange orphans'.[98] The parents of Inna Gaister (b. 1925) were both high-level Party workers and totally dedicated to the Soviet state. By the late 1930s, the family was living in the prestigious modern Government House on the riverbank near the Kremlin.[99] As was usual for the children of the Soviet elite, they had a domrabotnitsa, Natasha Ovchinnikova, a young woman who came from a village in central Russia.[100] She started looking after Inna right after she was born and then cared for her younger siblings as well. Inna's father was arrested first, and soon afterwards, the NKVD came for her mother too. Supported by a neighbour, Natasha refused to hand the children over that night. Their paternal grandmother eventually took legal responsibility for them. The grandmother also took in more nieces and nephews as other adults in the family were arrested. 'Grandmother's family kept growing,' Inna Gaister writes wryly, 'but it was an abnormal kind of growth'.[101] Inna and her younger siblings began years of wandering from apartment to apartment, seeking shelter and safety with different family members and friends, years of homelessness and precarity that melded into the evacuations and displacements of the Great Patriotic War.

Other children were rejected by their extended family, too scared to be associated with them. Instead, their *domrabotnitsy*, family friends or even former work colleagues of their parents looked after them. Often they spent the rest of their childhood being passed on to different relatives and friends. They had to assume adult responsibilities for looking after other siblings, for keeping home and for working; the emphasis on early physical independence here must have helped. In November 1935 at the Congress for Outstanding Shock-Workers Stalin famously responded with the words, 'A son does not answer for his father', to a worker's complaint that he had struggled to receive recognition because he was the son of a kulak. Most children felt they had to deal with the stigmatization and marginalization from their membership of a repressed family. The state viewed the children of the repressed as potentially subversive and feared they could seek revenge for the way their parents had been treated. These children were often marginalized and shunned at school, although many recall the kindness of their teachers, many of whom tried to help them. They could be forbidden to join the Pioneers or the Komsomol, which meant they were excluded from everyday Soviet collectives. This could have a serious impact on their future lives. Such children had to reconcile two very different realities; the reality of their parents' experience of repression and the reality of Soviet life, to which they were forced to conform in order to survive.[102] This disconnect may have eroded their loyalty to the Soviet state, although much memoir literature surprisingly contradicts this. Loyalty was often encouraged by parents who had survived the Terror and returned to rebuild a family life. One woman remembered:

> My mother was terrified about her fate, and for that reason, she maintained a spirit of loyalty, allegiance. And that was why she was bringing us up in an atmosphere of loyalty. I was in the Pioneers. They accepted me to be a Pioneer. I became a Pioneer.[103]

Leonid Muravnik lost both his parents to the Terror when he was ten. Feeling that he was a burden to the relatives that had taken him in, he deliberately got himself arrested for petty crime and was sent to the Danilov Monastery, which was then the main Moscow reception centre for children. Staff there soon realized that Leonid was not a straightforward *bezprizornik* but a 'political'. He remained there several days with other scared and exhausted children, 'until they put us in a closed van and took us somewhere. It was dark in the van, the light barely penetrated the small barred window. And some girl suddenly asked: 'What? Are they taking us to be killed?!'[104]

Thousands of children did end up in orphanages, most (but not all) of which had the usual defects of Soviet children's institutions. Siblings were often separated. Very young children and infants placed in orphanages could lose their entire identity. Even as adults, some could never find out the story of who they and their families had been. One woman told the civil rights group Memorial how her father, an industrial worker in Kharkov, had been arrested in 1937 and disappeared entirely. Her mother was arrested six months later and sent to a camp in Kazakhstan for five years. Her older brother was thrown out of the Komsomol at school, and so decided to leave and went off to the Donbass in search of work. She only managed to keep up a permanent link with her younger brother. She concluded her family history with the words, 'That was how our large, honest, hardworking family, so devoted to our country, was broken into pieces, the family of a simple worker, not even a Party member.'[105]

Family legislation in the Stalinist period

By the 1930s, the Soviet government claimed they were providing a secure social, legal, and economic environment for child rearing and now the family, and particularly males, had to accept responsibility for their children. This claim that the state now provided a solid base for children's lives had a significant impact on attitudes to juvenile delinquency. Children and adolescents were no longer considered victims of capitalism in the transition period and criminal behaviour was increasingly viewed as an unnecessary and free choice. Levels of *bezprizornost* and juvenile delinquency had begun to rise again because of the chaos unleashed in the countryside by collectivization and the famine of 1933. In 1933, 400,000 children were in children's institutions in the Russian Republic.[106] Life in Soviet children's institutions was extremely difficult. Local authorities were regularly caught cheating children's institutions out of resources, infuriating the *Detkomissiya*, which demanded the Party take action. Nikolai Semashko, who had been Commissar of Health in the 1920s, became the Head of the *Detkomissiya* in 1930. He complained continually to *Sovnarkom* about what he called the 'criminal non-compliance' of local and regional authorities regarding budget allocations set by the centre, which left children hungry and filthy and contributed to their mass flight.[107] In the first six months of 1931 the Moscow militia rounded up 4,654 children in the *oblast'*. Around half had run away from children's institutions.[108]

As in the 1920s, most juvenile criminals apprehended were boys aged between twelve and fifteen.[109] In 1933, authorities in Moscow instructed the militia to apprehend child vendors, beggars, acrobats, singers or shoeshine boys found on the streets, around markets or in railways stations. It ordered that these children be sent to reception centres. In 1934, the NKVD took over the reception centres previously belonging to *Narkompros*, as well as all reception centres on transport networks. As stated earlier, reception centres were places from which children picked up from the streets were assigned their fates. Authorities made the decision to return them back to their families, place them in an orphanage or trade school, or in more serious cases, hand them over to the criminal justice system.

Cases of juvenile delinquency almost doubled between 1931 and 1934.[110] The Minors' Commissions, which had been set up in 1918, were abolished in the mid-1930s. Responsibility for juvenile crime was given back to the courts and the procuracy. However, it was decreed that Republic, regional and local procurators were to appoint special procurators for juvenile cases. Chaotic, unstable and 'backward' families with histories of alcohol abuse and poor employment records were now viewed as a major cause of juvenile crime, rather than poverty and the heritage of capitalism. There was still some empathy with juvenile criminals, who the Soviet government saw as victims of 'social neglect'. The courts rarely applied the full penalties of the law to them, although they did apply it to adults convicted of luring minors into crime. There was yet another crackdown on fathers who refused to financially support their children, as child poverty was associated with crime. The NKVD was responsible for finding men who did not pay and bringing them to court, where they were liable for two years imprisonment.[111] Minimum levels of child support were set at one-third of a defendant's salary for one child, 50 per cent for two children and 60 per cent for three or more children.[112]

In April 1935, the Soviet government issued the Decree 'Regarding Measures in the Fight against Juvenile Crime' (*'O merakh bor'by s prestupnost'yu sredi nesovershennoletnikh'*). All juveniles twelve years and older accused of serious crimes against persons or state property were now to be tried in criminal courts. Additionally, adults found guilty of involving children in prostitution, begging or 'speculation' would receive a five-year minimum sentence. The NKVD established Labour Colonies for minors aged between twelve and sixteen. These provided adolescents with vocational training as well as a general education and *vospitanie* in a communist spirit to turn juvenile delinquents into honest and productive socialist citizens. They were in actuality little more than penal colonies with appalling living conditions. By 1940 the NKVD was running fifty Labour Colonies which had held 155,506 twelve- to eighteen-year-olds and had 162 reception centres, through which almost a million children had passed.[113]

Throughout 1935, the state announced further measures to tackle the issue of child neglect and juvenile delinquency. A Decree of 30 May, 'On the Liquidation of Child Homelessness and Neglect' (*'O likvidatsii detskoi bezprizornosti i beznadzornosti'*), called for the improvement and extension of children's institutions and more work with young criminals to be undertaken by Residents' Committees and the Komsomol. Parental responsibility for juvenile crime was reaffirmed; the police could fine parents up to 200 roubles for their children's criminal behaviour and parents were financially responsible for any criminal damage caused by them. From the age of fourteen, children became jointly liable for criminal damages.

The large numbers of unsupervised children (*beznadzornost'*) was still identified as a major social problem and was also blamed on the inadequacies of local authorities, be they local Soviets, Party or Komsomol organizations or Trade Unions. It was also considered the fault of neglectful or indifferent parents. The state was empowered to remove children from inadequate parents, and place them in institutions at the parents' own expense or organize labour training for adolescents.

Placing the NKVD in charge of child homelessness was a sign that it was no longer seen as a primarily social problem which could be solved through education and support. The head of the NKVD, Genrikh Yagoda, told his officers that *bezprizornost'* was a matter of state security and counter-revolution.[114] Between 1934 and 1939, 876,530 children were processed through the NKVD reception centres. Around 10 per cent were sent to Labour Colonies for minors; the majority were returned to their families or placed in children's institutions.[115] The NKVD used the reception centres to identify the children of 'class enemies' and separate them out from the others. Categories for children's social origin were added to the record keeping of the reception centres: 'kulaks' and 'former people'.[116] Later in the Great Terror, the category of 'children of repressed parents' was added.[117]

Schooling and education under Stalin

In the Soviet Union, there is no capital except education.[118]

In 1927, a decade after the Russian Revolution, less than three quarters of school-age children were enrolled in schools.[119] The drive to expand children's education was part of the Revolution from Above and a major priority of the Soviet government. Between 1928 and 1930, the number of schools rose from 85,000 to 102,000 and enrolment grew from 7.9 to 11.3 million.[120] A Central Committee Decree of 25 July 1930 ordered that all children aged between eight and ten be enrolled in school for the upcoming year. All children in urban schools who had just completed four years of schooling were required to stay on for another year. Children aged between eleven and fifteen who had never received any primary education had to enrol in supplementary courses. In August 1930, a Decree ordered that all children from now had to complete four years of compulsory education.

The massive campaign to roll out and enforce primary schooling across the Soviet Union involved building – or finding – new schools and training teachers. Teacher volunteers came from the Komsomol. Schools in rural areas were often set up in the former homes of kulak families or exiled priests; this accounted for one-third of rural schools, around 7,000 in number in Soviet Ukraine.[121] Many schools, even in urban areas, operated on a shift system to make up for lack of buildings and inventory, a situation that carried on into the 1950s. In campaigns, priority was given to the enrolment of girls and by 1935; girls in rural areas were attending at the same rate as their male peers. The mass enrolment of peasant girls in schools was one of the factors that led to the dramatic lowering of the birth rate in post-war Russia. Once grown, these young women rejected their mother's lives of continual childbearing. It also may have helped with the drop in infant mortality, as young peasant girls were largely eliminated as a source of childcare.[122] Rural schools were often unheated, unlit and overcrowded, with little in the way of equipment and poorly trained teachers. Local authorities gave material assistance to help rural children attend schools, but lack of shoes and warm clothes and poverty still militated against regular school attendance for some time. On the other end of the scale to rural schools were the prestige urban schools for the children of the Soviet elites, such as Moscow's Model School No. 25, which Stalin's children, Svetlana and Vasilii attended. Model School No. 25 had a range of excellent teachers (many of whom had trained in the pre-revolutionary period), science laboratories, an array of after-school activities as well as a library consisting of 12,000 books.[123] In 1936, only 50 per cent of schools in the RSFSR possessed their own library.[124] Despite all the unevenness in provision, in a relatively short space of time the Soviet state had created a new legal category of child: eligible for compulsory schooling. The most significant element in the modern model of childhood was put into place; the child was to be above all constructed as a school pupil. At the same time, the creation and dissemination of school-themed literature with 'heroic teachers and model pupils' was prioritized by the Soviet state.[125] The official culture for children would celebrate the new 'Soviet school'.

In 1931, the Pioneer movement became embedded into the expanding Soviet school system, although the Party and the Komsomol tried to create the impression that children had retained their autonomy. The Pioneer movement now functioned as a peer pressure group ('stern judges') to encourage high achievement in the Soviet school and was the main vehicle for *vospitanie*. Pioneers were to police the behaviour of other children in school:

> Straighten out your comrade if he allows himself bad habits, if he answers back to the teacher, if he slouches with his hands in his pockets. Real Pioneers always sternly judge a pupil who disrupts a teacher with bad behaviour, slackness and lack of discipline.[126]

This continuous disciplinary rhetoric emanating from the children's press was usually aimed at boys. In 1941, *Pionerskaya Pravda* announced a new 'invention' (supposedly originating from Pioneers themselves) an 'All-seeing Machine' (*Vezdezor*). This 'machine' was capable of seeing 'everything that happened in class, in the Pioneer troop, outside, on the streets, at home ... everywhere, where Pioneers and school children are, however distant, our machine hears everything, notes everything down, sketches, photographs, telephones, records and broadcasts'.[127] Early use of it 'discovered' a girl refusing to remove her hat in the classroom, while another pupil was 'seen' tearing up a book in frustration. The *Vezedor* column was dropped quite quickly, but gives some idea of the general tone of the Pioneer press in the 1930s and 1940s, which was in any case packed with naming and shaming letters from children criticizing their peers' behaviour in school. That the most important duty of a Pioneer was to excel at school did not contradict the general Soviet collectivist ethos, as the individual excelled for the collective, revealing the 'dual goals of Stalinist pedagogy: to control the individual's behaviour by a strict regime of rules and to encourage the realization of individual productivity'.[128]

As well as being involved with the Pioneers through school, from the 1930s more children now spent their summers in Pioneer camps, usually organized by their parents' workplaces. These camps offered a range of activities such as swimming, hiking and games, always culminating in the evening campfire. Although they were subjected to socialist messages and political content, many children still found these camps enjoyable for the activities and friendships. The summer Pioneer camp strengthened the idea of childhood as a collective experience and separated the family unit in potentially private times. From 1934, children who had excelled at school could be rewarded by a trip to the elite Pioneer camp, Artek in the Crimea, as a 'gift' from the Soviet state.

In general, children were encouraged to spend time 'rationally' and, in addition to cultural and sporting activities, were encouraged to join various hobby groups and circles dedicated to popular science, nature and technology. From the 1930s, Pioneer Palaces and clubs were organized where children could attend a range of cultural and sporting activities outside school. All these activities were not just to demonstrate how privileged children were in the Soviet Union, but also aimed at tackling the issue of *beznadornost'* and the state's fear of an unsupervised childhood.

From the end of the 1920s, previously tolerated non-Bolshevik progressive educationalists were attacked and their theories were rejected. In 1929, Stanislav Shatskii was accused of being an 'ideologue of the right wing of Moscow pedagogues' and of being influenced by Tolstoy and Rousseau.[129] Lunacharsky was removed as Commissar of Enlightenment in 1929 and

Narkompros was purged of employees who were considered ideologically unreliable. The children of 'class enemies' were meant to be expelled from schools, while anti-religious campaigns for children were given top priority.[130] A Central Committee Decree of 25 August 1931 put an end to progressive experimental forms of teaching, now described as 'thoughtless scheming'. As already noted, the most influential Soviet educationalist from the 1930s onwards was Anton Makarenko. In his practice as noted earlier. Makarenko rejected the progressive pedagogical theories of the 1920s, such as the idea that children were capable of self-organization and needed maximum autonomy. His educational theories were instead based on ideas of collective training, military-style discipline and the value and necessity of productive work. In his view, the aim of the Soviet school should be to create a strong disciplined collective, based on mutual respect and obedience, but should also allow for the full development of the human personality in the traditions of Marxism and the ideas of the Russian intelligentsia. The teacher, or the adult, was key in guiding the formation of the collective. The year 1936 saw an attack on the previously dominant discipline of pedology, and the same year Makarenko moved to Moscow to eventually become the leading 'All-Union' pedagogical authority, dying shortly afterwards in 1939.

The decision was made to return to classroom-based instruction by a single teacher with a uniform, standardized curriculum based around the acquisition of subject-based knowledge, approved textbooks, regular examinations and competitive grading. More traditional pedagogical methods, such as memorization and dictation, returned to the classroom. This was no longer a child-centred approach, but a teacher-centred pedagogy. The new Soviet school also drew on the Tsarist educational heritage. In 1935, a disciplinary code was introduced. Regulations attempted to control behaviour and movement in schools, as they had done in the classical *gymnazia* of the Tsarist period. Pupils stood when teachers entered the room or when answering the teacher's questions. They had to raise their hands in order to be allowed to speak. Pupils were to be tidy, obedient and clean inside and outside the school. The school day and pupil's movements around the spaces were heavily regulated and monitored by staff and other students. Soviet law forbade punishment within the school, both corporal and non-corporal. There were still major discipline issues in Soviet schools, judging by inspectors' reports, educational department documents, parents' letters and teachers' own accounts.[131] In one example, a pupil threw a book at a teacher and then said 'Ok, I'm going, it looks like you are in a state. What are you going to do with me? This is not the Tsarist-era.'[132] As noted earlier, strategies of collective responsibility, supported by the Pioneer movement, created discipline, using peer pressure and surveillance. In the Soviet school, 'teachers encouraged pupils to take on the operation of power by seeing themselves as subjects of a total system of surveillance, normalisation and discipline'.[133]

Children were also meant to be under the surveillance of their teachers outside the classroom. Rules of Conduct governed how pupils were to behave away from school. Aleksandr Kosarev, the head of the Komsomol in the 1930s, declared that teachers were obligated to 'interfere in the lives and souls of their pupils', visiting them at home and knowing all the details of their family background.[134] School uniforms were reintroduced, modelled on pre-revolutionary traditions; the normative uniform and appearance for girls became again a dark brown dress with white collar, and with hair tied in braids. From 1932, annual oral examinations became the sole criteria for pupil advancement. The Tsarist five-grade system was reintroduced and pupils' grades were widely publicized inside and outside the school. In 1944, the once much-coveted gold and silver medals were reintroduced for those who came top of their final year in secondary schools.

In the 1943/4 school year, gender-segregated schooling was introduced in urban secondary schools. Around 3 to 4 million children attended separate schools every year.[135] In Moscow and Leningrad, 97 and 93 per cent of pupils were attending separate secondary schools by 1952. This was a major attempt by the Soviet state to deliberately gender the experience of childhood, although it made the argument that as Soviet women had achieved full equality there was no longer any particular need for coeducation. The majority opinion, as far as can be traced, was against separate schooling. Girls in particular rejected it. Many historians have viewed the introduction of this policy as part of the cultural and social conservatism of Stalinism with its rejection of earlier Bolshevik commitments to gender equality. Others argue that the main rationale for separate schooling was not preparing girls for a future revolving around motherhood; the policy had been conceived before the Great Patriotic War and was an outcome of the growing militarization of society and concerns about the behaviour of Soviet boys. Young males were to be prepared for the military as well as the labour force and needed to be obedient. While girls were viewed as model Soviet pupils, quiet, calm, disciplined, hard-working high achievers, boys were problematized as needing greater control and authority. It was felt that additional resources for military training, physical education, technology clubs and male teachers should be given for boys' education.[136] The standard image of the Pioneer was more often female than male, and girls appeared more frequently with in public images with Stalin. They were extolled for their educational achievements, whereas boys were often presented as badly behaved, disruptive and problematic. Girls 'became icons for innocence, preservation, and the ordered defensive mobilisation of the population … the figurative bride for the Stalinist marriage between the leader and his feminized, infantalized population'.[137] In the case of the People's Republic of China, Orna Naftali argues that in cultural productions for children, girls were more closely linked with the figure of Chairman Mao than boys, although this may have been a way of 'subsuming the militant girl' under the power of a patriarchal figure.[138]

There were few changes to the curriculum for girls' schools and the commitment remained to a rigorous academic syllabus of core subjects and the promotion of the ideal of higher education and professional careers for women. There was a negative reaction to the suggestion that the aim of education for girls should be primarily to prepare them for motherhood. Official descriptions of the aims of educating girls were that they should wish to be future mothers, while still developing a long list of gender-neutral moral qualities such as patriotism, commitment to the motherland, love of labour, selflessness, honesty, modesty, courage, seriousness and thoughtfulness.[139] Ewing notes the 'ambivalence of Soviet maternalism, which simultaneously assumed girls would become mothers and expected them to fulfil the same roles as boys'.[140] Paradoxically, under Stalinism, mothers had primary responsibility for childcare while 'encouraging daughters to reject traditional roles'.[141] Svetlana Gouzenko, who came from an intelligentsia family, recalled the attitudes of her and her Moscow school friends in the late 1930s: 'Not one of us intended to become "wives". Most of us hoped to become engineers. A few wanted to be doctors, and some "queer" ones wanted to be teachers.'[142] When the director of Moscow's Educational Department asked a girl about her wish to become a mother in the future, she apparently replied, 'Curse that tongue of yours, for I am a citizen with equal rights,' while another girl told an inspector that 'if they want to lock us up in a tower, it will not work'.[143] The director of a girls' school wrote,

> Our primary task is to educate a Soviet citizen, a new person who should, just as much as a boy, acquire a high degree of culture, an advanced general education, a resolute sense of purpose, and great courage. ... Teaching housekeeping is an unnecessary waste of time and effort.[144]

A letter signed by thirty-five pupils from Sverdlovsk Girls' School No. 12 declared, 'We, Soviet female pupils, did not aspire to be like Natalia Rostova or Dolly Oblonskaia. ... We want to become not just mothers, but also public figures and scientists; in a word, we want to serve wherever we can be most useful to our country.'[145] Fifteen recent graduates of a girls' school in Molotov asked rhetorically, 'Are the new generation of young Soviet women really supposed to be satisfied with just motherhood? No!!! Never!!!'[146] Female role models in Soviet schools were usually scientists or political activists such as Sofia Kovalevskaya, Marie Curie or Nadezhda Krupskaya. Others were Stakhanovite super-achievers from the working class or peasantry like Pasha Angelina, famous as one of the first female tractor drivers in the Soviet Union. There was a broad commitment to gender equality in education, at least that separate schooling contradicted, although the policy was abandoned due to a lack of improvement in discipline in boys' schools. Secondary schools were reintegrated in 1954. Ludmila Petrashevskaya wrote of her shock when she first attended a reintegrated school, underlining that, in fact, there were still strong gender differences in pupil behaviour and appearance:

> The school stank like a menagerie, if animals could smoke. ... In my new co-ed class, fifty percent of the students brayed, spat at long distance, looked insolently with unfocused eyes, wore army crew cuts, chewed their nails, and had great difficulty speaking without swearing. In the evenings, some of them walked to the military barracks to fight with soldiers. The other fifty per cent adorned their uniforms with white lace, wore long braids, read Dreiser, Balzac, and Romain Rolland, attempted to wear bangs, and believed that not a single kiss should be given without love (not that anyone asked).[147]

Children and childhood in the Great Patriotic War, 1941–5

In the early morning of 22 June 1941, the Germans launched their surprise invasion of the Soviet Union along its western frontier, breaking the Non-Aggression Pact signed in 1939. The invasion, and subsequent collapse and retreat of the Red Army all along the front lines came as a terrible shock to Soviet society, in spite of the fact that there had been a build-up to the war throughout the second half of the 1930s.[148] For a decade, Soviet children had learnt not only about the superiority of the Soviet way of life but also about the territorial integrity of the Soviet Union. Throughout the 1930s, children also had been mobilized to prepare for war and military games. Subjects likely to be useful in wartime, such as topography and foreign languages, had more prominence in the curriculum. From 1930, adolescents had to do military training in school for two hours a week.[149] Pioneer groups had organized military preparation games and the children's press always carried information on military preparedness. 'Defence Badges' for participation in military-oriented fitness programmes were awarded by the Pioneers. The Pioneers also established the Young Friends of *OSOAVIAKhIM*, the Volunteer Society for Cooperation with the Army, Aviation and Navy, which had been set up in 1927 to train reserves for the Red Army, with the participation of over a million children.[150] In 1939 the All-Union Defence Championships was organized for twelve- to seventeen-year-olds, with around a million participants; there were 1.5 million the next year in 1940.[151] That year Moscow's educational authorities also set up summer military camps, which around 6,000 children attended.[152] In January 1941, the All-Union Military-Physical Culture Pioneer and Schoolchildren Competition (*Vsesoyuznie voenno-fizkul'turnykh sorevnovanii pionerov i shkolnikov*) was inaugurated, which involved the mastery of military skills such as putting on gas masks, defusing explosives, map reading, understanding camouflage, orienteering, topography and signalling with flags.[153] In 1940, Marshal Voroshilov informed children that the qualities common to a Soviet childhood would be more important than ever in the preparation for war:

> Discipline and organisation in labour, in daily life, in your studies, in your relationships, in your behaviour in the street and public places, in your free time – everywhere and always, discipline and organisation. They are as necessary to us as the air that we breathe.[154]

Expectations of participation in military games differed somewhat by gender; girls were assigned tasks relating to nursing and first aid. These gendered divisions would continue in wartime propaganda; young naval cadets were shown how to use weapons, while girls were seen gathering medicinal plants in a field.[155] Although tasks were gendered, desired behaviours were not; qualities valued in all children in this time of danger were 'bravery, persistence, strong character, truthfulness, the ability to work in teams and to be useful to the homeland'.[156]

When the war did come, it dramatically transformed childhood and children's lives during the war and long into the post-war years.[157] A third of Soviet citizens were fourteen or younger during the Great Patriotic War.[158] Children felt the impact of the loss of so many male lives and the myths of the war would become a framework for their understanding of their society and history and their own lives. Children in the Soviet Union were mobilized into the war effort in a way unparalleled in other belligerent states. Olga Kucherenko argues that the basis for this successful mobilization was Soviet ideology and shared values inculcated through the school system, the Pioneer movement and official children's culture. Almost perpetual hunger was a defining experience of the war years for all children, whether in occupied territories or in the cities and rural areas in the rear. *Bezpriznost'* returned yet again as children ran away from institutions or their own families to try to survive the poverty and hunger as best they could alone. As the Red Army pushed out the Germans and liberated Soviet territory, the NKVD took responsibility for dealing with the multitude of homeless, orphaned and displaced children, pulling more of them into its sphere and subjecting them to what has been described as 'relief combined with surveillance and control'.[159]

In the conditions of total war, children's well-being was put further down the list of state's priorities. In the words of Julie DeGraffenreid, Soviet childhood once privileged and valourized, was now was to be 'sacrificed' by the Soviet state, and she argues that children were left in danger. One aspect of the Soviet war effort that specifically affected children and has come in for some criticism was the civilian evacuations from the front lines to the rear. Civilian evacuations were chaotic and incompetent and initially were given a lower priority than the evacuation of industry and its personnel, which was clearly to be essential to any ability to fight the war. However, it is not true that the state did not include the evacuation of children or that did not make provision for children a priority.[160] The urban evacuations of civilians, including in Moscow and Leningrad, were ordered and enforced by the state often against popular resistance from families who did not want to separate from their children or leave the cities themselves. An estimated 7 to 8 million Soviet children were evacuated during the Great Patriotic War.[161] Children were evacuated with family members or collectively with workplace crèches, kindergartens, childcare institutions, children's homes, schools and Pioneer units. Evacuating children from the front line was presented not only as saving children and preserving Soviet childhood but also as a way of raising the morale of the Red Army ('we are looking after the children of front line soldiers') and keeping up the bonds between the front and the rear, which would be so crucial to the eventual victory. Additionally, it was hoped the evacuation of children and adolescents would mitigate the issue of *bezprizornost'* and its twin, juvenile crime. In many ways, it had the opposite effect; the difficult life evacuated children faced in institutions added to the problem. In Chelyabinsk, a large city in the Urals, almost 1,000 homeless children were picked up by the police in a ten day campaign in August 1944 including many child evacuees who had run away from institutions or their families.[162]

There were many problematic aspects to the evacuation of children. The extensive journeys to the Soviet rear often proved fatal to children, many of whom were already ill and undernourished. The children of employees of Leningrad's prestigious museum, the State Hermitage, for example, were initially evacuated to the Yaroslavl' region, but had to be evacuated further east to the Urals as the Germans advanced closer. They had to walk several days in winter to reach the Volga, where they waited for a week with thousands of other civilians in unheated buildings before being crammed onto an overcrowded steamer, which then ran aground. They were refused permission to disembark at the city of Gorky, but were eventually allowed to come off the steamer in the small town of Gorodets and were billeted in local schools. Here, their group leader was informed that there was a measles epidemic in the town, at which point as she wrote in her diary she 'finally lost whatever remained of my composure'.[163] Four children in the group died on this journey, including her own daughter.

While the wartime press, perhaps understandably, emphasized the warm welcomes and happy lives of the children in evacuation, in reality the situation was very different. Children evacuated in groups from Soviet cities were usually placed in rudimentary homes on collective farms in the Urals or Siberia. They were expected to not only become economically self-sufficient, cultivating land and keeping livestock, but also help with local agricultural needs. Komsomol activists were given the task of supplying children's homes in the rear for the evacuated, which were also supposed to be looked after by local factories and enterprises as well as Red Army units through the system of *shefstvo*. Often far from any railway station or urban settlement, they were dependent on the goodwill of whatever over-stretched and exhausted community they found themselves in. Evacuated children's homes suffered from the same problems as all other Soviet children's institutions: shortages of food, clothing, bedding, furniture and basic inventory, unsanitary and unsafe conditions and often indifferent or exploitative staff. Evacuated homes that were staffed by teachers and carers who had come with the children seem to have sustained some kind of supportive spirit, despite all the difficulties of life. Others found a less welcoming environment. Elena Kozhina was evacuated as a nine year old from Leningrad to the Kuban region in southern Russia with her mother.[164] They were placed in a Cossack *stanitsa*. Generally, as a social group, the Cossacks remained hostile to the Soviet state. The local community refused to help them at first, as they associated Elena and her mother with the Soviet regime due to their provenance from Leningrad, a quintessential Soviet city, and to their open support for the Soviet war effort.

Life under German occupation

Between 1941 and 1944, about 85 million Soviet citizens lived under German occupation at some point. The brutalities of the German occupation, which was characterized from the beginning by widespread atrocities against civilians, did not spare children. Jewish children in Russia, Ukraine, Belarus and the Baltic states were victims of the Nazi mobile killing squads, massacres, liquidation of the ghettos and transfers to concentration camps of the developing Holocaust.

Children and adolescents were tortured and executed for involvement in the partisan movements. Axis forces raped, beat, humiliated, exploited and abused Soviet children. They sent adolescents west to Nazi-occupied Europe to work as slave labourers. Children were killed during military action, tried to survive in destroyed villages and besieged towns or fled to an uncertain future in the rear. There was starvation in major cities due to deliberate German requisitioning policies and pitiful rations, part of the 'Hunger Plan'. The occupying forces dismantled the welfare state and social provision for children and closed down schools. In 1943, only 13 out of the 138 schools in Kharkov, a major city in German-occupied Ukraine, were still functioning.[165]

War and crisis challenge the boundaries between childhood and adulthood so painstakingly marked out since the Enlightenment. A small number of children and adolescents were directly involved in military combat. Possibly around 25,000 minors served in the armed forces, 5,000 in the navy and around 35,000 in the partisans.[166] Other estimates suggest that of the 250,000 partisans, possibly around 10 to 16 per cent were of school age.[167] More may have aided partisan groups with reconnaissance missions, cleaning shells and handling munitions, bringing the post and passing on messages, helping the wounded and delivering supplies. There were partisan camps that consisted of families, as whole communities sought escape from the brutalities of the German occupation. The Soviet state encouraged children in the occupied areas to carry out activities in support of the partisans. Arkady Gaidar told Soviet children in Ukraine that they should 'tear along like an arrow, crawl like a snake, fly like a bird, warn your elders about the enemy'.[168]

Images of child soldiers proliferated in Soviet propaganda, although the official enlistment age was eighteen. Many adolescents, both male and female, wanted to fight in the war and begged local and central authorities to let them sign up despite their ages. One woman told of her desire to fight:

> We were brought up this way! We read Gaidar, Ostrovskii. Those were not just books to us. We imagined ourselves those heroes, that's why we yearned for a fight, but once we got in the midst of it, there was very little romance.[169]

Older adolescents tried to attach themselves to military units, both at the front and in the rear. Those successful were known as *vospitanniki* or *syn polka* (sons of the regiment) and performed a variety of auxiliary duties, occasionally seeing combat. This became an 'unspoken tradition' in Soviet forces.[170] The Red Army, in particular, attracted children, mainly young boys, often those whose own families had died or disappeared, as it started moving westward after 1943 liberating Soviet lands. The 13th Guards Rifle Division picked up sixteen boys on its way from Stalingrad to Prague.[171] In December 1944, an officer in a Red Army division stationed in Lithuania wrote to the authorities in Leningrad enquiring if they could provide any details about the family of a twelve-year-old *vospitanniki*. They said that the boy had been staying with his grandmother outside Leningrad when the war broke out in 1941 and had eventually ended up spending the war years in German-occupied Lithuania. The Leningrad Soviet managed to establish that, in a rare piece of good fortune, the boy's parents were still alive, having survived both fighting with the Red Army and the Siege. They wrote to the army commander that the boy's mother 'asks us to pass onto you her deepest gratitude. She is beside herself with joy at the unexpected news that her son has been saved.'[172] Many of these boys later recalled that they were treated with great affection by the military units who rescued them. Red Army officers sometimes adopted these children after the war.[173] The Soviet navy was an exception to the call-up age. In 1942 the pre-revolutionary naval rank of 'ship's boy' (*junga*) was reinstated for boys aged between twelve and seventeen. Cadet schools and training units were established in the naval bases of the Soviet Union. There were around 5,000 *junga* and many saw combat; around a third died.[174] Suvorov Cadet Academies and military schools for adolescent boys were founded in 1943, partly to deal with juvenile delinquency, *bezprizornost'* and *beznadornost'*.

During and after the war, stories about children and adolescents who joined the partisans or helped the Red Army were promoted heavily, out of proportion to the actual numbers of those who had done so. Stalin Prizes for literature went to these mythologizing books about adolescent heroes, which continued the Russian tradition of education and *vospitanie* through the study of literary character. These texts of Pioneer heroics remained in the school curriculum throughout the Soviet period. These include Lev Kassil and Mark Polianovsky's *Street of the Youngest Son* (*Ulitsa mladshego syna*) (1949) the story of Volodya Dubinin, who helped partisans in Kerch until he was killed by a landmine in 1942 at the age of fourteen; Valentin Kataev's *Son of the Regiment* (*Syn polka*) (1945) about an orphaned peasant boy who is adopted by a front-line Red Army unit and Valentina Osseva's *Vasek Trubachev and his Comrades* (*Vasek Trubachev ego tovarishchi*), written across 1947 to 1951. The classic of the phenomenon is Alexander Fadeev's *Young Guard* (*Molodaya gvardiia*) (1946), a fictionalized account of the actions of partisan Komsomol members in Krasnodon, most of whom were killed by the Germans in 1943. In contrast to the wartime media which often had presented children as helpless victims, particularly in the first stages of the war, these literary works foregrounded children's agency and conscious sacrifice.

Children in the Soviet rear

The war utterly disrupted normal life, which for most children was now increasingly associated with school and its extension, the strange Soviet combination of 'organized leisure'. Attendance at schools dropped by over half in the first years of the war, as schools were destroyed, closed by the Germans or in the rear requisitioned for use by the Red Army (although this was illegal). The Soviet state tried to ensure that schools were kept running in the unoccupied areas. Schools that continued were short on supplies and usually offered shift schooling and a disrupted form of education. Evacuated children placed in remote areas had virtually no chance of receiving a formal education. The Soviet state was alarmed by the reversal of the educational achievements of the 1930s and in the early post-war period; the reconstruction of the education system was one of its chief priorities. The Pioneer movement, so closely attached to the school, was also disrupted by the war. Its leadership, which was drawn from the Komsomol, focused on other priorities in the first war years. In a meeting in September 1942 the then secretary of the Komsomol, Nikolai Mikhailov, concluded that the Pioneer movement was losing its focus and it should be directing and inspiring children's war work.[175] The first eighteen months of the war also saw the drastic curtailment of funding for official Soviet children's culture.

Despite the positive images of Soviet propaganda, the government feared that Soviet children in the unoccupied areas were out of control. One of the priorities of the Soviet state as far as children were concerned was to prevent the return of *bezprizornost'* and *beznadornost'*. Crime became a way to survive the appalling conditions of life in the rear. Most resources went to the Red Army and the front. A recent study of a group of people who were from Leningrad during the war as children revealed that memories of hunger and death were as strong for them as for those who stayed in the blockaded city.[176] Around 2.4 million children may have died in the rear during the war years.[177]

Many children stopped going to school and ran wild around the cities of the rear. The state introduced an array of measures to look after children who had become orphaned or separated from their families. *Sovnarkom* issued four Decrees between January 1942 and April 1943 establishing regulations for looking after homeless and abandoned children. The Commissariats of Health, Enlightenment, Justice, the NKVD and local authorities all had responsibilities for dealing with this issue. The policy was to place over-fourteens into work and younger children in institutions. The number of child reception centres under the control of the NKVD expanded. Now nationality became an important category for the NKVD to record, as it sought to separate out children from

Soviet nationalities suspected of collaboration with the Germans. In 1942, the NKVD arrested and sentenced 351,473 minors and detained 286,467 street children.[178] New reception centres were set up, as were City Commissions for Children without Parents. In starving, blockaded Leningrad, Komsomol members, teachers and janitors did regular search and rescue missions in apartments to find any children left alone after the death of adult family members. The notes of a young girl Tanya Savicheva (b. 1930), recording the deaths of each member of her family during the winter of 1941–2, ending with the words 'Only Tanya is left', were turned into an iconic image of child victimhood in the Soviet Union. Soviet authorities rescued Tania and she was placed in an orphanage and evacuated out of the city, but tragically died of tuberculosis in 1944. Another young Leningrad girl, who also features in the St Petersburg City Museum alongside Tanya, was Ida Bogacheva. In early 1942, a Komsomol activist found her alone in her flat; her mother and grandmother had died. She went to a children's home and then was evacuated. As an orphan, Ida was not initially allowed to return to Leningrad after the war. However, a staff member at the children's home helped her trace some friends of her grandmother's, who agreed to adopt her and helped her get back to the city.[179]

As the Red Army moved westward and began liberating Soviet territory, the NKVD was responsible for keeping children in order. In June 1943 a Decree, 'On the Strengthening the Arrangements against Child Homelessness, Neglect and Hooliganism', was published. The NKVD set up a Department for the Struggle against Child Homelessness and Neglect. Stalin also authorized the NKVD to expand places in their Labour Colonies for an additional 50,000 eleven- to sixteen-year-olds; in July 1944 places were to be increased again by 10,000.[180] Only a minority of minors apprehended by the NKVD ended up in these colonies; 25,140 children in 1944 and 23,066 in 1945.[181] The majority of those caught by the NKVD were placed in children's institutions, trade or factory schools or sent back to their families. In 1944, NKVD reception centres processed around 350,000 children.[182] In 1945, 638, 208 juvenile offenders and 185,543 children were taken 'off the streets' and out of public spaces.[183]

The Soviet mobilization of children and adolescents during the war played an important role in the victory. At the war's outbreak, Soviet children were told that their duty was to preserve their self-discipline (*distsiplinnost'*) and provide necessary help to adults. There were many ways in which children and adolescents could be mobilized to support the war effort, many of which built on activities in the 1930s. A Pioneer radio broadcast asked its listeners:

> Children! ... What are you doing? How are you helping to destroy the Hitler-following bandits? How are you helping the motherland which is wounded by the brutal beast? Maybe you are sitting, doing nothing, and waiting for

the Victory? Eating, partying, thinking only about your own benefit and about your own life?[184]

In the 1930s, the Pioneer Oath had been altered to include loyalty to Stalin. During the war, the following lines were added:

> I hate the fascist invaders with all my heart and I will tirelessly prepare to defend the Motherland. In this, I swear by the names of the former soldiers who gave their lives for our happiness. I will always remember that their blood burns on my Pioneer tie and on our Red Banner.[185]

The Pioneer Commandments also changed to further emphasize both patriotism and physical fitness: 'The Pioneer has a sharp eye, muscles of iron and nerves of steel' and 'The Pioneer fervently loves his motherland and hates its enemies.'[186]

Rural children and those evacuated to rural areas worked in agriculture. Child and adolescent part- or full-time labour made substantial contributions to agricultural output during the war.[187] An average of 5 million children worked each year, contributing 760 million labour days between 1941 and 1944 and making up between 20 per cent and 23 per cent of the workforce, respectively.[188] They also aided the general agricultural economy in other ways, such as animal husbandry, repair work, chopping wood, clearing snow, pest control and the ubiquitous provision of childcare to free up female labour. Protective labour legislation for adolescents was modified; fourteen became the minimum age for full-time industrial work and twelve for agricultural work although even these laws were often violated. Adolescents (twelve- to eighteen-year-olds) made up 10 to 18 per cent of the workforce.[189] Many worked to get rations, to keep warm or to stay close to trusted adults.

Under direction from adults, children were to assist during air raids, keep order in the cities and put up blackout curtains, put out fires, participate in sanitary brigades, carry sandbags and water and gather medicinal plants and berries (rosehip, camomile for vitamin C, nettles, pine needles, mushrooms, etc.). The latter was a major area for children's work and children apparently contributed 78 per cent of the total collected.[190] They helped in hospitals and collected scrap metal and paper. The state used children to link the rear and the front. They visited or wrote to Red Army soldiers and tended their graves. The Komsomol asked that Pioneers send every soldier a tobacco pouch and decorated handkerchief.[191] Ludmila Petrushevskaya recalled how when a military plane passed overhead, the children in her kindergarten group were told to look up and name a member of their family fighting in the war. The majority of adult males in her family had been arrested or executed during the Terror, but her aunt eventually rustled up some suitable name for her so that she could participate in this collective experience.[192] Helping the families of Red Army soldiers in the rear was one of the main activities of the *Timurovtsy*. As discussed earlier, the movement seems to have arisen spontaneously and seems to have been genuinely popular, before being incorporated into the Pioneer movement and inevitably controlled from the centre. *Timurovtsy* substituted at home for absent adults, volunteered in hospitals and collected money and clothes for evacuated children as well as for tanks and military hardware. This mass child mobilization movement was unique among the belligerent states.[193]

Particularly in the first disastrous period of war, state media (newspapers, posters, films, news reel, and radio broadcasts) portrayed children under attack by the Germans – vulnerable, helpless, tortured, dying or dead, a visual and aural propaganda that has been described as 'pervasive and intense', graphic and highly emotive.[194] The heroic child of the Stalinist 1930s temporarily disappeared and was replaced by the child as victim, as part of the 'hate-and-revenge' mobilization campaign. Marina Balina suggests that the deployment of the figure of the child as victim was a permissible way of expressing the generalized trauma caused by Operation Barbarossa and the catastrophic early defeats and retreats of the Red Army.[195] Of the one hundred essays, editorials, and reports in *Pravda* on children and the war published between May 1942 and May 1944, only eight featured children fighting back against the actions of the Germans. The majority were filled with gruesome and detailed descriptions of tortured and murdered children, whose terrible fates the adult population was called upon to avenge.[196]

The deployment of these violent images was perhaps specific to the Soviet Union and shows the intensity of mobilization efforts, particularly at times of extreme military crisis in the early years. Ludmilla Petrushevskaya was both shocked and fascinated as a child by the enormous painting in Kuibyshev train station of a fascist soldier dying alone in the winter steppe watched by a wolf.[197] A Pioneer Dawn broadcast from partisans for New Year 1943 told its listeners that 'Kolya, the littlest, is a partisan on our team. His heart is full of burning hatred for the German perverts. He remembers how the fascists drowned his mother and sister in a river.'[198] Films such as Mark Donskoi's *The Rainbow* (1943), and Fridrikh Ermler's *She Defends the Motherland* (1943) viscerally underlined the messages of unbearable child suffering. These scenes of the violation of children had great resonance due to the state's earlier valorization of childhood and its insistent claim that it had ensured a 'happy childhood'.

State media for children, rather than for adults, meanwhile emphasized their agency and dynamism, rather than their victimhood, and sought to empower children within acceptable bounds. The catastrophe of the war meant that there could be little room for age-graded expectations, blurring again the world of the child and adult. As noted earlier, many children responded to the call for mobilization. The state published the words of children who wanted to inscribe themselves in the heroic national epic. A twelve-year-old boy wrote in an school essay:

> I am sorry about one thing only. The Nazis will be beaten before I get a chance to grow up. I'll have no chance at all to put my hands on them. I did put out some incendiary bombs but that doesn't count. I didn't have a chance to hit them and probably never will. I won't be grown up enough.[199]

In reality, the Soviet state did not want thousands of children and young people running away to complicate the Red Army's struggle on the front line. Children and adolescents were encouraged to vocalize their desires to join in the war, while focusing on studying at school as a form of patriotic activity and assisting in the war effort behind the front lines, particularly by helping out soldiers' families. Arkady Gaidar made this clear to children in his speech on the radio on 30 August 1941, which was simultaneously published in *Pionerskaya Pravda*, informing his listeners, 'Your country has always taken care of you, she brought you up, she taught you, she indulged and often even pampered you. Now it is time for you, not by word, but by deed, to show how you value, care for, and love her.'[200]

The winner of a school essay contest in 1943 expressed perfectly this expectation: 'I know now what hard work means, and I feel responsible for the work I do. I feel I am not a child schoolgirl anymore, but a school girl warrior. I have worked for the city and for the Front.'[201]

The impact of the war on family legislation

On 8 July 1944, the Presidium of the Supreme Soviet of the USSR issued the Decree 'On Increasing State Aid to Pregnant Women, Mothers with Many Children and Single Mothers, Strengthening the Protection of Motherhood and Childhood, and Establishment of the Mother's Glory Order and the Medal of Motherhood'. State support for pregnant women, large families and single mothers was increased. The Decree, which had been drafted by Nikita Khrushchev, had pro-natalist aims to try to compensate for the massive wartime population losses. The state provided financial incentives to encourage families to have more than two children, providing subsidies for additional children. The Soviet state also threw its full weight behind official marriage and now repudiated de facto marriages, a total reversal of the approach of the early Soviet period: 'Only registered marriage generates rights and obligations between spouses.' Complex and expensive hurdles were placed on the path to divorce. Anyone who desired to dissolve a marriage had to submit a petition to a court for an expensive fee and summon the other spouse and witnesses. They also had to publish a paid announcement on the case in the local newspaper, appear at a People's Court hearing to discuss the possibilities of reconciliation before a higher court made the decision and pay 300 to 1,000 roubles to register the divorce. A note of any divorce was recorded in the Soviet passport, the main identity document. The whole procedure was meant to be accompanied by a round of public condemnation at Party, trade union or workplace meetings.

As far as children as a social group are concerned, one of the most far-reaching and disastrous effects of this new Decree was the reinstatement of illegitimacy as a legal category, again a total reversal from the radical ideas of the 1920s, when children had not been discriminated against by the circumstances of their birth. The aim was to encourage unmarried women and their male partners to have children outside marriage by, in theory, removing the financial cost of raising the child from both parents and displacing it onto the state. The law only recognized official marriages and so unmarried mothers no longer had any right to claim paternity for their children and the consequent child support payments. Instead, they were to receive financial support from the state until the child reached the age of twelve. Alternatively, if they so wished they could give up their children to be cared for in children's institutions without any financial cost, a feature of Soviet life that lasted until 1991. Single motherhood had become a legitimate 'site of reproduction', but in reality, the low financial support from the state condemned their children to poverty.[202] This legislation affected a large number of children. In the early post-war period, around 15 per cent of families were single-parent households, overwhelmingly headed by women.[203] It was estimated in 1947 that there were 11 million children classified as illegitimate and 3,312,000 unmarried mothers receiving benefits for them.[204] Other estimations are that the Soviet state created 8.7 million new 'fatherless' children between 1945 and 1955.[205] This legislation was controversial and unpopular and came in for sustained criticism after Stalin's death. The extreme preconditions for divorce were only mitigated in 1965 while the status of illegitimate children remained in force until 1968.

After decades of ambiguity towards adoption, the Soviet state heavily encouraged during and after the war. *Narkompros* launched national adoption and fostering campaigns under the general slogan 'Let there be no orphans among us!' In state propaganda, the ideal adopter was a mature woman who already had children, to keep the pressure to increase the natural birth rate. The state presented adoption as both a patriotic act and a source of personal joy for adults and children. Adoption law was modified, giving adoptive parents greater rights, no doubt to encourage the process. From 1943, for example, adoptive parents could put their names on the child's birth certificate and give children their patronymic and last name.[206] As earlier, children over the age of ten had to give consent to their own adoptions as well as to any changes to their names.[207] Adoptions could be reversed; there were to be many custody battles as biological parents or other relatives gradually re-emerged from the displacements of the war years. Local Soviet officials, the NKVD and the Union of Societies of the Red Cross and Red Crescent did everything they could to reunite families dispersed by the war, instigating and carrying out exhaustive enquiries as to the whereabouts of missing family members. If adoptions had taken place without the consent of the family, the courts usually upheld the rights of biological families. Workplaces adopted the children of colleagues who had died in the war, in part to circumvent the regulations forbidding the return of any evacuated children who were now orphaned. In May 1945, the Proletarian Victory Shoe Factory requested permission from the Leningrad Soviet to

> bring back along with the children's home from the Kirov region, 12 orphans, the children of our workers who were killed at the front or perished in the Blockade. ... The factory pledges that it will find somewhere for the children to live, guarantees that it will clothe the children and provide carers for them and will partially feed them from its own allotments.[208]

This form of fostering must have been unique to the Soviet Union and one wonders how widespread it was and what mixture of formalism and social solidarity determined these children's future fates.

Post-war childhoods

Of the estimated 27 million Soviet citizens who died during the Great Patriotic War, 76 per cent were men, most of the age of parenthood achieved or potential.[209] In rural areas, there were only 28 men for every 100 women in the eighteen to forty-nine age category.[210] Millions of children would grow up in homes without any adult males. Larisa Miller's father had died at the front in 1942 when she was two years old. Hardly any of her classmates in post-war Moscow had fathers living with them. She lived with her mother and both maternal grandparents, which by the standards of the day was considered a large family. Even though she knew her father was dead, she still longed for him:

> And yet, I was waiting for him to come back, I searched for him everywhere, I composed stories about him. I missed him most acutely when quarrels

broke out in the family, and also when mother was dismissed from *Red Army Men* newspaper, when she and I roamed the streets, reading 'Help Wanted' notices, and when I was harassed by the children in the yard.[211]

The state praised children and teenagers in the war's aftermath for the contributions they had made to the victory; 200,000 Pioneers had received awards and medals for the Defence of the Motherland.[212] Soviet child psychiatrists asked the state to support children who had trauma caused by their wartime experiences, while medical professionals recommended therapists should work in schools.[213] Yet the overall tone was victorious and the state soon monopolized the collective memory of the war, excising individual memories of pain and loss. The child who suffered had been a useful 'accusatory fact' during the war, but was no longer required in the victorious aftermath.[214]

The restoration and triumph of the Stalinist political order and the Soviet system was linked to the 'happy childhood' model. The state presented victory over Nazi Germany and the liberation of occupied Europe as justifying the Soviet system. The education and *vospitanie* of Soviet children was considered an important element in that system. 'Pedagogically abandoned' children, whose lives the war had disrupted, had to be re-disciplined, particularly in the areas that had come under German occupation. There were concerns at every level that children and adolescents had become more independent and assertive.[215] The state wanted to re-establish control over children in public places. 'Order and heroism' had to be reconciled.[216] Fears about the war's negative influence on children and adolescents led to an increase in school discipline, as in other aspects of Soviet life. Ludmila Petrushevskaya described herself as coming from that generation of 'post-war children, who grew up in conditions of total famine and old-school discipline'.[217] Teachers' Congresses demanded the application of stronger measures of discipline. In February 1944, the general secretary of the Komsomol complained that some teachers were taking discipline to extremes, placing children in isolation cells, escorting them with armed guards and having them arrested by the local police.[218]

The state tried to control the return of evacuated children to cities to avoid the disruption to the female labour that it was relying on for reconstruction and having to deal itself with problems caused by unsupervised children. The state ordered in 1944 that all childcare facilities were to be started again, but it is unlikely this happened. Children who had been orphaned or who had no relatives living in the city were forbidden to return with the rest of the group.[219] In 1945, Leningrad police processed 76,787 children who had been picked up for various reasons; only 8,752 were categorized as homeless.[220] Memoirs from early post-war period talk of the street culture of unsupervised children roaming destroyed and chaotic cities.[221] As usual, the behaviour of boys was considered as most problematic – smoking, drinking and getting drawn into juvenile crime. Citizen activists in various grassroots bodies were to keep children away from the 'lure of the streets'. A night-time curfew was imposed for under-sixteens. School-age children were forbidden to visit the cinema on their own. It was illegal to buy anything from a child unless they were selling items on behalf of their schools.

As elsewhere in Europe, states and societies viewed children outside kinship groups not only as victims of war, but also as potential carriers of disorder and crime. The Soviet state was embarrassed by the presence yet again of hundreds of thousands of orphaned and abandoned children in the cities and on transport networks, which contradicted its self-image as emerging victorious from the war.[222] The 'happy childhood' model had to be swiftly reinstated and those who disrupted it, marginalized. A major part of post-war reconstruction involved rebuilding, restocking and re-staffing schools. Local authorities vigorously pursued new school enrolment drives. In August 1945, the Soviet government published a resolution ordering house managers in apartment blocks to draw up lists of all school-age children living there.[223] Workplaces were encouraged to adopt (shefstvo) schools to help rebuild them, while Komsomol members were meant to help. Extra lessons were put on for children who had missed out on years of schooling. The high normative standards of Soviet education are revealed by one teacher's comment that she was shocked to discover that only a few evacuated children had read Charles Dickens, most only knew Shakespeare by hearsay and none had even heard of the German poet Friedrich Schiller.[224] On a more general level the Soviet behavioural norms of self-discipline and kulturnost, so painstakingly instilled by the state over the previous decades, had to be re-imposed.[225] There was little relaxation of military tensions. The early Cold War period saw continued emphasis on military preparedness and defence. The MVPO Local Anti-Air Defense, which offered military training, had 13 million child members in 1947.[226]

Conclusion

In 1949, 2,000 Pioneers held a ball in honour of Stalin's seventieth birthday, with the theme 'Thank you Stalin for our Happy Childhood!'[227] What kind of childhood had he created for them? In the 1930s and 1940s the qualities desired in a Soviet child were to be hard-working, honest, organized, highly disciplined and devoted to the collective, while simultaneously showing physical and mental independence and a capacity for self-development and activism. The Soviet model of childhood at this period was still influenced by the agricultural model, which viewed the child as a worker and contributor to the family economy rather than an object of care and attention by parents. Children in the first few decades of the Soviet period were expected to be physically self-reliant from a very young age, and were not quite yet the 'priceless child'.[228] Independence, of a certain kind, was highly valued.

The child's framework went well beyond the immediate family: 'How should one live to be useful to one's homeland?' was a question they were supposed to ask themselves. Yet Geiger's analysis of interviews from the Harvard Project seemed to suggest that the child-oriented family was well developed in certain social groups by the 1930s. From the 1930s, to be a Soviet child was to be excited by technology, science and progress and to reject religion. The future communist society would be technologically advanced, so mastery of the sciences was to be essential. Children were associated in this way with rationalism, rather than romanticism. However, childhood remained heroic and revolutionary. Children were becoming the 'new person'. Stalin and the Soviet regime linked childhood with the great transformations of industrialization and the bringing of 'modernity' to the Soviet Union, attracting the loyalty of a new generation. Lisa Kirschenbaum writes, 'Positing the identity of the child's … deepest desires and the state's interests made it possible to turn obedience to the great father into a revolutionary act.'[229] Revolutionary transformation and generational conflict were linked to the state's ends and the everyday, even for children, could become heroic.

Perhaps, the greatest change in the Stalinist years was the expansion of education. Like other transformers, the Bolsheviks understood that children's education would be a weapon for the remaking of society and for economic development and social modernization. Like other states, the Soviet state used the education system to regulate society by forging its future citizens. The expansion of compulsory education anywhere is part of the process of state formation and the extension of state power. Article 121 of the 1936 Stalin Constitution stated that 'citizens of the USSR have the right to be educated'. Between the school years of 1927/28 and 1938/9, total enrolment in the Soviet school system grew by 19 million pupils, 11 million more in primary schools, 8 million more in secondary schools, with the numbers in education rising from 11.3 million to 31.4 million.[230] This change was not simply about increases in literacy and numeracy and the acquisition of academic knowledge. Set days and demarcated periods of time were to be celebrated, observed and shared across the Soviet Union through the school network, which drew in virtually all children by the end of the 1930s. This was reiterated through the Pioneer and Octobrist movements in schools and in children's magazines and journals such as *Pionerskaya Pravda*. Some of these important days were 22 April, Lenin's birthday; May 1st, the worker's holiday and the day of the All-Union *Subbotnik*; 19 May, The Day of the Young Pioneers. May and June was the exam period, followed by the weeks of summer camp. The start of the new school year on 1 September (Day of Knowledge/*Den Znanie*) was celebrated with parades and ceremonies, although this did not become a formal holiday until 1984. Winter was for skiing, skating and putting up the New Year's tree, re-legalized from 1934. Lenin's birthday and the day of the All-Union *Subbotnik* were usually the dates on which children were inducted at school into the Pioneers. This ritualistic sameness enabled the creation of the idea of a standardized, normative childhood across the Soviet Union. We can compare this cyclical routine of Soviet childhood with that of the Don Cossack boy in late imperial Russia at the end of Chapter 3.

Politics saturated childhoods. Cathy Frierson estimates that around 10 million children (under-sixteens) had parents targeted by one of Stalin's campaigns from the 1930s to his death in 1953.[231] Frierson and Vilensky argue that children suffered along with their parents who were repressed by the state and also suffered because of deliberate Soviet policies which placed them in danger.[232] Terror was aimed at family groups and children were also 'collateral victims of political repression and terror'.[233] The Soviet state under Stalin strongly differentiated its treatment of children of 'class enemies' from the children of acceptable social groups.[234]

Despite children's seeming power and status in the Soviet Union, the educational system under Stalin reinforced hierarchy, discipline and the personalized authority of the adult. The concept of discipline in Russian (*distsiplina*) did not mean teaching children to be obedient or simply the exertion of control over their behaviour. It was instead a 'desired attribute ... an end in itself, something to acquire and master' for children themselves.[235] In this way, just like adults, the state incorporated children into the Stalinist practices of self-fashioning, restraint and the acquisition of *kul'turnost*.

Despite all the talk of a 'happy childhood', it can be argued that although the child had symbolic value in the Soviet state, there was little concept of the 'child as child' or childhood as precious and valuable for itself, in the European tradition begun by Rousseau in the late eighteenth century.[236] In the post-Stalin years, there would be a turn to that during the relaxation of tensions under Khrushchev (the Thaw). However, many of the structures, constructs and features constitutive of a 'Soviet childhood' were laid down in this period, remaining influential until the 1980s and even beyond.

6

Post-war Soviet childhoods, 1953–91

Introduction

Children are our future, our joy and happiness. Our first thoughts are about them. Theirs must be a life of smiles. For their sake, we are fighting and working. Our children are destined to live in a communist society and in the Soviet Union everything is being done to give them a happy life so that they should grow up to be healthy, vivacious citizens of the state, its future masters.[1]

The Stalinist period was key to the creation of a new and stable model of Soviet childhood, although it did incorporate some of the aspects of the revolutionary child of the 1920s. It was in the period after Stalin's death in 1953 that a modern model of childhood became something approaching the reality of most children's lives. The 1950s and 1960s were decades of great change in the Soviet Union. Universal schooling, a functioning welfare state and medical infrastructure, and a clear advance in standards of living transformed the lived experience of children and the structures of childhood from the 1950s. Children remained at the symbolic centre of Soviet life. The state described children as the 'only privileged class'. One of the obligations of a Soviet citizen outlined in the 1977 Constitution was 'to bring up children, train them for work and raise them as worthy members of society'.[2] The programme of the CPSU declared: 'To ensure that every child will have a happy childhood – that is one of the most important and noble tasks of the building of a communist society.'

Nikita Khrushchev (1956–1964) gradually emerged as Stalin's successor as Secretary General of the Communist Party. He initiated an era of reform, known as the Thaw, to improve the daily lives of Soviet citizens and reduce state terror but also to reinvigorate the commitment to a communist future. Khrushchev launched a de-Stalinization campaign, most famously in his 'Secret Speech' to the 20th Party Congress in February 1956. At the 22nd Party Congress in 1961, Khrushchev introduced the *Third Party Programme* of the Communist Party and promised that communism would be built by 1980. Those who were children then, those born in the 1950s and early 1960s, would complete this task, making them a vital social group for the state. The state constantly pushed the message of their importance to them, although the reception was mixed. Many recall the enthusiasm of the early 1960s and the shared belief in a future scientific and humanistic utopia:

> Our teachers and the whole atmosphere of school life undoubtedly, was pushing the childish organism of the pupils to the discovery of some kind of new hormone, some new kind of energy, beyond the human. We felt this energy around us and within us and not only at school but also at home as we had to participate in the life of adults with almost obligatory marches during the demonstrations on the 'red days' of the calendar and then the evenings around the table as state holidays turned into family ones.[3]

One woman, a child in the early 1960s, recalled how mortified she felt when her teacher expressed her dislike for her by saying to the rest of the class, 'Well, we won't be taking *her* into communism with us!'[4]

Others had doubts; a woman born in 1950 recalled of Khrushchev's predictions:

> But people didn't think it was possible. Even children. How could we? Because suddenly we didn't have bread here in Saratov. There was no milk. What kind of communism could there be when they passed out bread in school?[5]

Between 1956 and 1962, the state raised the minimum wage and social security benefits were also improved.[6] Of greater significance, Khrushchev – and later Brezhnev – prioritized the provision of mass urban housing. From the late 1950s onwards, more children would grow up in small private flats in modern purpose-built neighbourhoods, living only with their immediate family members. This new development, which could have heralded a 'retreat' from collective life, was offset by a commitment to providing more collective public spaces for children – kindergartens, Pioneer Palaces and sports grounds – as well as continuing to try to regulate the courtyard and other urban spaces children played in. This development had an impact on the structures and experiences of childhood. This increased privacy for family also paradoxically spurred further state intervention in the family sphere. While family life was now protected from state terror, new attempts were made to regulate it through the enforcement of standards of 'communist morality' by groups of professionals and volunteers (*obshchestvennost'*) in an array of grassroots organizations.[7] All family decisions were held to have ramifications for the state, and the family was subject to social intervention.

The cultural values of the Thaw included more concern for the individual development of the child and respect for the child's supposed natural proclivity for creativity and self-expression. Children were once again associated with play and fantasy. In her study of the construction of a new Pioneer Palace in Moscow, Susan Reid has argued that the Khrushchev period was characterized by a notion of childhood as more distinct from adulthood than under Stalinism, closer to nature and with direct access to the world of imagination.[8] This was a return to the influences of Rousseau and romanticism. Official childcare practices, child literature and psychological theories about children were framed in a humanistic paradigm which 'partially legitimized the notion of the "being child"'.[9] In some ways though, this 'romanticization' of the construct of the 'Soviet child' can be explained by Khrushchev's desire to return to the 'sources of the revolutionary fervour' of the 1920s and reject Stalinism. Therefore, in this sense it was still a political shift.[10]

In fact, the extreme politicization of childhood continued into the Cold War. Soviet children were encouraged to participate in the Soviet peace movement and express solidarity with global anti-colonial struggles. The Soviet Union in the 1960s and 1970s was at the height of its international power. It supported decolonization and national liberation movements across the Global South as part of its strategy of competitive coexistence with the United States. The pressure was kept up on children to identify as both revolutionaries and peace activists. When Pioneer rallies were reintroduced in 1962 the prescribed programme included a 'Day for the Defence of Peace'. Children from other socialist countries were invited to these events in practices of transnational solidarity.[11] In this period of competitive coexistence, the Soviet state continued to extol its treatment of children and provision of a 'happy childhood' as one of the elements of its superiority to capitalist states. Just as foreign visitors to the Soviet Union had been taken to see Model Schools in Moscow in the 1930s, now purpose-built Pioneer Palaces were placed on tourist itineraries.

Reforms in education directly impacted the lives of children, although there was much continuity as Soviet education remained openly committed to inculcating values and beliefs about the benefits of collectivism, dedication to 'socially useful labour' and the development of moral character (*vospitanie*). Even kindergartens for preschool children left little space for the free play that had become prevalent in contemporary West European educational theory by the 1960s. They followed a standardized, rigid and highly controlled schedule as outlined in *The Programme: Upbringing and Instruction in the*

Kindergarten.[12] At the other end of the age range, childhood was extended from fourteen to sixteen as the age for leaving compulsory education rose.

Families became smaller. The Soviet birth rate dropped from 44.3 per thousand in 1928 to 24.9 in 1960, one of the most rapid drops in recorded history.[13] By 1974, it was at 18.2 per 1,000 of the population.[14] A small family of one or two children became the cultural ideal, although not necessarily the ideal of the state. Soviet educators worried about whether the 'only child' was capable of being a proper socially active member of the collective. Makarenko had earlier warned of potential problems caused by presumably spoilt and selfish only children. The decision to limit fertility, combined with the extension of medical services and drop in infant and child mortality, meant that the frequent death of siblings, which had been a defining feature of childhood for centuries, had now become a highly unusual and traumatic life event.

Under Brezhnev (1964–82), the Soviet state prioritized the provision of consumer goods and families spent their budgets on toys and games and music lessons, particularly as there was now usually only a single child. Natalya Chernyaeva, who grew up in the Soviet Union in the 1970s, recalls that low-middle-class intelligentsia families like hers

> developed a distinctive pattern of consumption, in which all the family's scarce resources were lavished on a precious child, and it was not unusual for children from families of very modest means to live in a 'bubble' of relative prosperity.[15]

Urbanization and the 'privatization' of family life continued. Between 1965 and 1978, 10.5 million people moved into private flats every year.[16] By the time of 'really existing socialism' in the 1970s and 1980s, state and society began to see childhood and adolescence as complex and unique periods of life. More emphasis was put on the emotional value of the individual child and its emotional needs; the era of the 'priceless child' had finally arrived.

By the late Soviet period, the state's promise of universal and accessible childcare made in 1917 had largely been fulfilled, at least in urban areas. In 1960, only 14 per cent of children had attended Soviet preschool institutions, but by 1985 two-thirds – around 17 million children – did.[17] Soviet children in the post-war period were perhaps all 'children of the state', as they spent more time in kindergartens, schools and clubs than with their families. Time budget studies from the early 1980s showed that women had only 25 minutes a day to spend with their children during the week, rising to 50 minutes on the weekend.[18] In the early 1980s almost 11 million children stayed in school until 7.00 pm, where they had their evening meal and help with homework.[19]

From the outset, the Soviet government had encouraged children to believe that they could and would have a radically different life from their parents and a life better than that lived by children in the capitalist world. The notion that Soviet children were far better off than children in capitalist societies carried on throughout the Cold War, but as life in the Soviet Union became more difficult in the 1980s and society became more open, these claims rang increasingly hollow and contributed to the general sense of malaise. By the 1980s, childhood itself seemed under threat.

Developments in Soviet education in the post-war period

By the 1950s, 57 million children were enrolled in school, compared to the 8.1 million in late imperial Russia.[20] Since the Revolution, Soviet education had shifted from an emphasis on vocational training, pedagogical experimentation and the 'liberated child' to the highly academic curricula and strictly disciplined schools of Stalinism. In the post-war decades, the state recognized that Soviet education needed to be more imaginative and creative and that there should be a shift away from the Stalinist model of a teacher-centred pedagogy. Despite this, most of the structures and approaches remained the same until 1991. Under Khrushchev, there was a return to a vocational emphasis in education, as part of his overall efforts to rejuvenate enthusiasm and mobilize society for the transition to communism. Khrushchev wanted to make sure that Soviet children were preparing themselves for a future of work.

In 1954, lessons in basic manual skills had been introduced in primary schools. In 1955, two hours of practical work a week became mandatory in the final years of secondary school. In 1958, the Memorandum 'On Strengthening the Link between School and Life and Further Developing the System of Public Education' declared that 'the most important task in education is that all children should be ready for useful work, ready to take part in the building up of Communist society'. A Decree of December 1958 further reiterated that the purpose of education was to prepare pupils for socially useful labour. All fifteen- to sixteen-year-olds should be taking part in 'socially useful work suitable to their age, and all their further education should be combined with productive work in the national economy'.[21]

In 1959 the RSFSR curriculum was reformed and the time allocated to manual skills rose by two or three hours a week for the first years of secondary school and as much as twelve hours a week for the later years, taking up around one-third of the timetable. Pupils were sent into factories for training.[22] These reforms were opposed by both factory and plant managers, who did not want to incorporate adolescents into the workplace and by the

Soviet elites who wished to transmit their status to their offspring and were not interested in them spending time in factories. These particular changes were abandoned after Khrushchev was deposed in 1964. However, some degree of vocational training was compulsory in primary and secondary schools until the end of the Soviet Union and the instillation of a love of labour remained theoretically one of the most important tasks of the Soviet education system.

Khrushchev also promoted the expansion of state boarding schools (*internaty*). Initially he envisaged that the number of pupils in them would be 2.5 million by 1965. State boarding schools would be built in state-of-the-art facilities and staffed by expert pedagogues. One target group for Khrushchev's boarding school plan were the children of unmarried mothers, the category of child created by the 1944 Family Law discussed earlier. The 'fatherless' children of the early post-war period were now reaching school age. Between 1947 and 1957 there was a tenfold increase in single mothers receiving child allowances, when they peaked at 2.8 million.[23] Many of these were only children, a 'suspect' sub-category of child seen as in need of support with a suitable collective upbringing. Khrushchev launched his boarding school project in the Central Committee's Report to the 20th Party Congress in 1956 as part of his optimism about the future transition to communism. In his view, too many children were being brought up by widows, single parents and working parents while they could instead be placed in 'model institutions raising model citizens'.[24] Khrushchev's boarding school project never worked out in practice, mainly due to the usual reasons of state underfunding. However, it also came up against strong parental reluctance to the idea of sending children away. Most of the pupils who did attend state boarding schools came from disadvantaged backgrounds and ended up there because of their poverty. The schools' function became that of social welfare, rather than the provision of advanced socialist education for the new generation. There were 980,000 pupils in boarding schools in 1963, which accounted for 2 to 3 per cent of school-age children.[25] There was a peak of 1.6 million children at the end of the 1960s but the numbers went into decline after that.[26] Khrushchev's boarding school policy was one last attempt at imposing a collectivist ideal of state upbringing for children, at a time when actually most children were moving into private flats designed for nuclear families. Soviet society rejected his vision.

Khrushchev was unhappy that only around 30 to 40 per cent of students at Moscow University were of working-class or peasant origins, despite these social classes being numerically overwhelming.[27] To increase the chances of social mobility for working-class and peasant adolescents he abolished the fees for upper-level secondary schooling introduced under Stalin and larger quotas were set for working-class children to go to university. This measure was to mitigate the increasingly stratified childhoods, as the Soviet elites had become more entrenched. The Brezhnev years saw an immediate return to a competitive secondary education system for access to higher education. Khrushchev's other educational reforms were later partially reversed as well. In 1966, the number of hours of vocational training in secondary schools was cut back to two hours practical work and only a third of secondary schools offered any vocational training. Boarding school numbers were frozen.

There was no streaming in Soviet schools and children studied a set national curriculum. As part of the Pioneer collectivist ethos, children who performed better than their peers were supposed to help those who were struggling and exert peer pressure on the recalcitrant. At the same time, from the mid-1950s, a network of specialist schools were established for children who showed high levels of ability in foreign languages, mathematics, science, art and music. The state selected pupils to attend these prestigious schools through open competitions or by entrance exams, though in reality entrance was weighted heavily in favour of the children of Soviet elites, who either had the ability to pay for extra tuition or used their connections to gain access to opportunities.[28] By the late 1960s, there were 50 specialist art and music schools and 700 specialist language schools.[29] Prominent examples of science-oriented specialist schools include the FMSh (*fiziko-matematicheskaya shkola*), a physics and mathematics boarding school for fifteen- to seventeen-year-olds attached to Novosibirsk University and the *Kolmogorovskaya shkola* in Moscow. By the 1980s, 2 to 3 per cent of schoolchildren identified as particularly gifted were attending specialist schools.[30]

As well as changes, there were continuities in Soviet post-war education. Makarenko's work was still the normative pedagogical approach in the post-war decades, emphasizing self-discipline and the primacy of working in the interests of the collective. Teachers were still expected to have relationships of benign surveillance with their school class and were meant to visit pupils in their homes at the beginning of every school year to monitor the family dynamic. Discipline remained strict in appearance and behaviour; unacceptable behaviour was recorded in Disciplinary Books. As in the Stalinist period, the school was meant to be the object of deep loyalty and emotional attachment. Children were encouraged to have a positive view of school and education and view their teacher as a 'friend'. Schools developed their own traditions and songs. Historical and political events were closely interwoven with the life of the school. When Yuri Gagarin's successful space flight took place on 12 April 1961, schools across the Soviet Union finished early for the day to celebrate the event that for many who were children at the time encapsulated the Soviet link of utopia with childhood. A man who had been a child then recalled:

In 1961 Gagarin flew into the cosmos. There was not the slightest doubt that he could only have made this flight from our country – the best country in the whole wide world! It wasn't for nothing that we beat our drums and blew our Pioneer bugles, was it? It was like some kind of crazy cosmic joy – totally unforgettable.[31]

From 1962, the Day of the Cosmonauts on 12 April became another celebration day to add to the Soviet children's calendar. Cosmonauts replaced football players and aviators as children's heroes. In the Soviet period, schools were sponsored (*sheftsvo*) by local military units, factories, plants or enterprises. This had been formalized in 1932 during the expansion of the school system. One woman recounts how in the 1960s her school was sponsored by DOSAF (The Voluntary Society to Aid the Army, Aviation and Flotilla). The school had an old MiG-17 Soviet fighter plane placed at the front, which she and her friends were once allowed to sit in as a reward for winning a cross-school competition.[32] Their school song was the 'March of the Aviators', the official song of the Soviet Air Forces and one that was played to greet Soviet cosmonauts. Summarizing the atmosphere of those times, and indeed the emotional tenor of a proper 'Soviet child', she writes how as they sang the famous lines 'We were born to make fairy tales come true/to overcome vastness and expanse', 'our voices flew upwards and harmonised in an ecstasy that was simultaneously life-affirming and self-sacrificial'.[33]

Differences in rural and urban schooling remained and these differences were heightened by the depopulation of the villages. By the 1970s, most primary schools in rural areas had less than twenty-five pupils.[34] In 1973 in the hope of reanimating rural schools, the state promised the provision of more housing for pupils and teachers, as well as more school buses and equipment. This was an attempt to raise their standard closer to that of urban schools and halt the depopulation of the countryside.[35] Rural adolescents who boarded at secondary schools in towns rarely returned to settle back in the villages.

As well as excelling individually and being self-reliant, Soviet children were meant to accept responsibility for the success of their collectives ('the link' or subgroup within the class, the class, the school) and offer help and support to weaker members on whom their own status depended. They were expected to evaluate and criticize each other's behaviour from the point of view of the group, as well as share cooperatively operating with the principle of 'what's mine is ours, and ours is mine' – '*Moe eto nashe; nashe moe*'.[36] They were taught to be loyal to the Party and be prepared to protect the USSR from its enemies. Many responded to Soviet patriotism, for example, a woman who went to school in the late 1970s declared: 'That is the way we were raised: first comes social responsibility, before the personal!'[37] Another who went to school in the 1980s commented, 'When we were at school we really believed that we were living in a great and happy land with bright futures. … Perhaps because we had nothing to compare it to?'[38] Others found the values and practices of the Soviet school stifling and hypocritical.

In their study of early literacy textbooks in the late Soviet period, Silova and Palanjian describe how the Bolshevik 'temporal blurring' of the child and adult continued right into the late Soviet period. Emphasis was placed on children's participation in work ('socially useful labour'), even for the very smallest children.[39] The strong emphasis on early physical independence and acceptance of responsibilities remained. In the normative Soviet childhood, in the first year of primary school (aged seven) children were expected to help out with housework and childcare, be able to behave properly in public places, obey all adults and explore and interact with their local area. 'Communist morality' for this age encompassed a sense of good and bad behaviour, truthfulness, honesty, kindness, an understanding of atheism, self-discipline, diligence, friendship and love of neighbourhood and country.[40] In terms of 'socially useful labour', by the first year of secondary school, children were expected to chop wood for school if needed, keep the school clean, clear snow, act as a monitor, help out weaker classmates, help in the school garden, supervise younger children, do simple repairs, have a proper posture in class and communicate well with other pupils. Outside of school, they were to help at home, be able to do basic cooking, tidy the garden or courtyard, show care for others, help in kindergartens and crèches, show cultured behaviour, look after public places and heritage sites and perform socially useful work such as collecting scrap metal.[41] At the other end of the school system, communist morality for sixteen- to eighteen-year-olds encompassed collectivism, duty, honour and conscience, development of will, patience and perseverance, a communist attitude to work and public property, socialist humanism and proletarian internationalism.[42]

In the Soviet school, emphasis remained placed on obedience, academic excellence and self-regulation. As throughout Russian history since the Enlightenment, the school's role was not just to educate and impart academic knowledge but also to engage in *vospitanie*, political education and guidance to develop communist morality. As Thomas Ewing comments:

> *Vospitanie* in official educational discourse included the maturation of the child, the formation of a worldview, the development of character, socialization into customs and the habits of the established order, and the acquisition of knowledge and skills.[43]

In the school curriculum, the study of literature was still a main conduit for *vospitanie* and teaching communist morality, as well as where the lessons of Soviet patriotism were learnt. Although the secondary school literature syllabus did include Western writers such as Homer, Cervantes, Shakespeare, Hans Christian Andersen, Moliere, Goethe, Byron and Balzac, the focus was on Russian and Soviet literature. The classic Soviet texts from or about the Great Patriotic War were at the heart of the literature curriculum. Children were encouraged to identify with the sacrificial child and adolescent heroes, as well as the adult positive heroes. Typical texts studied were Kataev's *Son of the Regiment*, Gaidar's *Timur and His Team*, Boris Polevoy's *Story of a Real Man (Povest' o nastoyaschim cheloveke)* about the Soviet fighter pilot Aleksei Mares'yev who fought on in the war despite having his legs amputated, and Aleksandr Tvardovsky's *Vasilii Tyorkin* about an ordinary soldier in the Great Patriotic War. These books had a deep imprint:

> In those days, [late 1960s and early 1970s] our favourite pastime was reading. The heroes of A. Gaidar, L. Kassil', A. Rybakov, A. Fadeev and M. Sholokhov raised us to be responsible, brave, honest, to show initiative, called us to good deeds and taught us the value of friendship.[44]

There was concern in the late Soviet period that the heavily didactic and teacher-centred school system was stifling creativity and initiative in children, with worrying implications for the Soviet future. In the 1970s, the state made a conscious decision to move away from the Stalinist model of pedagogical teacher-centred didacticism.[45] However, the state monopoly on historical truth made this very hard to carry out in the humanities. When Gorbachev became General Secretary in 1985, like Khrushchev he wanted to reinvigorate Soviet society's commitment to building communism. The 1980s saw major educational reforms, with renewed emphasis on labour training and work experience, strengthened by further stress on political education and an attempt to promote more active forms of learning. As the Soviet system started falling apart in the late 1980s, the Soviet school lost its prestige and there was a call for a *perestroika* (restructuring) in education.

The Octobrist and Pioneer movements in late Soviet society

As earlier, the Pioneer and Octobrist movements bore responsibility for carrying out *vospitanie*. *Vospitanie* in late Soviet socialism meant raising children to be politically aware, ethical and patriotic internationalists and cultured atheists, with a desire to carry out socially useful work, an appreciation of beauty and a love of sport.[46] From the late 1950s, there was an attempt by the state to reinvigorate the Pioneer movement and move it away from its auxiliary role of supporting performance in the Soviet school system. The function of the movement was reconceptualized as a return to the Russian progressive educationalist aim of the 'harmonious development of the individual personality'. More emphasis was also placed on the encouragement of greater initiative and self-direction in children. Pioneers were meant to remain politically active though, particularly on the international level, as will be discussed later. This and other developments in the late Soviet period have been interpreted as a move away from the Stalinist model of a grateful and dependent childhood.

Pioneer Palaces were built in greater numbers in the 1960s and 1970s, funded by the Komsomol. In 1958, Artek became the official Pioneer headquarters. It was also expanded in the early 1960s when it became an 'international children's camp', on the front line of the battle for competitive coexistence and for hearts and minds in the Cold War. Another prestigious Pioneer Camp on the Black Sea, *Orlyenok*, was opened in 1960 to reward high-achieving children. On the 1 June 1962, the Day of the Protection of Children, Khrushchev opened a new Pioneer Palace in Moscow.[47] The Palace was designed using modernist principles, a children's 'city of the future' rejecting the monumentalism and neoclassicism of Stalinist architecture.[48] The larger Pioneer camps and Palaces had swimming pools, planetariums, cinemas, cosmonautic museums and sports grounds and functioned as international showpieces for the concern the Soviet state had for children and for the privileges it gave them. More modest city camps expanded in number from 185 in 1965 to 324 in 1976.[49] By the 1960s, the majority of Soviet children attended some kind of summer camp, even if this just meant a few weeks hiking and camping outside the city limits. As noted earlier, the closer association of children with nature (rather than with industry) foregrounds a later Soviet notion of childhood, which was influenced by Rousseau and romanticism.[50] Many post-Soviet life writings emphasize how much as children they enjoyed the Pioneer camps, not for direct political indoctrination but for the sociality, play and activities: swimming, the cosmonautic clubs and the campfire at the close of the day.[51] A recent study of online post-socialist childhood memory work shows that this connection between childhood, nature and the conviviality of the Pioneer camp forms a major part of the collective emotional memory of the late Soviet period.[52]

Another significant collective memory of late socialist childhood is the *Zarnitsa,* a military-oriented competitive game for Pioneer-aged children with manoeuvres, reconnaissance, ambushes and mock battles, which was introduced across the Soviet Union in 1967. Participants were divided into green and blue teams, distinguishable by coloured armbands. The aim was to try to capture the 'enemy' flag, while avoiding being taken 'prisoner', a fate achieved when an armband had been ripped off by the other team. As with the Pioneer camp, the day would end with a campfire and communal celebration.

There was a great expansion in membership of these organizations, plus the facilities and activities that they could offer. By the late 1960s, around 15 million children were part of the Octobrist movement for six- to nine-year-olds.[53] Their 'Little Red Star' initiation ceremony took place on 7 November, the anniversary of the Revolution. This was preceded by a period of learning about Lenin and the Revolution, accompanied by a lot of game playing. At the ceremony, which was led by older children in the Pioneers, new Octobrists were given a badge of a five-pointed star with a picture of Lenin as a child in the middle. The normative guidance for Octobrists in the 1980s was that they were meant to love work and school and respect their elders as well as being friendly, honest, creative and life affirming.[54]

In 1960, the Pioneer movement had 15.4 million members out of a cohort of 16.6 million in the age group. In 1970, the equivalent figures were 23 million out of a cohort of 25 million.[55] In 1977 Moscow had 7 Pioneer Palaces and 32 Pioneer Houses, which ran more than 4,300 clubs with 75,000 child participants.[56] Pioneer initiation ceremonies took place in the week of Lenin's birthday in late April. Many of those who had been schoolchildren in the later Soviet period still remember how thrilled they had been when they were allowed to join the Pioneers, even when membership was almost universal. Children were inducted in groups, and to be chosen for one of the first groups based on good school performance and behaviour was considered a great achievement:

> I was bursting with pride when I was one of the first to have the red kerchief tied round. The first few days I went everywhere in it and never took it off. … I felt part of something large and grand. When I would whisper the oath to myself, I could barely hold back the tears.[57]
>
> And while everyone eventually became Pioneers, it was an honor to be inaugurated first. I earned that honor and I was particularly proud to be a part of the Communist future. We marched in circles around the school as the songs of the Great Patriotic War blasted on school speakers. Our pledge was 'Always Ready'. We were the future believers. We were the future sacrifice. As the old Soviet joke went, 'What is the difference between a Pioneer and a boiled egg? A Pioneer is always ready and the egg takes five minutes.'[58]

The Pioneer Laws changed again during the period of 'really existing socialism', with war remembrance and love of nature now added in:

1 A Pioneer honours the memory of those who have given their life in the struggle for freedom and the flowering of the Soviet Motherland.

2 A Pioneer is a friend to children of all the nations of the world.

3   A Pioneer studies diligently, is disciplined and courteous.

4   A Pioneer likes to work and takes good care of public property.

5   A Pioneer develops courage and does not fear difficulty.

6   A Pioneer tells the truth and treasures the honour of his unit.

7   A Pioneer develops his physique, does physical exercises every day.

8   A Pioneer loves nature; he is a protector of green plants, useful birds and animals.

9   A Pioneer is an example to all children.[59]

Children's lives within the family

From the 1950s, a Soviet notion of a personal life took shape, which included the right to family apartments and family holidays. In 1960, the Soviet economist Sergei Strumilin relaunched the original revolutionary call for public child rearing, prophesizing that

> every Soviet citizen, upon emerging from hospital as a baby, will go to a crèche, from there to a nursery school maintained day and night or to a children's home. From there, he will go to a boarding school, from which he will depart with a ticket into independent life.[60]

In this view, the Soviet family was essentially reduced to the adult couple. The 1961 Party programme did not support this approach however and Khrushchev restated that the family would grow stronger under communism, despite his own commitment to boarding schools. The introduction of the five-day working week at this time was meant to enable parents to spend more time with their children. In 1960, the Supreme Soviet decreed a seven-hour day and the free time gained was meant to be spent as a family.[61] In reality throughout the late Soviet period, adults worked long hours and women then spent more time on shopping and chores. Even for the generation born after the war, grandparents and particularly grandmothers remained key figures in children's lives, often looking after children full time while their parents worked or studied. 'Children with grandparents had better a childhood than those without', recalled one woman born in 1950.[62] The practice of hiring a peasant *domrabotnitsa* for urban families persisted into the early post-war period as well.

The 1960s saw the introduction of fifteen days paid holiday leave as well as the five-day week.[63] From its inception, the Soviet state provided holidays for both adults and children. These were intended for medical and health purposes, for cultural improvement or for the development of a Soviet identity by visiting other Republics. The state presented them as part of the benefits of socialism. In the Stalinist period, state-subsidized holidays were for work collectives, aiming to strengthen work-based identities, not the family as a unit.[64] The reluctance to sanction 'family holidays' reveals the ambiguity the Soviet state felt towards families and any claims to personal interests. An extensive tourist infrastructure of health spas, resorts, nature walking holidays and standardized travel itineraries across the Soviet Union was developed for adults, excluding children, who instead went to Pioneer camps and health spas of their own. Public opinion surveys in the 1960s though seemed to reveal a desire to holiday with one's own family. From the 1960s, the state showed a grudging official acceptance of family holidays and called for the expansion of family vacation facilities in tourist camps and resorts. The state now built 'family friendly' hotels and developed a family-oriented tourism on the Black Sea. Many Soviet families holidayed together anyway. In 1961, the Krasondar region hosted 170,000 vacationers through the workplace voucher system and a further 1.5 million who came outside these schemes on their own.[65]

Families were getting smaller, and most children now had only one sibling, if any. In the 1970s, the average family had 2.39 children but in urban areas, it was 1.68.[66] Female participation in higher education and the labour market, urbanization, divorce and education were all contributing factors to this low birth rate. By the late 70s, 86 per cent of women of working age had an occupation outside the home.[67]

One major change in the post-war decades was that of where children lived. The 1950s and 1960s was an era of mass residential construction, when many families in urban areas finally moved out of communal apartments in the city centre into private flats in four or five storey apartment blocks, often in newly developed *mikro-raions* on the outskirts of the city. The city centred emptied of children. These mass housing areas became known as *khrushchoby*, a play on Khrushchev's name and the Russian word for slums. Between 1955 and 1970, more than 35 million family apartments were built and 130 million Soviet citizens moved into them.[68] Many children welcomed this as a dramatic and exciting improvement in living conditions. 'A tramline rumbled along outside our windows', remembered one woman who grew up in Gorky (Nizhni Novgorod), 'but nobody minded as this was considered a distinguishing marker of urban civilisation. Beyond the tramline were garages, and gardens that blossomed in the spring. We were children of the sixties living in Gorky ... and we were happy.'[69] The street that her apartment block was on and her Pioneer Group were named after the cosmonaut Valentina

Tereshkova, who had become the first woman to fly into space in June 1963. The local children's club she attended was called *Chaika* (Seagull), which had been Tereshkova's call sign on her flight. Urban planning in the period of late socialism was generally non-hierarchal and *mikro-raiony* were built with the perceived needs of children in mind, including schools, children's clubs, sports facilities and parks and other spaces where collective activities could take place. By 1970, just over half of Russia's families lived in towns, mostly in private apartments. It was still relatively common for the grandmother to live with the family, or live close by, to look after the children and keep the household running while both parents worked or studied. In Leningrad in 1970, a quarter of families were still three-generational.[70]

The Party adopted the 'Moral Code for the Builders of Communism' in 1961 at the XXII Party Conference. This consisted of twelve tenets, one of which was 'mutual respect in the family, concern for the upbringing of children'.[71] It has been argued that rather than a signal of a new post-Stalin era, The Code was lifted from the values embedded in 1930s Stalinist children's literature and therefore was meaningful to the generation that had been socialized by these texts.[72] Parents were meant to raise a child as 'a true patriot, an honest labourer, a good collectivist, a worthy successor and continuer of our great Revolutionary task'.[73] They were encouraged to take an interest in their children's education and focus on 'enrichment' in their free time. Maternal care was seen as most valuable for very young children; fathers came into their own with education and *kul'turnost, vospitanie*, hobbies and excursions.[74] As it had done since the 1930s, the state insisted it had provided the prerequisites for a happy, stable family life and therefore deviations from the norm were due to personal failings. An expert warned:

> There can be no 'difficult children' in families where the parents take the upbringing of their children seriously, visit the school often, constantly watch over the success and accomplishments of their children.[75]

A range of official and voluntary bodies monitored children's lives within the private family setting. Factory Committees, the Voluntary People's Militia (*druzhiny*), Resident's Committees (*domkomy*), Comrades' Courts, Trade Unions, Party Committees and Parent-School Committees were all empowered to intervene in the family. Parent-School committees established ties between the school and the family and got parents involved in their children's education. In Residents' Committees, volunteers organized after-school activities, helped with homework and supervised parenting. Workplaces monitored the school performance (including behaviour) of employees' children and even posted school marks on their bulletin boards.[76] The Komsomol took an interest in 'problem children'. The *Komissiya po rabote s naseleniem* (Commission for Work with the Population) in the local Soviets offered family seminars on such topics as 'Life is not a Personal, Private Affair'.[77] In the early 1960s, Moscow had 80,000 'parent activists' on voluntary committees in schools, housing and workplaces.[78]

A Russian Republic law of 1957 and an All-Union law of 1961 reintroduced Minors' Commissions, which Stalin had abolished in 1935. The use of these expanded greatly in the 1970s. Minors' Commissions consisted of teachers and representatives from the Party, trade unions, doctors, lawyers, the Komsomol, Soviets, the police and local educational authorities. Minors Commissions dealt with cases of juvenile delinquency and could petition courts to remove children from neglectful or abusive parents. Even though they were not part of the court system, they could send children to Children's Educational Colonies. Parents were blamed for either spoiling or neglecting their children. In one meeting of a Minors Commission, the father of a disruptive boy was asked, 'Did you go with your son to the theatre, to the cinema, did you discuss readings with him? How did you help him gain an understanding of life?', revealing the ideal role of the father and the ideals of a Soviet childhood.[79]

Comrades' Courts held discussions with troubled families and brought legal cases against neglectful parents.[80] Comrades' Courts were heavily relied on in the Brezhnev years. These were lay bodies which 'entitled unskilled personnel to deal with complex childcare problems…[with] the deliberate use of public censure and shaming'.[81] Many Soviet families still lived in communal apartments, which increased both the surveillance and safeguarding of children. Neighbours stepped in to care for, or report, neglected children. Surveillance and safeguarding were everybody's responsibility.

Although the Soviet state had tried to justify the 1944 Family Law that freed fathers of financial responsibility for children born outside of official marriage as progressive, it was always deeply unpopular. In 1956, the Soviet luminaries Samuil Marshak, Ilya Ehrenburg, Dmitrii Shostakovich and leading paediatrician Georgy Speranskii had written to *Literaturnaya gazeta* criticizing the law.[82] Some adjustments were finally made in the late 1960s. The 1968 Basic Principles of the Legislation of the USSR and Union Republics on Marriage and the Family allowed for the establishment of paternity and rights to child maintenance outside marriage. The subsequent 1969 RSFSR Family Code allowed courts to establish paternity by considering evidence of cohabitation, the forming of a common household, joint upbringing or recognition of paternity.[83] This also allowed the father's name to be on the birth certificate in cases of de facto marriages.

After the 'Happy Childhood' of Stalinism and the cosmic utopian childhood of the 1960s, childhood became increasingly problematized in the 1970s and 1980s. Children were becoming regarded not just as self-sufficient future citizens, but also as vulnerable, unique individuals in need of special psychological protection.[84] The state viewed alcoholism and family breakdown (two closely linked and widespread phenomena) as damaging to children.

By the 1980s, around 400,000 children a year were becoming part of single-parent households.[85] Research on family behaviour, child development and social problems was prioritized. The results seemed to point to negative educational and psychological outcomes for children growing up in single-parent families, as well as the clear link between single-parent families and child poverty.[86] A new course was introduced into Soviet secondary schools for years nine and ten, 'The Ethics and Psychology of Family Life', to try and combat potential future family breakdowns. Juvenile delinquency was on the rise again. At the same time, there was greater emphasis on the role of the family in knowing what was best for the child. There was increased public debate by economists, sociologists and demographers over whether Soviet women's double (or triple) burden was damaging children's well-being and whether or not women with young children should be supported more to stay at home to care for them, rather than work outside the home. Paid and unpaid maternity leave and child benefits gradually increased across the 1970s and 1980s to facilitate this, despite the seeming contradiction with Soviet theories on female emancipation.[87]

By the 1980s, feelings of decline in the quality of childhood the Soviet state could offer children encouraged feelings of a general sense of decline. The explosion of journalism under *glasnost'* from the mid-1980s allowed a more open discussion of issues of child neglect and abuse and homelessness. One particular area of national concern was the scandal of closed children's institutions, where orphaned or handicapped children were left to experience miserable and isolated lives. A 1987 Resolution of the Central Committee 'Measures for fundamentally improving upbringing, education and material provision for orphans and children without parental care' echoed past denunciations of Soviet institutions:

> All these deficiencies have resulted in disgraceful anti-pedagogical practices, undermining of children's feelings of self-worth, abuses, embezzlement, the grossest violations of financial and labour management and sanitary conditions.[88]

Economic decline and then collapse affected most the children of single parents and children in large families. In 1990, the year that the Soviet Union signed the UN Convention on the Rights of the Child, 10 to 12 million children in Russia were living in poverty.[89]

Children and politics

Across the Soviet period, the state positioned children as militant activists against capitalism and fascism and advocates for international peace and decolonization. Soviet children were encouraged to see themselves as part of a global socialist and anti-colonial struggle. From the 1950s the Pioneer movement promoted a 'new vision of the child that was an international participant in the Cold War effort, committed to creativity and personal responsibility in work, engaged in "peaceful competition with the West" and the international promotion of Soviet-led "peace" abroad'.[90] In the post-war period *Pionerskaya Pravda* regularly carried reports on political events and struggles abroad; Churchill's 'Iron Curtain' speech, the Civil War in Greece, the division of Germany and anti-colonial struggles in the Dutch East Indies in the 1940s. This continued; in 1970 the publication covered among other topics incursions by Israel into Egypt, the beginnings of the 'years of lead' (*Anni di piombo*) of labour unrest and strikes in Italy and the extension of the Vietnam War into Cambodia.[91]

A state radio broadcast in 1955 for the International Day of Youth informed its listeners:

> You live in Soviet society where the government constantly worries about its children. Everyone here can study and become what they want to be. Right now it is summer and almost all Soviet children are vacationing either at Pioneer camps, at children's sanatoriums, or at their dachas. ... Many children of capitalist countries know about the Soviet Union and dream about the life that you children lead. They strive to have a life similar to yours.[92]

Childhood had always been a major arena in which the Soviet Union displayed the superiority of the socialist way of life, and in the post-war era of mass media and national liberation movements, it now commanded an international audience. When in 1959 the United Nations drew up the Declaration of the Rights of the Child, the Soviet government tried to get the right to free medical care for children written into the Convention as it could demonstrate that it offered this. The US government had to oppose this, as the Soviets knew they would.[93]

Soviet children showed solidarity with black children in the United States during the Civil Rights movement in the early 1960s. 'Who are these child killers?' asked one Soviet radio broadcast about the bombing of the Baptist Church in Birmingham, Alabama that had resulted in the deaths of four black girls.[94] Some of those who were children in the 1960s remember the strong impression made by the charismatic and energetic Fidel Castro on his visits to the Soviet Union. Children were encouraged to identify with Freedom Island (Ostrov Svobody), as Cuba was known in the Soviet Union. One woman remembered they had a special school assembly and a 'teacher got on the stage and said "Children! A wonderful thing has occurred in Cuba". The insurgents, the revolutionaries, have won! We gave a standing ovation, we were so happy. Although, we understood very little. We always loved Cuba.'[95] Soviet children sang 'Cuba – My Love' the wildly popular song of revolutionary solidarity, composed for Fidel Castro on his visit to the Soviet Union in 1962.[96]

As well as the usual Pioneer work campaigns for domestic purposes – collecting scrap metal to use for trains and tractors, cleaning up urban spaces and parks – Pioneers now worked on an international scale. They collected donations for the victims of Hiroshima, wrote letters to US politicians about nuclear disarmament and learnt Vietnamese. Young Pioneers had 'Aid Vietnam' campaigns, sent gifts to children in Vietnam and collected medicinal herbs for the Hanoi Children's Hospital.[97] Children in Odessa (twinned with the city of Haiphong) constructed 'Vietnam Corners' in classrooms with materials and documents about North Vietnam.[98]

The showcase Pioneer camp and Pioneer headquarters, Artek, was opened to children from socialist and developing countries. 'Camp is full of colour but race is one colour we do not see', were the words of a Pioneer in a radio broadcast to Angola in 1961, then beginning the armed struggle to overthrow Portuguese colonialism.[99] Anti-colonialism had an appeal of moral clarity to some Soviet children:

At that time, they taught us that Africa had awoken. It had cast off the yoke of colonialism, and all the countries on the dark continent in a wink became socialist. I really didn't understand who Patrice Lumumba was in the Congo. I read the papers and thought that colonialism was a very bad thing and that Africa became free and that everything was instantly good there.[100]

Throughout the twentieth century, states have deployed children in their own interests for their associations with peace, and the Soviet Union was no exception. Dove-shaped pins were placed on Pioneer badges. Children participated in activities organized by the Soviet Peace Committee and joined International Friendship Clubs (kluby internatsional'noi druzhby) in schools and Pioneer Palaces. There were 700 of these clubs in Moscow.[101] Children were encouraged to write to pen pals in other socialist countries. Although this correspondence seems to have been highly regulated and censored it may still have been meaningful.

In the Soviet child calendar, 10 November was 'Youth Peace Day'. In 1978, a 'Disarmament Week' was inaugurated in the Soviet Union; apparently, 90 million people, including children, took part in activities during this week in 1984, at the height of the new Cold War.[102] From 1983, the first lesson of school for every year was a Peace Lesson (*Urok mira*) where children were taught about the dangers of the arms race, the causes of war and the importance of remembering Soviet sacrifices in the Great Patriotic War.[103] In the 1980s, peace campaigns in Leningrad's schools and Pioneer camps encouraged children to write letters to their American counterparts on the need for nuclear arms control.[104]

The peace movement in the Soviet Union was not motivated by pacifism, but aimed at the avoidance of military conflict. Acknowledging that this was not always possible, children and adolescents remained mobilized for action in the Cold War. One woman recalled of her childhood in the late 1960s that 'fear was absolutely part of our lives, so much so that we did not even notice it'.[105] After the Sino-Soviet split in the 1960s, and particularly with the Ussuri River Crisis in 1969 when Soviet and Chinese troops had a military clash, China was a source of fear, though also condescension. The main source of fear was the United States, particularly during the tense 1980s. Children had nightmares about nuclear war and were fully mobilized into Cold War fears and threats. Marina Levina remembers:

> My school was holding a 'Raising Communist Consciousness' event that week and we heard terrifying stories how President Reagan would drop nuclear bombs on our country, killing our mothers, fathers, and siblings. If we were left alive, we would wander the nuclear hellscape only to be arrested and tortured by the invading American troops. I remember how angry I was at the United States in that moment.[106]

At secondary school, children had basic civil defence classes. Those not inspired by Soviet patriotism remember being politically apathetic and un-enthused by their war preparation classes, in which they had to put together and dismantle a Kalashnikov in under 4 minutes. Many adolescents shared their parents' increasing disillusionment. Marina Levina recalls it was the nuclear explosion at Chernobyl in 1986 (or rather the lies that the Soviet state initially told about it) that finally ended for her even the performance of loyalty at the age of twelve: 'The surveillance apparatus had faltered and with it so did our careful performances. My friends and I started to make fun of the same rituals we once worshipped.'[107]

Childhood remained highly politicized on the domestic level as well. Once Stalin had been dethroned, there was a major cult of Lenin aimed at children. A picture of Lenin appeared on the first page of primary school textbooks. His image as a boy was in the centre of the Octobrist star. A 1986 Ukrainian textbook for seven- to eight-year-olds urged them to protect the homeland as Lenin had done and be a model pupil like him.[108] Lenin was associated not only with the Revolution and the founding of the Soviet state, but with literacy and learning, hard work and self-discipline; a true Soviet role model. A woman who was at school in the early 1960s recalled that as young schoolchildren, 'We looked upon him as a member of the family, as a protector, as a teacher, and as a person to imitate.'[109]

Atheism as well was one constant feature of a Soviet childhood, although grandmothers or other older relatives may have had children baptized when they were very young. Children in the 1970s and 1980s were still expected to create 'atheists corners' at home and school and organize 'anti-religious' evenings for their parents and the local community. A Soviet atheistic education was meant not simply to consist of crude anti-religious propaganda or mockery of 'backward' beliefs but to include, according to the *Pioneer Leader's Handboo*k:

> discussions, interesting science and technology evenings, questions and answers on atheistic subjects, observations of nature and explanations of natural phenomenon, thematic film festivals, debates, quizzes on natural science subjects, young atheist clubs, excursions to museums and planetariums, reading and discussion of books on leading scientists and naturalists.[110]

Children's culture in the late Soviet period

An official culture for children remained one of the state's priorities and reading literature remained the highest form of activity for the Soviet child. Soviet film was an enormous part of popular culture in the later Soviet decades. After Stalin died, the focus of Soviet official culture shifted from the 'big family' of Soviet collectivism to the normative nuclear family. The figure of the 'child hero' had also disappeared from the screen by the later Soviet period.[111] Characters that were more believable were portrayed as in ordinary recognizable environments. There was a preoccupation with the individual. The adolescent (usually male) who had lost his father in the war and become attracted by 'false mentors' was a staple of crime melodrama in films such as *The Rumiantsiev Case* (*Delo rumyantsev*) (1955) and *Case 306* (1956).[112] Children were often portrayed as isolated, rather than in united collectives.[113] Films such as Marlen Khustiev's *Two Fedors* (1958), Tengiz Abuladze's *Someone Else's Children* (1958), Tarkovsky's *Ivan's Childhood* (1962), Georgy Daneliya and Igor Talenkin's *Seryozha* (1960) and Alexander Mitte's *Someone*

Is Ringing, Open the Door (1965) showed children and adolescents that had been abandoned and let down by adults.

More playfully, Elim Klimov's 1964 popular comedy, *Welcome, or No Trespassing!* (*Dobro pozhalovat', ili Postoronnim vkhod vospreshchyon!*) satirized Soviet official culture in the figure of a young boy subverting order in a Pioneer camp. The pomposity of the Stalinist era was overturned. During the Thaw:

> Concern with the specificity of children's cognition, combined with the idea that children's culture had different aims and requirements than grown-up culture, placed it in the vanguard of reformist efforts to dismantle the dogmatic norms of Stalinist realism and reclaim the right of art to fantasy.[114]

The science fiction film *Amphibian Man* (*Chelovek-amfibiya*), based on a story by Alexander Beliaev, was the most popular Soviet film of 1962, selling 65.5 million tickets.[115] By the early 1960s around forty children's films were made annually, as well as family films.[116] The family melodrama and the school film were popular genres, including *Clouds over Borsk* (*Tuchi nad borskom*) (1960), *And What if its Love?* (1962), *My Friend Kolka!* (*Drug moi Kolka!*) (1961), *We'll Live until Monday* (1968) and *Man Follows the Sun* (*Chelovek idyot za solstem*) (1961). Later as childhood was intertwined with fears of social crisis, the idea of the 'happy childhood' and the prestige of the Soviet school was problematized further. The film *Chuchelo* (1981), based on a 1962 story by Vl. Zhelezhnikov, showed the hypocrisy and conformist nature of the Soviet school.

A rich and creative approach to culture for younger children continued in the Soviet Union. In 1964, the popular children's television show *Goodnight, little ones! (Spokoynie nochi, malyshi!)* began broadcasting. Soviet children's animation (*mult'filmy*) from the 1970s and 1980s was of a universally acknowledged high standard and many of the series from this time, such as *Well, Just you Wait!* (*Nu, pogodi!*) featuring a wily wolf and a hare and *Cheburashka,* about the strange little creature who comes to live with Gennady the Crocodile, are still much loved in Russia today and part of every Russian's cultural universe. Even in children's cartoons though, such as *Three from Prostokvashino (Troe iz Prostokvashino)*, 'the child's loneliness becomes a focal point. Children are viewed as isolated and misunderstood, both by society and by their parents, and are comforted by magic creatures, pet animals and toys.'[117]

Conclusion

After the Revolution, the state viewed the family as the 'diversion of loyalty, as the carrier of an antagonism between the individual and revolutionary society'.[118] However, the 1960s saw the final formation of a 'personal sphere'.

The family was viewed as the primary cell of Soviet society, responsible for child rearing as well as rejuvenating the Soviet project. This period was one of transition from the 'Great Family' of Stalinism to the small nuclear family.[119] By the late Soviet period, Soviet family life did not radically vary from other societies at a comparable stage of development. Special features were the employment of the mother in waged labour, the important role of the grandmother and the encouragement of early independence for children.[120] As already noted, the role of the grandmother was key in Russian childcare and the culture of childhood, and not only for children who had been deprived of their parents by the Terror. As one Displaced Person told the Harvard Project in the 1950s:

> I spent the whole day with my grandmother. In fact, I called her 'Mother'. She was the one who always asked where I went and why I went. She took the place of my mother. This is very characteristic in Russia. Mothers are usually young, they want to go out and they often want to work. But the grandmother always stays home to take care of the children.[121]

The population losses of the Great Patriotic War, which were predominantly of adult males, heightened the important role of the grandmother in children's lives. This continued into the late Soviet period. Although there was concern about family life, the family remained important as a source of stability, particularly in the increasingly difficult times of the late 1980s. The modern era of the 'priceless child' had arrived. Daily life had been so difficult for the majority of the population in the first half of the twentieth century that devoting significant amounts of time and energy to looking after infants and children had to come low down on the list of priorities. Child rearing had not been regarded as a primary task for rural women until the 1950s.[122] A welfare state arrived in the Russian villages in the 1960s and 1970s and this changed women's attitude to their children.

Provision of activities for children by the state was quite remarkable, although the *dvor* remained an important place of play, leisure and relationships into the late Soviet period. By 1980, there were almost 60,000 Summer Pioneer camps, 6,473 Sports Schools, 4,844 Palaces of Culture and 7,691 art, music and choreography schools.[123] In 1984, 19.5 million children were in the Pioneers.[124] The popularity of the Brezhnev era in the post-Soviet collective memory is partly due to this widespread provision for children. At the same time though, there was increased concern on the part of the state that society was not raising its children properly, that *vospitanie* was failing, as well as a build-up of economic problems and serious fault lines in the Soviet state and society. The Soviet healthcare model for children offered accessible and state-guaranteed free medical help and childhood was prioritized for protection. Yet by the 1980s, it was under-funded and slipping behind technologically.

As the Soviet economy and state started collapsing and unravelling in the 1980s under Gorbachev and perestroika, this Soviet model of children and children's lives and well-being came under threat. The Communist Party of the Soviet Union was dissolved in August 1991, followed by the Soviet Union on 26 December that year, an unexpected culmination of unleashed social and political forces for many Soviet citizens.[125]

The post-Stalin generation was the first Soviet generation to live in a period of relative stability. They were the promised generation, 'the generation of cosmic utopia, communal pedagogy, children of physicists and lyricists'.[126] In the 1960s, children were growing up in a future-oriented society, looking forward to new technological and social advances. Donald Raleigh suggests that the gradual disillusionment of the generation who grew up in the optimism of the Khrushchev years, believing that they would build the world of communism, contributed to the downfall of the Soviet system as 'unconscious agents of change'. One interviewee told him: 'We were the cynical generation because we knew. We had the opportunity to learn that what we were being sold as universal truths, were nothing like it.'[127] Another said: 'The tragedy of our generation is that we spent the best part of our youth going along that awful path to nowhere.'[128] In 1991, the framework that had protected, captured, shaped and dominated children's lives for seventy years had suddenly gone and the future was unclear. If children are the future, what happens to them and to ideas about them if the future is in doubt?

7

Postscript: Childhood in the modern Russian Federation

Vospitanie and patriotism

Childhood is still a serious business in the Russian Federation today where children are seen as, among other things, a source of national wealth. Recent years have seen an increasing interest on behalf of the Russian government in children and childhood, in large part due to perceptions of demographic decline. The modern Russian Federation has an extremely low birth rate and a high mortality rate. The birth rate has been below replacement levels since the 1970s and there was a particularly sharp drop during the difficult years of the 1990s. In 2006, the United Nations assessed that the projected Russian population in 2050 would be 31 million below its current size of 112 million, even with predicted increases in net migration, and male life expectancy and a rise again in the birth rate.[1] In May 2006, the Russian president Vladimir Putin's annual State of the Nation address to the Federal Assembly focused on this demographic crisis. Putin proposed a series of financial benefits to encourage women to have a second child and to support families. This included more state supported childcare, the encouragement of fostering and adoption as well as a new political focus on the home and the traditional family.

While using a 'family values' rhetoric, the Russian government has paid increasing attention to children's rights, signalling two approaches that can be in contradiction. In 2009, the state established a Federal Children's Rights Ombudsperson, under the urging of the UN Committee on Children's Rights. In 2010, there were fifty-nine Children's Rights Ombudspersons in the Russian Federation.[2] In 2012, the Russian government launched a five-year National Children's Strategy, confirmed by a Presidential Decree. The Strategy outlined state policies for improving children's lives ('childhood') and referenced international documents on children's rights, such as the Convention on the Rights of the Child, adopted by the General Assembly in 1989 and ratified by the Russian Federation in 1990, and the Council of Europe's Strategy on the Rights of the Child (2012–15). A children's rights activist who was one of the authors' of the Strategy has described it as a document 'being born not in the Cabinet of Ministers, but rather in the expert group' of Russian NGOs.[3] The state's rhetoric around the Strategy was somewhat different though. At its heart was the question of *vospitanie*, the correct upbringing of children in the modern globalized age, in the interests of both the child and society. Developing a strategy for *vospitanie* was, announced the Deputy Minister for Education and Science V. M. Kaganov, a 'state affair'.[4] The goal of the Strategy was conceived of as raising 'a highly educated and moral human being, imbued with a sense of patriotism and responsibility for the fate of the Fatherland (*Otechestva*) and capable of active cooperation and inter-cultural mutual influence'.[5]

Kaganov also argued that Russia's competitiveness and independence in a global world is dependent on the correct *vospitanie* and education of its children.[6] Furthermore, although the National Strategy drew on international conventions and global norms, he emphasized that Russian children are the inheritors of a 'unique mentality', formed over a thousand-year history. He described this mentality as one that prioritizes the spiritual over the material and is characterized by openness, collectivism and devotion to inter-ethnic cooperation and service to the Fatherland. In this view, Russian children should be raised in the spirit of their shared moral norms such as spiritual generosity (*velikodushie*), honour, conscience, justice, charity and respect for elders. The 'happy childhood' model has not gone away, but is written into the Strategy: 'In order for children to grow up as good people, they must be happy.'[7]

In addition to the National Strategy, the Federal Law 'On Education in the Russian Federation' guarantees that *vospitanie* is an inalienable part of education, just as Catherine and Betskoi had argued during the Enlightenment. The Federal Law characterizes *vospitanie* as:

> an activity aimed at the development of the human personality, the creation of conditions for the self-determination and the socialisation of the pupil on the foundation of socio-cultural, spiritual, and moral values and socially accepted rules and norms of behaviour in the interests of the individual, the family, society and the state.[8]

In 2015, the Russian government launched its 'Strategy for the Development of *Vospitanie* in the Russian Federation up until 2025' under the control of the Ministry of Education and Science (*Minobrnauki*).[9] The Strategy addresses issues of civic, patriotic, spiritual-moral and vocational upbringing; the promotion of family values; the inculcation of a culture of health for children and young people and the popularization of scientific knowledge and cultural heritage and safety guidelines. Again, the state's aim is the formation of a modern civic Russian identity, based on supposed Russian values of morality, conscience and spirituality that can withstand the forces of globalization and develop patriotism among children. The Russian language is to be a signifier of this identity, accounting for its place in the school syllabus and in children's culture, as was the case during late imperial Russian and Soviet times. Also included in the function of *vospitanie* is the strengthening of the family and improvement of the social status of parenthood.

As part of their role in strengthening a Russian civic identity, schools and other educational institutions are encouraged to promote the new post-Soviet national holidays: *Den' Rossii* (Russia Day) on 12 June, *Den' gosudartsvennogo flaga Rossiisskoi federatisii* (Day of the State Flag of the Russian Federation) on 22 August and *Den' narodnogo edinstva* (Day of National Unity) on 4 November. The largest role for *vospitanie* is given over to activities around *Den' Pobedy* (Victory Day) on 9 May. Pupils are meant to meet with veterans and lay wreaths and flowers. They also are encouraged to participate in the Immortal Regiment (*Bessmertnyi Polk*) marches with their families as well as take part in Memory Watch (*Vakhta pamyati*) events.[10] Most Russian schools continue to have their own museums that display the material and memory culture of the role of the locality in the Great Patriotic War. Embedding the emotional memory of the war in the consciousness of new generations is viewed as a way of achieving inter-generational unity, social cohesion and loyalty to the state.

Under its National Strategy for Childhood, the state supports the provision of more out-of-school activities (*dopolnitel'noe obrazovanie*) to try to extend its influence over childhood. One priority has been reviving and repairing the Soviet summer camp network. When the Soviet Union was dissolved, the new Russian Federation lost much of its child *sanatoria* and resort facilities, as many of these were in Ukraine, the Baltics and Central Asia. In 2014 Prime Minister Dmitrii Medvedev announced plans to create 52,000 summer camps to provide holidays for over 8 million children, many of which would be supported by the state. After the controversial annexation of the Crimea in March 2014, the Russian state has invested billions of roubles in redeveloping and expanding Artek, the former headquarters of the Young Pioneer movement on the Black Sea coast. Just as in Soviet times, the state 'rewards' children who have excelled in some way with free three-week stays. In 2015, Medvedev flew down to celebrate the 90th anniversary of the camp's founding and Putin has made well-publicized visits there as well. Another, less controversial aspect of the National Strategy is the discovery and encouragement of so-called talented children. In the Soviet period, Olympiads for school pupils began to be held in Moscow and Kiev in the 1930s and gradually spread out to other regions and were established at several levels of the Soviet administrative structure (school, district, city). All-Russian Olympiads are held for pupils in various subjects, showing the state's interest in identifying gifted children. A Presidential Decree founded the Sirius Educational Centre on the site of the Olympic facilities in Sochi for children aged between ten and seventeen who had excelled in classical music, ballet, fine art, figure skating, ice hockey, chess, the natural sciences, literature or technology. This has been seen by some outside Russia as part of an ominous 'authoritarian modernization' project.[11]

In September 2018, the Ministry of Education and Science sent a circular to all schools in the Russian Federation informing them that all pupils are required to participate in some form of after-school activity. Soviet era Pioneer Palaces have been renamed Youth Palaces and Palaces of Youth Creativity. As well as the usual artistic and sporting clubs, there are a wide variety of clubs and organizations devoted to civic activism. Just as they were in the Timur movement, children are encouraged to do good work in their communities, send packages to military conscripts, clean up their neighbourhoods, restore historical monuments and fight against alcoholism. Other clubs have a more specific focus such as the historical re-enactments of battles or the making of historical costumes. Clubs for adolescents can involve military training and extreme sports. The Russian state is funding what could be termed as patriotic clubs in schools, which are run by teachers in and out of school hours. Most focus on Russian history or on a subject known as *Obzh* (*Osnovy bezopasnosti zhiznedeyateli*), a subject in Russian schools that can include basic military training, safety and citizenship. An important focus area for school clubs is the local memory of the Great Patriotic War. Regional and local authorities organize patriotically themed summer camps. The United Nations Committee on the Rights of the Child has expressed concern at the number of children joining what it calls 'nationalist movements', some of which are involved in hate crimes against minority groups.[12] Commentators have seen these clubs as evidence of state control of children and youth. Marlene Laruelle's study of patriotic youth clubs argues that the activists who run them have different narratives and practices than those expected by the Kremlin. Their own patriotic engagement is in some sense 'private' and not a response to the state-sponsored ideological incentives. It is rather a result of 'evanescent and content-free' patriotism, usually focused on local communities and the transformation of individuals.[13]

Children's institutions in post-Soviet Russia

By the 1980s, Soviet children's institutions, to which hundreds of thousands of children were consigned, with very little hope of ever escaping, were considered a national and international disgrace. The 1995 Family Law had already encouraged the transition from residential institutions to family care settings. In 2004, however, there were still around 734,200 children in care, the majority in large institutions.[14] As in the later Soviet period, most children who went into care were 'social orphans', with at least one living parent. There has been an escalation of de-institutionalization in the last decade or so. The stabilization and growth of the Russian economy has meant families can afford to consider adoption and fostering. There has also been the political will to reform the child welfare system and bring it in line with international conventions and global norms. Since 2010, the Russian state has promoted domestic adoption, fostering and the creation of smaller family-like units for cared for children as well as developing early support services for 'problem' families.[15] The number of children placed in families is now ten times higher than in the early 2000s.[16] The Russian government has set the goal that 90 per cent of children in care will live in families.

The National Children's Strategy has a strong focus on adoption and fostering. Additionally the Presidential Decree 1688, issued on 28 December 2012, directed officials to begin work on fostering and adoption processes. The Deputy Prime Minister for Social Affairs is responsible for the protection of orphans and children without parental care.[17] A specific criterion for the evaluation of the effectiveness of Regional Governors has been added – the proportion of children living in the region in family care.[18] In 2014, the 'State Concept for Family Policy in the Russian Federation until 2025' was launched, which promoted foster care. In May 2014, mandatory reforms for children's institutions began with the Decree of the Russian Federation 481. Henceforth, the primary purpose of children's institutions was to be to place children in families. Institutions were to be changed into family support centres, working with biological and adoptive families.[19] The separation of siblings and strict age segregation of the Soviet period has been abandoned and children are to be educated as far as possible in mainstream schools.

Experts though point out that 'residential care still operates as the main strategy for solving the education of children with disabilities, intervening with minors in conflict with the law, and preventing abuse and neglect against children in families'.[20] In 2014, the United Nations Committee on the Rights of the Child noted that deinstitutionalization is not happening rapidly enough in the Russian Federation, particularly for disabled children.[21] Since the beginning of 2013, one of the routes out of children's institutions, adoption by Americans, has been deliberately closed off for vulnerable children by the Russian state.

International adoptions

The poverty of the 1990s led to a greater number of social orphans in Russian children's institutions. The Russian Federation began allowing the adoption of Russian children by foreigners in 1991. Around 8,000 Russian children were adopted abroad every year.[22] A significant number of those went to the United States; in 2005, the United States issued 4,639 immigrant visas to orphans from the Russian Federation.[23] The subsequent cases of abuse and murder of several Russian children in the United States, including Alexei Geiko in December 2003, Vika Bazhenova in 2005 and finally Dima Yakovlev, a twenty-one-month-old child who died in 2008 when he was left for hours inside a car by his adoptive father, outraged sections of the public in Russia. This outrage was encouraged by the Russian Orthodox Church and conservative Russian politicians, who claimed that foreigners were 'stealing' and abusing Russia's children. On 28 December 2012 Federal Law no. 272-FZ was passed, informally known as Dima Yakovlev's Law, which has banned American citizens from adopting Russian orphans. This law has come in for some criticism among sections of the Russian public, who claim it cruelly deprives some of Russia's most disadvantaged children of the chance of ever leaving institutions.[24] Although only 2 to 3 per cent of Russian children are born with developmental or sensory disabilities, they account for almost half of the children in Russian children's institutions. Parents are still encouraged to view disabled children as unteachable ('*neobuchaemy*') from birth and strong pressure is put on them to give them up; an astonishing 30 per cent of children with Down's Syndrome are consigned to institutions at birth. A 2014 report by Human Rights Watch describes the very distressing lives of disabled children in these institutions, which are still predominantly of the remote closed 'Soviet' type and offer little in the way of stimulation, education or treatment.[25] International children's rights organizations have been strongly critical of the actions of the Russian state. In 2017, the European Court of Justice ruled that the Dima Yakovlev Law had violated the human rights of forty-five US citizens who had already begun adoption proceedings at the time of its passing, in particular, their right to family life.

Family values, 'anti–juvenile justice' and moral panics

The Russian state's attempts to bring their policies on children and childhood in line with global norms and adhere to international conventions that protect children's rights has met with some resistance among certain sections of the Russian population. It has contributed to a series of recent 'moral panics' over perceived threats to Russian children and the Russian family from foreigners, 'foreign' ideas (homosexuality), the internet and the Russian state itself. As in other states, there is a bitter debate over who has rights over children – the state (and international organizations) or the family. A new grassroots parental movement, backed by sections of the Russian Orthodox Church, has arisen, which calls itself 'anti–yu yu' or 'anti–juvenile justice'.

One of the sparks for this development was the 2009 Ageyvys case (delo Ageyvysa). The Ageyvys parents were in the process of adopting two children. The two children they were hoping to adopt were removed from them in March 2009 when the boy was taken to hospital with what seemed to be non-accidental burn injuries. The adoptive parents were deprived of their parental rights and the adoption process was immediately revoked while criminal proceedings were still pending. In November 2010, one of the parents was acquitted of all charges, while the second was convicted of non-fulfilment of duties relating to the care of a minor and of the intentional infliction of mild harm to health. They were sentenced to one year and eight months correctional work and fined. The Ageyvys appealed to national and international courts. In 2013, the European Court of Human Rights upheld the parents' complaint that their right to a private life had been violated by the hasty revocation of the adoption, by the state's refusal to allow them to see the children for over a year, by the leaking to the media by hospital officials of details of the case and by intrusive and sensationalist media reporting.

The case caused wide debates in Russia. It fuelled the anger of the Russian Orthodox Church and the nascent grassroots Parents' Movement towards the supposed influence of international (that is, 'Western') institutions over the 'traditional' Russian family. They called for the upholding of parental rights within the domestic sphere. In addition to child protection cases within the Russian Federation, several cases in Finland and Sweden, in which Russian children were removed from their Russian parents by social services, received wide attention in the Russian media. These were presented as 'state kidnappings' that could eventually happen inside Russia. The diffuse Parents' Movement (roditel'skoe dvizenhie) and the 'anti–yu yu' campaign are grassroots mobilizations against a perceived Western conspiracy to weaken Russia via the implementation of international instruments such as the UN Convention of the Rights of the Child or the Council of Europe's 2011 'Draft Recommendation on the rights and legal status of children and parental responsibilities'. Russian state administrators and West-funded NGOs are seen as part of this conspiracy. Activists that are more radical see a plot to destroy Russia and its 'unique civilization' by wiping out the traditional Russian family via the spread of sexually transmitted diseases, abortion and homosexuality.[26] Adherents to such views spread lurid 'depravity stories' about children in Western countries being taught to masturbate at school, suing their parents or being removed from their parents and given to homosexual couples.[27] Adherents that are more moderate distrust the Russian state and the political elite and do not want them to intervene in family life. *Anti–yu yu* campaigners adhere to the pre-Enlightenment belief in children's innate wilfullness and uphold parental authority to punish children physically. They argue that children need hierarchy and discipline and that children's individualism should submit to the family unit. Campaigners formed a *Roditelsky Front* (Parent's Front), whose first Congress in 2013 was addressed by Putin.[28]

The Russian critique of the Convention on the Rights of the Child and other international instruments is similar to that arising in other societies. They claim that the Convention imposes a Western normative standard of childhood and an unproven theory of the 'autonomous child', ignores local cultural and social traditions as well as local living standards (often 'lower' than in Western states), and gives the state too much power over family life. The Association of Parental Committees and Societies (*Assotsiiatsiia Roditelskikh Komitetov i Soobshestv*) has proposed its own 'Family Code' to replace the one of the Russian state. In their view, children could be commanded to help with housework, to do their school work and to have compulsory religious study; and they should be subject to a series of incentives and punishments.[29]

Children's rights in the modern Russian Federation are not always clear or consistently applied in line with international norms. There are conflicting laws about the age a child reaches legal capacity, reflecting the difficulties in defining what is a child. Russian civil legislation states that under-fourteens are 'underage' and cannot carry out any significant acts; medical legislation calls for mandatory consideration of a minor's opinion from the age of fifteen; legislation on education gives the seventeen-year-old the right to education while the transition to secondary school at ten makes a child subject to disciplinary action.[30] At age ten, a child must give its consent to a change in name, the restoration of the parental rights of the biological parents, adoption and the appointing of a guardian. At fourteen years and older, children have to give consent for the obtaining or withdrawing of Russian citizenship. Sixteen-year-olds can organize political meetings and public gatherings. Meanwhile, the Family Code recognizes the child's right to express an opinion on any issue, which must be taken into account by parents, guardians, trustees and courts, without setting a minimum age limit. Unlike in most states, there is no separate family court system and there is no separate juvenile justice system. In 2003, Russia amended its Criminal Code Article 87, which placed priority on alternative methods for children who broke the law, but there is no autonomous juvenile justice system.

The United Nations Committee on the Rights of the Child has responded positively to recent Russian government attempts to introduce policies that adhere to the articles in the Convention on the Rights of the Child, such as the

National Strategy for Childhood.[31] However, the Committee expressed concern that children in marginalized and disadvantaged situations such as migrant, refugee, asylum seeking, indigenous and Roma children are not protected against discrimination by the Russian state. It also expressed concern that both the 2012 Federal Act which requires organizations who receive financial support from abroad to register as 'foreign agents' and recent amendments to the Criminal Code that expands the definition of the crime of state treason to include providing assistance to international organizations could impact the work of NGOs in the area of children's rights. Law no. 436, 'the protection of children from information which could corrupt their health and development' (*O zaschite detei ot informatsii, prichinyayushcei vred ikh zdorovyu i razvitiyu*) and Federal Law no. 135 which prohibits 'propaganda of unconventional sexual relations' censors information that children can receive about sexuality and leads to discrimination against LGBTI children or children from LGBTI families.[32]

Masha and the Bear

Post-Soviet Russian children's culture went global with the television series *Masha and the Bear*. Oleg Kuzukov created the animated character Masha based on a traditional Russian folktale. This cartoon series, which features a little Russian girl's adventures in the forest with a kindly bear, was first broadcast in Russia in 2009 and then began appearing on European children's television in 2011. It is broadcast in over 100 countries and has been released on Netflix. Masha is a global commercial and imaginative phenomenon, who has been watched by billions on television channels and YouTube; as well as the copious merchandise in shops and live spin-offs, there is an area of an amusement park built around her in Leolandia, Italy's most popular family theme park.[33] However, as children and politics are never viewed apart, Masha has come in for some criticism. Ukrainian and Baltic political figures and academics have described her as a 'tool for Russia's soft power', part of Russia's hybrid war against the 'West', 'a coded political message' and a 'Kremlin Trojan Horse'. There have been calls in these states to have her and her Bear (Russia) banned from screens and children's minds.[34] Masha has also been also criticized in Russia by adults because of her sense of freedom and rebelliousness. She is seen as a poor role model for creating obedience in Russian children. Masha may disturb some adults, as she is the return of the 'child in nature' of Rousseau, instinctive, unafraid, curious and exuberant. There are no visible adults in Masha's world. She is a 'being' child, liberated, 'autonomous, vital, determined to discover everything that reality has to offer'.[35] Networked globalized digital Masha returns us to where concepts of modern childhood began in Russia: the Enlightenment.

8

Conclusion

Constructions of childhood are produced within a specific political context and form part of the state's (and its opponents) political and national interests. Children are both an 'index of civilisation and modernity' and the 'key arena' in which to instil such civilization.[1] In Russia from the late eighteenth century, child welfare and the welfare of the nation became linked in the minds of natural scientists, writers, pedagogues, local officials, politicians, reformers and revolutionaries. Children and childhood became an object of their special interest. Children are agents of cultural reproduction, which is why so much attention is given to their education and upbringing. In late imperial Russia, many opponents of the Tsarist regime focused on education and child welfare in the hope that a new generation would one day change the social order. Russian reformers in the nineteenth century saw the expansion of education at primary level for peasant children as one of the ways to the 'bright path' that Russia should take out of Tsarism. Childhood education even at the earliest stages of kindergarten 'became linked to a more radical vision of individual emancipation from the authoritarian constraints of school and family'.[2]

Childhood was central to Bolshevik identity and the way it treated its children was an important marker for the Soviet state between 1917 and 1991. In the Soviet Union, where the state wanted the future to be very different from the present, children took on a role of even greater importance. Children were going to be used to create a social order rather than simply reproduce one. Not only this; they were to be an entirely new kind of person, unseen before in human history, the 'new Soviet person'. Childhood (and youth) was vitally important in the future-oriented Soviet Union. Stalin and other Soviet leaders liked to make public displays of taking children very seriously. Children were evidence of the success of Soviet socialism as well as the mechanism by which it would advance. They were future creators and inhabitants of a true communist society. Children's institutions were high up on the list of prestigious places for foreign and local visitors: Moscow's Model School No. 25, attended by the children of the Soviet elite, including some of Stalin's children, was visited by 5,000 people in the 1934–35 school year.[3] The Exhibition of the Protection of Motherhood and Infancy in Moscow's House of Health Education was another tourist destination in the 1930s.[4] Other spaces for children such as modern Pioneer Palaces were widely shown off in the Khrushchev era as markers of distinction. On the other hand, the anti-Bolshevik Russian émigré press focused on the supposed despair and corruption of children under the Bolsheviks as a way of criticizing them to an international audience, as well as highlighting the difficult conditions of refugee Russian children driven out by the Revolution.[5] Soviet leaders wanted to spread their own ideal of childhood globally, in particular to the 'Third World' during the Cold War as part of its competitive coexistence struggle with the West. Later, when the Soviet state weakened in the 1980s and then collapsed in the 'wild nineties', childhood itself seemed under threat.

After the Russian Revolution, the Soviet authorities committed to a modern view of childhood and created a set of expectations for children and childhood, building on the pre-revolutionary traditions and practices of Russian reformers and revolutionaries and drawing on many Western philosophers and educationalists from Jean-Jacques Rousseau to John Dewey. It has been argued that the model of childhood in the Soviet Union was similar to that of the Western one; 'different in terms of degree, rather than intrinsically different'.[6] In one view, the great change in ideas about childhood happened in late imperial Russia. The late Imperial period saw Russian society participate in and contribute to this creation of a modern notion of childhood with new pedagogical, psychological, medical and scientific views of childhood and child development, a rich children's culture and writings about childhood and a network of philanthropic institutions focusing on child welfare. Boris Gorshkov has argued that there was a heightened interest in childhood in Russia after the 1860s, similar to that seen in Britain and France at the same time and Catriona Kelly shows that in many ways the Russian model of childhood had become similar to that of other Western states by the 1890s.[7] Other historians have traced discontinuities or even ruptures over time, for example during the Great Patriotic War or between the Stalinist period and the post-war decades.[8] Others have argued that particularly in the early years, 'the Bolsheviks rejected some of the most cherished, naturalised and emotionally charged Western visions of childhood'.[9]

Childhood is connected to systems of power relations, and childhood in the modern model is meant to be characterized by dependency on adults. It has been constructed as a special protected but powerless space, free from politics, responsibility, and conceptually and often literally separated from the adult world. The Western modern model of a dependent childhood was precluded in the Soviet Union by Marxist-Leninist ideology, which took children seriously as revolutionary actors. In the Soviet Union, the child was meant to be a revolutionary, fighting against the remnants of Tsarist exploitation, interwar capitalism and fascism, Cold War imperialism, colonialism and racism, Western war mongering, the nuclear arms race and environmental destruction. Equally importantly, they were also meant to lead the fight against the vestiges of the old world at home – against religion, patriarchy, peasant mores and bourgeois attitudes in their own families. A study of Soviet primers in the 1940s argues that these depicted children as ideologically and politically well educated, 'essentially represented as adults'.[10]

A childhood of dependence was equally precluded by the model of childhood in Russia prior to the Revolution, which had been the lived reality for most children: the agricultural model. This model encouraged, in fact demanded, early physical independence. Further research can elaborate on the balance between the influence of specifically Soviet (Marxist) policies and attitudes and the influence of the model of agricultural childhood or even the spread of the agricultural model into the urban arena. Moshe Lewin, among others, has talked of the 'ruralisation of the cities' in the 1930s, as a result of the mass migration of the Russian peasantry to urban areas.[11] Any idea of a dependent and passive childhood was also challenged by the harshness of daily life and multiple periods of extreme crisis, including the two world wars and the Civil War, the collectivization of agriculture and the dekulakization in the early 1930s as well as the famines of 1921, 1933 and 1947. There were also many periods of terror and deportations between 1917 and 1953. All of this required children (urban and rural) to be contributors to family survival and communal life. Delayed physical independence is a post–Second World War development for most non-elite children in the West as well.

The Western model of modern childhood is associated above all with the replacement of labour by education in children's lives. In the Soviet Union, the key construction of the child above all as 'school pupil' took place in the 1930s and this is where it began to align more closely with the Western model. The Stalinist period in the 1930s which saw a dramatic extension of state power and the creation of institutions through which that power operated (schools, culture, medicine, welfare, law) in general was the exemplary period for the production of a 'Soviet childhood'. Compulsory schooling gave states great power to organize childhood. In the Soviet case, the use of standardized textbooks allowed the state to 'shape Soviet childhood by regulating children's minds, bodies, habits as well as "locating" them in the Empire's space and time'.[12] The Soviet Union was envisaged from the start as an 'education society'.[13] Education, and therefore children and childhood, had been increasingly important in the Russian Empire, where after the 1860s, 'national enlightenment, social modernization, and international security were interdependent'.[14] The extension of education in the 1930s in a state the size of the Soviet Union was one of the real achievements of the Soviet state, even if eventually the production of a modern educated society proved its undoing. The successful launch of Sputnik in 1957 led their US competitors to worry that Soviet education was better than they had thought. In 1958 Lawrence Derthick, the United States Commissioner of Education visited the Soviet Union and reported that 'we were simply not prepared for the degree to which the U.S.S.R., as a nation, is committed to education as a means of national advancement. [It is] a total commitment. We witnessed an education-centred economy. The privileged class in Russia is the children'.[15] By the late Soviet period, the equalizing effect of education was undercut by social differentiation, particularly between the chances of urban and rural children and entrenched positions of the Soviet elites, although nothing on the scale of the post-Soviet period. After the collapse of the Soviet Union, the much-vaunted Soviet school was criticized as having been part of the 'administrative-command centre', used to enforce obedience to the state.[16] One special feature of the Soviet case is that alongside the education system and indeed embedded in it, the Soviet state developed a powerful official children's culture which 'played a significant role in identity formation' among Soviet children.

In his study of revolutionary regimes in the first half of the twentieth century, Paul Ginsborg argues that the contestation of patriarchy and attempts to enforce gender equality were the most significant and long-lasting developments to come out of the Russian Revolution.[17] One of the aims of the Russian Revolution was to destroy the patriarchal family and liberate children as well as women. Through family legislation, the Soviet state tried to redress the power imbalance between children and adults. The state claimed that children were the 'only privileged class'. The complexity and paradox of historical processes is revealed by the study of a state where corporal punishment for children in schools was illegal, but millions of children suffered when their families were repressed, uprooted, deported, marginalized, starved and executed. A state that proclaimed children's liberation from their parents and at times appointed the political police as their protector. Soviet concepts of childhood saw children as powerful, but legislation viewed them as vulnerable, and despite claims of gender equality, it conceptually bound them closely to their mothers. It has been argued that the role of fathers in Soviet family life was diminished, as the state took on the role of patriarch.[18]

Theorists have pointed to the intimate relationship between 'the child' and social order. Everywhere, children are 'enjoined to speak, make themselves visible and to regulate their own behaviour, as well as be controlled by others'.[19]

Children pose a potential threat to the social order due to their presumed anarchy and resistance to intelligibility. They can be viewed as dangerous, carrying the threat of degeneration within them and a challenge to the future as well as the present. Childhood therefore is 'the context within which the otherness of the child is rendered safe'.[20] In the Soviet case, we can trace this idea in the attempts to capture and reform the *bezprizornyie* and the development of harsher attitudes to juvenile delinquency. We can see it also in the linkage of the Soviet political police, the Cheka and later the NKVD, with street children, the exile and forced resettlement of kulak children in the early 1930s and the removal of the children of 'Enemies of the People' to state institutions during the Great Terror of 1936–8. Children, it could be argued, were also made 'safe' in the Soviet period by having their childhoods contained in schools, clubs, Pioneer Palaces and camps, libraries, sports grounds and Parks of Culture and Rest and in the Octobrists and Young Pioneer movements.

Studies of the history of Soviet childhood show more of the complexities of the relationship between childhood and space. Childhood has been defined as 'that status of personhood which is by definition often in the wrong place'.[21] As already stated, one of the major characteristics of the Western model of modern childhood, following the tradition begun by Rousseau, is that the child's world should be separated from the adult world, while being regulated by it. Although the lines between the adult and child were blurred when it came to (unwaged) labour and politics, the Soviet state did concern itself with children 'out of place' – on the streets, in cinemas, at train stations, markets, in the unregulated yard (*dvor*). Such children were viewed as potentially threatening to the social order.[22] Again, one of the main examples of this is the *bezprizorniki* of the 1920s and 1930s. Not only were they 'out of place', they were also considered 'unchildish' in their actions to survive (crime), their appearance and in their expression of emotions such as hate and resentment, which are not considered appropriate for children in most models of childhoods, including the Soviet one. Only during the total crisis of the Great Patriotic War were such emotions considered acceptable for children. In China during the Cultural Revolution in the late 1960s, young primary age children were even encouraged to participate directly in violent political acts against their teachers and other authority figures.[23] Yet these acts were not meant to remove them from the category of 'child'. There as in the Soviet Union, children and youth were harnessed by the state to destroy vestiges of the old world.

Threats to the 'privilege' of an apolitical childhood are seen as deeply transgressive and children who have power over adults are often constructed as 'folk devils'.[24] Many observers at the time, and since, believed that the Soviet state was deliberately subverting the age-based hierarchy so it could use the younger generation to destroy the old world. 'Folk devils' such as the Young Pioneers ruled over their parents and other adults. The ultimate acts of the subversion of the age hierarchy was the denunciations of parents by their own children, such as that of Pavlik Morozov.[25] In this interpretation, the state was either brainwashing Soviet children into unthinking loyalty or unleashing children's inner wilfulness and propensity for evil, in line with the pre-Enlightenment idea of original sin.

Alternatively, other historians have stressed that the dominant emotional stance considered appropriate for Soviet children was actually that of gratitude and submission, rather than subversion and power. After the 1920s, hierarchy and obedience were important strictures on the lives of all Soviet citizens, including children. The 'privileges' of childhood can be limiting and at the same time disciplinary regimes are often presented as a privilege.[26] Children everywhere are meant to be happy, grateful, obedient and dependent. The most famous – or notorious – slogan of childhood in the Soviet Union was 'Thank you Stalin for Our Happy Childhood!' This slogan adorned posters, banners and books and is nearly always mentioned in memoirs and other life writings. Additionally some researchers have seen the Soviet family as an apolitical refuge from the outside world, rather than a place of conflict between children and their parents.

The status identity of a child in the Western model is connected with play and the binarism of work/play is mapped onto the adult/child. This conceptual and practical separation between these aspects of the worlds of adults and children was collapsed to a great extent in the Soviet Union. Throughout the Soviet period, peasant children worked and so did urban children. This was no longer the exploitative work of capitalism, but 'socially useful labour'; work for their families, their communities and the Soviet state. During the first Five Year Plan period (1928–32), 'Educators represented a program of intensive labour and immersion in the world of adults as the chief source of childhood delights' and even children of five and six were supposed to be interested in themes of 'productive labour'.[27] A promoter of the Soviet kindergarten wrote at this time that 'the chief task of the kindergarten is to … arm the child with the temper of Soviet communism, to kindle his love for and his devotion to factories, machine tools, our fields, our Red Army men'.[28]

In the Soviet Union, the state placed children in the public sphere to a far greater extent. Unlike in the Western model where the middle-class family was 'privatized', children were not placed inside the home until the late 1950s. When this key transformation happened, the state stepped up its surveillance and control of the family to mitigate this potential 'privatization'. Soviet children typically had both parents working in waged labour outside the home, so the role of the street, or in the Soviet case, the 'yard' (*dvor*) and the peer group, the school and organized youth movements was heightened in their lives.

Children's experiences depend to a large degree on the social groups into which they are born and those in which they move and interact. Childhood is both a collective and generational experience but it is also highly differentiated by class, gender, geography, ethnicity and social group among other categories. Children's experiences and the kind of childhoods they are meant to 'enjoy' (a historical notion itself). In late imperial Russia, society remained highly stratified which meant that children in different social groups (peasant, nobility, merchant, working class) had very different childhoods. In the Soviet period, a continuing urban/rural divide, which structured children's lives throughout the twentieth century minimized the initial general equalizing effect of post-revolutionary developments. Despite the early commitment to social mobility, the new Soviet elite began to replicate itself in the post-war era with membership in it becoming akin to hereditary status, and this also stratified childhoods.

Most recent work has looked at Soviet childhood and there has been less research done on the Tsarist period. Some approaches transcend the boundaries. There are strong continuities in approaches to children's education across the Tsarist and Soviet periods, for example. Catriona Kelly singles out the emphasis on rote learning, patriotic texts, and intensive discipline and points to the continuities between Catherine the Great, Nicholas I, Tolstoy, Lenin and Stalin.[29] The Tsars and Soviet leaders saw children's education as a social benefit, rather than an individual one and therefore sought to control it for the state. Catherine the Great saw education as a way to create a 'new race of men and women', while Nadezhda Krupskaya saw education as 'the training of many-sided men with conscious and organised social instincts. ... They should be able to build up a rational, beautiful, joyful social life.'[30] Later on, under Khrushchev, the 1959 Theses of the Central Committee of the Communist Party claimed that Soviet education would produce 'the new person, in whom spiritual wealth, moral purity, and physical perfection will be harmoniously combined'.[31]

The Enlightenment introduced the emphasis on *vospitanie* and moral upbringing and the development of character remained important across the centuries. It is still an ongoing state concern in Russia today. In terms of daily life as well, older traditions lived on long into the Soviet period. In his study of rural mothering across the twentieth century, which often took place in the absence of males due to war and social upheaval, David Ransel points to the 'generational chain of knowledge, norms and assistance that strongly reinforced inherited practice'.[32]

As noted throughout the book, one of the most important stories that the Soviet state told about itself to its own citizens and the world was that it was providing children with a uniquely 'happy childhood', a childhood that was far superior to that offered in capitalist states. Researchers have challenged this claim by focusing on recovering and representing unhappy childhoods and the suffering of Soviet children. Privileges can be denied, as well as granted. On the other hand, terror, repression and social and economic catastrophe are often considered to have impacted so greatly on children and family life that many researchers find the idea of a 'Soviet childhood' an oxymoron, at least for the first decades of Soviet power. Frierson accuses the Soviet state of 'discriminatory neglect' towards millions of children whose families suffered under Stalin.[33] During the early Soviet decades, the state denied millions of children the privilege of childhood due to their membership of social and national groups targeted for punishment. These include the children of the 'Whites', the 'bourgeoisie' and peasant insurgents during the Russian Civil War; the children in kulak families during the collectivization and dekulakization drives of the early 1930s; the children of victims of the Terror; the children of deported national minorities such as the Chechens and the Crimean Tatars in the 1930s, 1940s and 1950s. When looking at this violence and repression, researchers have asked whether the Soviet state deliberately victimized children in this period. Cathy Frierson and Simon Vilensky argue that right from the beginning of their rule, the Bolsheviks established 'key values, practices, vocabulary and economic problems that would threaten children over the next four decades'.[34] These included the deliberate use of state violence, population displacement as a policy, the refusal to allow private initiative in social welfare, the encouragement of class hatred and stigmatization, the search for enemies and a belief in collective guilt. They also outline how the hyper-masculization of the Soviet state and the dominating Bolshevik quality of *tverdost'* ('hardness': presumably opposing this last quality to the 'softness' of children) precluded a humanistic social policy towards the vulnerable.[35] Childhood though as a state of privilege was only ever available to a minority of children across the Western world well into the twentieth century. For many children even in the most economically developed states, it was not accessible until after the Second World War. One example would be, black children in the American South, whose own struggles for civil rights were closely followed by the Soviet press in the 1960s. Historians have recently focused on the exploitation and abuse of working-class children forced into child migration schemes from the United Kingdom to the colonies and the Commonwealth right up until the late 1960s. The appalling conditions and experiences of children kept in closed Catholic institutions in Ireland and the United Kingdom until very recently could be mentioned. Across the modern world, many children would have repeated the lines so often found in the life writings of those who were children in Russia in the first half of the twentieth century – 'And so, at the age of X, my childhood ended.'

Historians like to see children as agents and competent social actors who shape circumstances as well as experience them. Recent studies foreground their agency in social action and show an interest in 'the life-worlds of childhood, the daily lived experience of children, their experiences and understandings, their interactions with each other and with adults, their strategies and tactics of action'.[36] The study of childhood during the Soviet Union contributes towards debates about how far children are resourceful social actors or passive recipients of policies and programmes designed by adults. In the Soviet Union, children could be flexible and capable of employing a variety of modes of agency. At one extreme is the phenomenon of the *bezprizorniki* of the 1920s, the millions of vagrant children who survived the social, economic and demographic catastrophes of their time through crime and group solidarity. At the other end perhaps is the testimony of how children participated in everyday practices through which society negotiated its relationship with the state and social reality. Larissa Miller (b. 1940) recalled how she and other children in post-war Moscow would play truant from school and hire themselves out to adults to stand in queues for flour.[37] Children had an important role in accessing goods throughout the Soviet period and helped the family economy. Marina Levina, born in Odessa in 1975, writes:

It is perhaps a cliché, but I spent a substantial portion of my childhood waiting in lines for everything from salami to underwear. This was an elaborate process, one that could occupy the entire day. My grandmother started the day visiting the shops and finding out what was being waited for in each one. She would then double back and ask acquaintances to hold her a place in the line. In return, she would hold their place in a different line. Without mobile phones, the system required massive coordination based on experiential estimation of timing and length of each line. It was a masterful exercise in planning. I was dragged along and often asked to hold a place while she looked around. I hated the entire practice with the passion of a seven-year-old asked to stand still for hours at a time.[38]

Svetlana Gouzenko (b. 1923) wrote in her memoirs how she and her siblings would deliberately repeat the positive statements they learnt at school about Stalin and the Party in front of visitors, to help deflect criticism away from their father's refusal to join the Party.[39] Many though retell their childhood stories as ones of victimhood or suffering due to the catastrophic impact of state policies on their family lives. Historians of childhood have recently begun to question the idea of 'agency', which has so far privileged opposition and public acts.[40] Agency can mean support, and compliance can be a form of agency. Perhaps this concept of agency may be more helpful in the Soviet case.

Children were a significant social group in both Tsarist Russia and the Soviet Union, which was a young society: under Stalin, children under sixteen formed 38 per cent of the population.[41] Including children's accounts and experiences enriches the understanding of historical events and developments: the Russian Revolution and the Civil War, the great transformations under Stalin, the civilian experience in the Great Patriotic War, the change in living standards from the 1950s and the culture of the Cold War and the collapse of the Soviet state in the 1990s. The life writings of young Russian refugees in Europe recalling the years of revolution and Civil War reveal a new visceral and emotional side to those experiences. Memories of those who experienced dekulakization show how the intimate violence unfolded on the ground.

The structures and experiences of the early decades of Soviet power had a powerful socializing impact on children and accelerated the transformations of Russian childhoods begun in the late nineteenth and early twentieth centuries. The Soviet state created spaces real and imaginary for children: childcare and educational institutions, sanatoria, literature and media, after-school and leisure networks. It also created an entire official culture for them, which was rich and varied. It projected itself, its values and its power through childhood. As in the Western model, it finally turned children into pupils. However, even in the post-Stalin years, it is not clear how much childhood was valued for itself, rather than being viewed as a period of forward movement to historical progress and a way of strengthening the state. In the Soviet Union as elsewhere in the modern age, childhood was understood as both a 'privilege' and a 'province of state power'.[42] From Catherine the Great, through to Nicholas I, Alexander II, the Bolshevik leaders and Putin today, the Russian state sought and seeks to place Russian children in a Russian childhood of its own making. Real, live children will no doubt at certain times and in their own ways enjoy, take advantage of, create, challenge, frustrate and escape this Russian childhood that adults have imagined for them.

Notes

Chapter 1

1 Ransel, D. (1988) *Mothers of Misery: Child Abandonment in Russia*, Princeton: Princeton University Press, 10.

2 Ransel, *Mothers of Misery*, 12. See also Glagoleva, O. E. (2005) 'The Illegitimate Children of the Russian Nobility in Law and Practice, 1700–1860', *Kritika: Explorations in Russian and Eurasian History*, vol. 6, no. 3. For the *Ulozhenie,* see https://pages.uoregon.edu/kimball/1649-Ulj.htm#ch22

3 Riasanovsky, N. (2005) *Russian Identities: A Historical Survey*, Oxford: Oxford University Press, 76.

4 Mintz, S. (2012) 'Why the History of Childhood Matters', *Journal for the History of Childhood and Youth*, vol. 5, no. 1, Winter, 15.

5 Ariès, P. (1965) *Centuries of Childhood: A Family History of Social Life*, London: Random House. (Originally published as *L'enfant et la vie familial sous l'ancien regime*). Since its publication, historians have challenged his ideas and there is now a greater consensus that medieval societies did have conceptions of childhood, albeit different to the later modern one.

6 Heywood, C. (2002) *A History of Childhood: Children and Childhood in the West from Medieval to Modern Times*, Cambridge: Polity, 2.

7 See Zelizer, V. (1985) *Pricing the Priceless Child: The Changing Social Value of Children*, Princeton: Princeton University Press.

8 See Marshall, D. (1999) 'The Construction of Children as an Object of International Relations: The Declaration of Children's Rights and the Child Welfare Committee of League of Nations, 1900–1924', *The International Journal of Children's Rights*, vol. 7, no. 2, 103–48.

9 Fass, P. (2015) 'Is There a Story in the History of Childhood?', in P. Fass (ed.), *The Routledge History of Childhood in the Western World*, Abingdon: Routledge, 2.

10 Quoted in Jablonka, I. (2015) 'Social Welfare in the Western World and the Rights of Childhood', in P. Fass (ed), *The Routledge History of Childhood in the Western World*, 380.

11 Stearns, P. (2011) *Childhood in World History*, Abingdon: Routledge, 73.

12 Rose, N. (1991) *Governing the Soul: The Shaping of the Private Self*, London: Routledge, 121.

13 In this book, I use both 'noble' and 'gentry' interchangeably. There were enormous differences within the noble class in imperial Russia, from the

small number of fabulously wealthy noble elite families in St Petersburg to thousands of moderately well-off gentry in the provinces and many impoverished nobles who lived barely better than peasants.

14 Kirschenbaum, L. (2001) *Small Comrades. Revolutionizing Childhood in Soviet Russia, 1917–1932*, Abingdon: Routledge, 13.

15 For more on birth and babyhood see Kelly, C. (2005) *Children's World: Growing Up in Russia, 1890–1991*, Yale: Yale University Press; and Ransel, D. (2000) *Village Mothers: Three Generations of Change in Russia and Tataria*, Bloomington: Indiana University Press. Also Kuxhausen, A. (2013) *From the Womb to the Body Politic: Raising the Nation in Enlightenment Russia*, Madison: University of Wisconsin Press. For Soviet adolescence and youth see: Fürst, J. (2010) *Stalin's Last Generation: Soviet Post-War Youth and the Emergence of Mature Socialism*, Oxford: Oxford University Press; Neumann, M. (2011) *The Communist Youth League and the Transformation of the Soviet Union*, London: Routledge; Tsipursky, G. (2016) *Socialist Fun: Youth, Consumption, and State-Sponsored Popular Culture in the Cold War Soviet Union*, Pittsburgh: Pittsburgh University Press; and Gorsuch, A. (2001) *Youth in Revolutionary Russia: Enthusiasts, Bohemians, Delinquents*, Bloomington: Indiana University Press.

16 See Ball, A. (1996) *And Now My Soul Is Hardened: Abandoned Children in Soviet Russia, 1918–1930*, Berkeley: University of California Press; Kucherenko, O. (2016) *Soviet Street Children and the Second World War: Welfare and Social Control under Stalin*, London: Bloomsbury; and Harwin, J. (1996) *Children of the Russian State, 1917–1995*, Aldershot: Avebury and Ashgate.

Chapter 2

1 Okenfuss, M. (1980) *The Discovery of Childhood in Russia: The Evidence of the Slavic Primer*, Newtonville, MA: Oriental Research Partners, 5. The *Domostroi* is a book of household rules and advice for Muscovite elites. It later became the exemplary text supposedly revealing of Muscovite patriarchal tyranny for generations of Russian reformers and revolutionaries. The text can be seen as a religious homily, rather than a normative or descriptive document. See Grant, S. (2012) 'The Russian Gentry Family: A Contrarian View', *Jahrbücher für Geschichte Osteuropas*, Neue Folge, Bd. 60, H. 1, 1–33 for scepticism about the influence of the *Domostroi*. Grant also suggests that a change in ideas about childhood in Russia took place in the seventeenth century.

2 Cotta Ramusino, P. (2005) 'How to Behave at Home and in Society: Karion Istomin's *Domostroj* and Its Possible Sources', *Studi Slavistici* II, 53–65; Kosheleva, O. (2015) 'What Should One Teach? A New Approach to Russian Childhood Education as Reflected in Manuscripts from the Second Half of the Seventeenth Century', in *Word and Image in Russian History: Essays in Honor of Gary Marker*, M. Di Salvo, D. H. Kaiser, and V. A. Kivelson (eds), Boston, MA: Academic Studies Press.

3 Okenfuss, *The Discovery of Childhood*, 19.

4 Khromov, O. R. (2015) 'The Primer of Karion Istomin with Handwritten Additions by Diomid Yakovlev syn Serkov as a Monument of XV11-Century Russian Book Culture', *Russian Education and Society*, vol. 57, no. 12, 1023.

5 Kosheleva, 'What Should One Teach?', 279.

6 Voskoboinikov, V. (2013) 'Children's Literature Yesterday, Today … and Tomorrow?', *Russian Studies in Literature*, vol. 49, no. 3, 65.

7 Cotta Ramusino, 'How to Behave at Home and in Society', 63.

8 Kosheleva, 'What Should One Teach?', 291.

9 Okenfuss, *The Discovery of Childhood*, 31.

10 Bushkovitch, P. (2001) *Peter the Great*, Lanham: Rowman and Littlefield, 69.

11 Glagoleva, 'The Illegitimate Children of the Russian Nobility', 470.

12 Alston, P. L. (1969) *Education and the State in Tsarist Russia*, Stanford: Stanford University Press, 4.

13 Matveenko, V. E, Nazartseva, E. A., Zharkova, E. Kh. (2018) 'State Policy of Russia in the Field of Science and Education (the End of 17th–early 18th Centuries)', *Journal of History, Culture and Art Research*, vol. 7, no. 1, 93.

14 Alston, *Education and the State,* 5.

15 Fedyukin, I. (2016) 'Nobility and Schooling in Russia, 1700s–1760s: Choices in a Social Context', *Journal of Social History*, vol. 49, no. 3, 561.

16 Alston, *Education and the State,* 5.

17 De Madariaga, I. (1979) 'The Foundation of the Russian Educational System by Catherine II', *The Slavonic and East European Review*, vol. 57, no. 3, 370.

18 Okenfuss, 'The Jesuit Origins of Petrine Education', 125.

19 Cracraft, J. (1973) 'Feofan Prokopovich', in *Russia in the Eighteenth Century*, 95–101.

20 Cracraft, 'Feofan Prokopovich', 99.

21 Fedyukin, I. (2018) 'Shaping Up the Stubborn: School Building and "Discipline" in Early Modern Russia', *The Russian Review*, 77, 200–18.

22 Fedyukin, I. (2018) 'The "German" Reign of Empress Anna: Russia's Disciplinary Moment?', *Kritika: Explorations in Russian and Eurasian History*, vol. 19, no. 2, Spring, 363–84.

23 Fedyukin, 'Shaping Up the Stubborn', 211.

24 Fedyukin, 'Shaping Up the Stubborn', 211.

25 Fedyukin, I. (2016) 'Nobility and Schooling in Russia, 1700s–1760s: Choices in a Social Context', *Journal of Social History*, vol. 49, no. 3, 558–84.

26 De Madariaga, 'The Foundation of the Russian Educational System', 371–2.

27 Fedyukin 'Nobility and Schooling in Russia, 1700s–1760s', 579.

28 De Madariaga, 'The Foundation of the Russian Educational System', 373.

29 This educational project outlined in *Émile* was for a male child. Rousseau believed in essential differences between men and women and proposed a limited educational agenda for his female character Sophie, Émile's future wife.

30 Kelly, C. (2001) *Refining Russia. Advice Literature, Polite Culture and Gender from Catherine to Yeltsin*, Oxford: Oxford University Press, xvii.

31 Kelly, *Refining Russia*, 19–20.

32 Dukes, P. (1982) *The Making of Russian Absolutism, 1613–1801*, Harlow: Longman.136. *Dvorianstvo* is Russian for the nobility.

33 See Ransel, D. (1980) 'Ivan Betskoi and the Institutionalization of the Enlightenment in Russia', *Canadian-American Slavic Studies,* vol. 14, no. 3, 327–38.

34 Quoted in De Madariaga, 'The Foundation of the Russian Educational System', 373.

35 Fedyukin, 'School Buildings', 215.

36 De Madariaga, 'The Foundation of the Russian Educational System', 373.

37 Blakesley, R. P. (2014) 'Ladies-in-Waiting in Waiting: Picturing Adolescence in Dmitry Levitsky's Smolny Portraits, 1772–76', *Art History*, vol. 37, February, 29.

38 Kosheleva, O. (2009–10) 'Educational Models for Enlightened Eighteenth-Century Russians', *Russian Studies in History*, vol. 48, no. 3, 56.

39 'O smysle slova vospitanie', *Sobesednik lyubitely rossiyskogo slova*, 1, part 2, St. Petersburg, 1783, 12–13, quoted in Raeff, 'Home, School and Service', 302.

40 De Madariaga, 'The Foundation of the Russian Educational System', 386.

41 Betskoi, I. (1766) *Kratkoe nastavlenie, vybrannoe iz luchshikh avtorov s nekotorymi fizicheskimi primecchanami o vospianie detei ot rozhdeniia do ikh iunoshestva.* St. Petersburg.

42 Blakesley, R. (2014) 'Ladies-in-Waiting in Waiting: Picturing Adolescence in Dmitry Levitsky's Smolny Portraits, 1772–76', *Art History*, 37, February, 15.

43 Raeff, M. (1962) 'Home, School, and Service in the Life of the 18th-Century Russian Nobleman', *The Slavonic and East European Review*, vol. 40, no. 95, 295–307.

44 Alston, *Education and the State*, 18.

45 Ransel, *Mothers of Misery*, 3.

46 Hartley, J. (1989) 'The Boards of Social Welfare and the Financing of Catherine II's State Schools', *The Slavonic and East European Review*, vol. 67, 211–27.

47 Alston, *Education and the State*, 19.

48 See Kuxhausen, *From the Womb to the Body Politic*, for the impact of the Enlightenment on medical practices in Russia.

49 Fedyukin, 'School Buildings', 559.

50 Kosheleva, O. (2009–10) 'Educational Models for Enlightened Eighteenth-Century Russians', *Russian Studies in History*, vol. 48, no. 3, 50–62.

51 Kelly, *Refining Russia*, 11–12; Kosheleva, 'Educational Models for Enlightened Eighteenth-Century Russians'.

52 Raeff, 'The Enlightenment in Russia', 42–3.

53 Pankier Weld, S. (2018) 'Paradoxes of the Russian Empress Catherine the Great's Writings for Children', *International Research in Children's Literature*, vol. II, no. 2, 147–59

Chapter 3

1 Glagoleva, 'The Illegitimate Children of the Russian Nobility', 476.

2 Czap, P. Jr. (1978) 'Marriage and Peasant Joint Family', in D. Ransel (ed.), *The Family in Imperial Russia: New Lines of Historical Research*, Urbana: University of Illinois Press, 103–23.

3 Czap, 'Marriage and Peasant Joint Family', 110.

4 See for example Raeff, M. (1962) 'Home, School and Service', 295–307; Dunn, P. (2006) ' "That Enemy Is the Baby": Childhood in Imperial Russia', in L. deMause (ed.), *The History of Childhood*, Oxford: Rowman and Little, 383–405; Tovrov, J. (1978) 'Mother-Child Relations among the Russian Nobility', in D. L. Ransel (ed.), *The Family in Imperial Russia. New Lines of Historical Research*, Urbana: University of Illinois Press, 15–43.

5 Raeff, 'Home, School and Service', 296.

6 Grant, S. (2012) 'The Russian Gentry Family', 15. Dunn, 'That Enemy Is the Baby', 383–405.

7 Grant, 'The Russian Gentry Family', 8.

8 Kelly, *Refining Russia*, 52–3.

9 Pickering Antonova, K. (2017) *An Ordinary Marriage: The World of a Gentry Family in Provincial Russia*, Oxford: Oxford University Press, 153–4.

10 Antonova, *An Ordinary Marriage*, 159.

11 Antonova, *An Ordinary Marriage*, 132.

12 Kelly, C. *Refining Russia*, 40–1.

13 Tovrov, 'Mother-Child Relations among the Russian Nobility', in Ransel (ed.), *The Family in Imperial Russia*, 15–43.

14 Randolph, J. (2007) *The House in the Garden: The Bakunin Family and the Romance of Russian Idealism*, Ithaca and London: Cornell University Press, 151. Randolph shows the tension in their lives caused by their attempt to avoid this fate while staying loyal to their parents and wider family.

15 Alston, *Education and the State*, 19.

16 Nikitenko, A. (2001) *Up from Serfdom: My Childhood and Youth in Russia, 1804–1824*, London and New Haven: Yale University Press.

17 Nikitenko, *Up from Serfdom*, 84–5.

18 Nikitenko, *Up from Serfdom*, 87. Nikitenko's father was a teacher, clerk and estate manager who had himself received formal schooling, having been selected as a boy to sing in Count Sheremetev's famous serf choir.

19 Hans, N. (1963) *The Russian Tradition in Education*, London: Routledge & Kegan Paul, 21.

20 Unnerved by the Decembrist Revolt and the state's severe reaction to it, Mikhail Bakunin's father quickly packed him off at age of fourteen to St Petersburg to enrol in the Artillery School, while his mother wrote to Admiral Shishkov, the new Minister of Enlightenment, asking for advice and approval for her educational plans for the remaining Bakunin children. See Randolph, *The House in the Garden*, 127–9, 141–5.

21 Hans, *The Russian Tradition in Education*, 27.

22 Alston writes that there was a contraction of around 17 per cent of children attending *gymnazium* for three years after the Circular was issued, but it was largely ignored after that. Alston, *Education and the State*, 129.

23 Saunders, D. (1992) *Russian in the Age of Reaction and Reform 1801–1881*, Harlow: Longman, 152.

24 See Wachtel, A. (1990) *The Battle for Childhood: Creation of a Russian Myth*, Stanford: Stanford University Press for the impact of Tolstoy on literature about childhood in Russia.

25 Shelgunov, *Vospominaniia* I, 137, quoted in Engel, B. A. 'Mothers and Daughters', in Ransel (ed.), *The Family in Imperial Russia*, 58.

26 Waldron, P. (1997) *The End of Imperial Russia, 1855–1917*, London: Palgrave, 38.

27 Waldron, *The End of Imperial Russia*, 81.

28 Cuvillier, J.-P., (1980) 'L'Enfant dans la tradition féodale germanique', *Senefiance*, 9, 49, quoted in Heywood, *A History of Childhood*, 18. See Stearns, P. (2011) *Childhood in World History*, Oxford: Routledge, 17–27 for a broad discussion on agricultural childhoods.

29 See Shanin, T. (1985) *Russia as a 'Developing Society'. The Roots of Otherness: Russia's Turn of Century*, vol. 1, Basingstoke: Macmillan for a comprehensive description of peasant structures in the post-Reform era.

30 Mironov, B. N. (2016) 'Long Term Trends in the Development of Family Structure in Christian Russia from the Sixteenth to the Twentieth Centuries: An Analytic Overview of Historiography', *Journal of Family History,* vol. 41, no. 4, 357. Likewise, the words 'family' (*sem'ya*) and 'household' (*dvor*) were used interchangeably.

31 Mironov, 'Long Term Trends', 355–77. Mironov argues that extended and multiple family households were frequently found in urban areas as well. The 1897 Census showed that 46 per cent of town dwellers in European Russia lived in these structures.

32 Czap, 'Marriage and Peasant Joint Family', in Ransel (ed.), *The Family in Imperial Russia,* 121.

33 Mironov, 'Long Term Trends', 363.

34 Mironov, 'Long Term Trends', 363.

35 Ginsborg, P. (2014) *Family Politics: Domestic Life, Devastation and Survival 1900–1950*, New Haven: Yale University Press, 9.

36 Gorshkov, B. B. (2009) 'History of Child Labour in Imperial Russia', in *The World of Child Labour: An Historical and Regional Survey*, Armonk, NY: M.E. Sharpe.

37 Gorshkov, B. B. (2009) *Russia's Factory Children: State, Society and the Law, 1800–1917*, Pittsburgh: University of Pittsburgh Press, 15–16.

38 Gorshkov, *Russia's Factory Children*, 21.

39 Gorshkov, *Russia's Factory Children*, 16.

40 Ransel, *Village Mothers*, 37.

41 Gorshkov, *Russia's Factory Children*, 20.

42 Gorshkov, 'Child Labour in Imperial Russia'.

43 Eklof, B. (1986) *Russian Peasant Schools: Officialdom, Village Culture and Popular Pedagogy, 1861–1914*, Berkeley and Los Angeles: University of California Press, 103.

44 Hans, *The Russian Tradition in Education*, 146.

45 Hans, *The Russian Tradition in Education*, 145–6.

46 See Timberlake, C. (1993) 'N. A. Korf (1834–83): Designer of the Russian Elementary School Classroom', in B. Eklof (ed.), *School and Society in Tsarist and Soviet Russia*, New York: St. Martin's Press, 12–35. Many primary schools did not have purpose-built premises but used peasant huts or other existing rural buildings.

47 Kelly, *Children's World*, 522.

48 Eklof, *Russian Peasant Schools*, 267.

49 Eklof, B. (1993) 'Worlds in Conflict', in B. Eklof (ed.), *School and Society in Tsarist and Soviet Russia*, 98.

50 Alston, *Education and the State*, 69.

51 Hans, *The Russian Tradition in Education*, 72.

52 Kirschenbaum, *Small Comrades*, 19–23.

53 Eklof, B. (1993) 'Worlds in Conflict', in B. Eklof (ed.), *School and Society in Tsarist and Soviet Russia*, Basingstoke: Macmillan, 106–9.

54 Eklof, 'Worlds in Conflict', 100–01.

55 N. Remorov, *Na nive narodnoi* (St. Petersburg, 1906), 26, quoted in Eklof, 'Worlds in Conflict', 100.

56 Eklof, *Russian Peasant Schools*, 269–78.

57 Eklof, *Russian Peasant Schools*, 253.

58 Andreev, A. L. (2013) 'On the Modernization of Education in Russia: A Historical Sociological Analysis', *Russian Social Science Review*, vol. 54, no. 5, 8.

59 Eklof, *Russian Peasant Schools*, 265.

60 Eklof, *Russian Peasant Schools*, 301.

61 Eklof, *Russian Peasant Schools*, 303.

62 Eklof, *Russian Peasant Schools*, 294.

63 *Realschule* were established in Prussia from the mid-eighteenth century as a practical and scientifically oriented alternative to the classical *gymnazium*. They became one of the main forms of secondary education in modern Germany.

64 Alston, *Education and the State*, 95.

65 Alston, *Education and the State*, 97.

66 Alston, *Education and the State*, 97.

67 Kelly, *Children's World*, 501.

68 Alpern Engel, B., *Women in Russia, 1700–2000,* Cambridge: Cambridge University Press, 70.

69 Rogers, R. (2005) 'Porous Wall and Prying Eyes: Control, Discipline, and Morality in Boarding Schools for Girls in Mid-Nineteenth Century France', in *Secret Gardens, Satanic Mills. Placing Girls in European History*, Bloomington: Indiana University Press, 113–30.

70 Veremenko, V. A. (2015) *Deti v dvoryanskikh sem'yakh Rossii (vtoraya polovina XIX- nachalo XXv.)*, St Petersburg: Leningradskii gosudarstvennyi universitet, 136.

71 Fen, E. (1970) *A Girl Grew Up in Russia*, London: Andre Deutsch, 19.

72 Rogers, 'Porous Wall and Prying Eyes', 127.

73 Dobrenko, E. (2005) ' "The Entire Real World of Children": The School Tale and "Our Happy Childhood" ', *Slavic and East European Journal*, vol. 49, no. 2, 228.

74 Alston, *Education and the State*, 173.

75 Alston, *Education and the State*, 167.

76 Alston, *Education and the State*, 176.

77 *Russkaya Shkola*, March 1905, 60–5 in Alston, *Education and the State*, 177.

78 Nabokov, V. (2000) *Speak, Memory. An Autobiography Revisited*, London: Penguin, 138.

79 Nabokov, *Speak, Memory*, 10.

80 Nabokov, *Speak, Memory*, 53–4.

81 Hellman, B. (2013) *Fairy Tales and True Stories: The History of Russian Literature for Children and Young People*, Leiden: Brill.

82 Kelly, *Children's World*, 450.

83 Veremenko, *Deti v dvoryanskikh sem'yakh*, 87.

84 Philipponnat O. and Lienhardt, P. (2011) *The Life of Irène Némirovsky*, London: Vintage.

85 Fen, *A Girl Grew Up in Russia*, 50.

86 Fen, *A Girl Grew Up in Russia*, 90.

87 Obolensky, D. (1999) *Bread of Exile. A Russian Family*, London: Harvill Press, 4–5.

88 Nabokov, *Speak, Memory*, 26.

89 Fen, *A Girl Grew Up in Russia*, 71.

90 Fen, *A Girl Grew Up in Russia*, 167–8.

91 Obolensky, *Bread of Exile*, 5.

92 Obolensky, *Bread of Exile*, 10.

93 Petrushevskaya, L. I. (ed.) (1997) *Deti russkoi emigratsii: Kniga, kotoruyu mechtali no ne smogli izdat' izgnanniki*, Moscow: Terra, 114. A *tropar'* is a short religious hymn in Eastern Orthodoxy.

94 Chernyaeva, N. (2009) 'Childcare Manuals and Construction of Motherhood in Russia, 1890–1990', PhD (Doctor of Philosophy) thesis, University of Iowa, https://ir.uiowa.edu/etd/344/, 20, 34.

95 Ransel, *Village Mothers*, 32.

96 See Pollock, L. (1990) *A Lasting Relationship: Parents and Children over Three Centuries*, University Press of New England, for an early corrective to this view.

97 Ransel, *Village Mothers*, 183–7.

98 Ransel, *Village Mothers*, 271.

99 Stearns, *Childhood in World History*, 65.

100 Kelly, *Children's World*, 161.

101 Kirschenbaum, L. (2001) *Small Comrades*: *Revolutionising Childhood in Soviet Russia*, New York: Routledge, 29.

102 Chernyaeva, 'Childcare Manuals', 32–3.

103 The first formally recognized children's hospital was the *Hôpital des Enfants Malades*, founded in Paris in 1802. The Great Ormond Street Hospital was opened in London in 1852. A department of paediatrics was opened in Moscow State University in 1888.

104 Chernyaeva, *Childcare Manuals*, 44.

105 Chernyaeva, *Childcare Manuals,* 54.

106 Chernyaeva, *Childcare Manuals*, 41, 44–5.

107 Chernyaeva, *Childcare Manuals*, 48.

108 Ransel, *Village Mothers*, 40.

109 Kelly, *Children's World*, 297.

110 Lindenmeyr, A. (1996) *Poverty Is Not a Vice*: *Charity, Society, and the State in Imperial Russia*, Princeton: Princeton University Press, 182.

111 Lindenmeyr, *Poverty Is Not a Vice*, 146.

112 Lindenmeyr, *Poverty Is Not a Vice*, 162

113 Kelly, *Children's World*, 162. Maria Fyodorovna (1759–1828) was the spouse of Paul I, who had managed imperial philanthropic structures and institutions during her life.

114 Rose, N. *Governing the Soul*, 121.

115 Kelly, *Children's World*.

116 Alston, *Education and the State*, 230.

117 Alston, *Education and the State*, 232–3.

118 Alston, *Education and the State*, 230. See also Byford, A. (2016) 'V.M. Bekhterev in Russian Child Science, 1900s–1920s: "Objective Psychology/ Reflexology" as a Scientific Movement', *Journal of the History of the Behavioural Sciences*, vol. 52, no. 2, 99–123; and Byford, A. (2017) 'The Imperfect Child in Early Twentieth Century Russia', *History of Education*, vol. 46, no. 5, 595–617.

119 Kelly, *Children's World*, 40; Chernyaeva, 'Childcare Manuals', 77.

120 Gorshkov, *Factory Children*, 29.

121 Gorshkov, *Factory Children*, 28–9.

122 Pretty, D. (2009) 'Child Labour in the Russian Textile Industry', in *The World of Child Labor: A Historical and Regional Survey*, Armonk, NY: M.E. Sharpe.

123 Pretty, 'Child Labour in the Russian Textile Industry'.

124 Gorshkov, *Factory Children*, 80.

125 Gorshkov, *Factory Children*, 48.

126 Gorshkov, *Factory Children*, 67.

127 Gorshkov, *Factory Children*, 123.

128 Gorshkov, *Factory Children*, 138.

129 Gorshkov, *Factory Children*, 130, 133.

130 Gorshkov, *Factory Children*, 164.

131 Gorshkov, *Factory Children*, 140.

132 Gorshkov, *Factory Children*, 151.

133 Gorshkov, *Factory Children*, 154.

134 Eklof, *Russian Peasant Schools*, 371.

135 Gorshkov, *Child Labour*.

136 Gorshkov, *Factory Children*, 167.

137 Wagner, W. (1995) 'Family Law, the Rule of Law, and Liberalism in Late Imperial Russia', *Jahr-bucher fur Geschichte Osteuropas*, vol. XLIII, no. 4, 519–35.

138 Butler, *Russian Family Law*, 20.

139 Kelly, *Children's World*, 182–5. The first juvenile court was established in Illinois in 1899. In Great Britain special courts for minors were established with the passing of the Children Act of 1908, followed by Portugal, Belgium and France in 1911–12. See Jablonka, 'Social Welfare and the Rights of Children', in P. S. Fass, *A History of Childhood in the Western World*, New York: Routledge, 384.

140 Andreev, 'On the Modernization of Education in Russia', 4.

141 Eklof, *Russian Peasant Schools*, 311.

142 Andreev, 'On the Modernization of Education in Russia', 5.

143 Eklof, *Russian Peasant Schools*, 90.

144 Hans, *The Russian Tradition in Education*, 149.

145 Eklof, *Russian Peasant Schools*, 293.

146 Eklof, *Russian Peasant Schools*, 287.

147 Gorshkov, *Factory Children*, 165.

148 Eklof, *Russian Peasant Schools*, 184.

149 Kirschenbaum, *Small Comrades*, 8.

150 Veremenko, *Deti v dvoryanskikh sem'yakh Rossii*.

151 Byford, A. (2013) 'Parent Diaries and the Child Study Movement in Late Imperial and Early Soviet Russia', *Russian Review*, 212–41.

152 Veremenko, *Deti v dvoryanskikh semei*, 121.

153 Fass, 'Is There a History in the History of Childhood?', in *A History of Childhood in the Western World*, 12.

154 Ransel, *Village Mothers*, 265.

155 Kirschenbaum, *Small Comrades*, 27.

156 Alston, *Education and the State*, 170.

Chapter 4

1 Sovnarkom Decree 31st December 1917, cited in Baron, N. (2016) 'Placing the Child in Twentieth-Century History: Contexts and Framework', in N. Baron (ed.), *Displaced Children in Russia and Eastern Europe, 1915–1953*, Leiden: Brill, 32.

2 See Byford, A. (2017) 'The Imperfect Child in Early Twentieth Century Russia', *History of Education*, vol. 46, no. 5, 595–617 for developments in 'child science' in the early Soviet period.

3 Baranov, A., Namazova-Baranova, L. and Albitsky, V. (2015) 'Paediatrics in Russia: Past, Present and Future', *Archives of Diseases in Childhood*, vol. 102, no. 8, 774–8.

4 Kelly, *Children's World*, 76.

5 Chernyaeva, *Childcare Manuals*, 134.

6 See Goldman, W. (2008) *Women, the State and Revolution: Soviet Family Policy and Social Life, 1917–1936*, Cambridge: Cambridge University Press, 29–43 for a fuller discussion on Marxism and the family.

7 Marx, K. and Engels, F. (2012), *The Communist Manifesto: A Modern Edition*, London: Verso, 56.

8 Geiger, H. K. (1968) *The Family in Soviet Russia*, Harvard: Harvard University Press, 11.

9 Marx and Engels, *The Communist Manifesto*, 57.

10 Choe, H. (2014) 'Marx on the Family and Class Consciousness', *Rethinking Marxism*, vol. 26, no. 2, 262–77.

11 Engels, F. (1847) *The Principles of Communism*. Written in 1847, the draft was first published in 1914. https://www.marxists.org/archive/marx/works/1847/11/prin-com.htm.

12 Kelly, *Children's World*, 63.

13 See Bukharin, N. I. and Preobrazhensky, E. (1920) *The ABC of Communism*, Chapter 10. Communism and Education, Part 79: Preparation for School Life, https://www.marxists.org/archive/bukharin/works/1920/abc/10.htm

14 Geiger, *The Family in Soviet Russia*, 72.

15 Geiger, *The Family in Soviet Russia*, 47–8.

16 Geiger, *The Family in Soviet Russia*, 48.

17 Butler, W. *Russian Family Law*, London: Wildy, Simmonds and Hill Publishing, 70.

18 Kelly, *Children's World*.

19 Kopelev, L. (1980) *The Education of a True Believer*, London: Harper Collins; Bonner, E. (1992) *Mothers and Daughters*, New York: Alfred A. Knopf, 40.

20 Chernaeva, *Childcare Manuals*, 97. In the 1920s, advice on childcare by medical experts in general remained within the paradigm of the non-productive, breastfeeding mother performing all the care, in contradiction to stated Bolshevik revolutionary ideals.

21 Slepkov, A. (ed.), (1926) *Byt i molodezh*, Moscow, quoted in Geiger, *The Family in Soviet Russia*, 45

22 Petrushevskaya, *Deti russkoi emigratsii*, 160.

23 See White, E. (2013) 'The "Struggle against Denationalisation" in Europe: The Russian Emigration and Education in Europe in the 1920s', *Revolutionary Russia*, vol. 26, no. 2, 128–46.

24 These essays are published in Petrushevskaya, L. (1997) *Deti russkoi emigratsii*. For a contemporary analysis of the essays and the state of childhood in the emigration, see Zenzinov, V. (ed.) (1925), *Deti emigratsii. Sbornik statei*, Prague: Pedagogicheskoe buiro po delam srednei i nizhshei shkoly zagranitsei.

25 The majority of the children in the schools came from the middling gentry, Cossack or the families of Imperial Army Officers. See also White, E. (2017) 'Relief, Reconstruction and the Rights of the Child: The Case of Displaced Children in Constantinople', in N. Baron (ed.), *Displaced Children in Russia and Eastern Europe, 1915–1953*, Leiden: Brill.

26 Petrushevskaya, *Deti russkoi emigratsii*, 42.

27 Petrushevskaya, *Deti russkoi emigratsii*, 167.

28 Petrushevskaya, *Deti russkoi emigratsii*, 143.

29 Petrushevskaya, *Deti russkoi emigratsii*, 230.

30 Petrushevskaya, *Deti russkoi emigratsii*, 185.

31 Petrushevskaya, *Deti russkoi emigratsii*, 312.

32 Petrushevskaya, *Deti russkoi emigratsii*, 89.

33 Petrushevskaya, *Deti russkoi emigratsii*, 137.

34 Petrushevskaya, *Deti russkoi emigratsii*, 161.

35 Petrushevskaya, *Deti russkoi emigratsii*, 160.

36 Petrushevskaya, *Deti russkoi emigratsii*, 174.

37 *Listovki grazhdanskoi voini v SSSR, 1918–1922 gg*, Moscow: Gospolizdat, 1942, 39.

38 'Iz listovki politupravleniya revvoensoveta respuliki k trudyashchimsya. June 1919', 'Obrashchenie politupravleniya revvoensoveta respuliki k krasnoarmeitsam', in *Listovki grazhdanskoi voini v SSSR*, 47, 56.

39 'K voiskam, oboronyayushchim Petrograd!', in *Listovki grazhdanskoi voini v SSSR, 1918–1922*, 39.

40 See Materialy o vzyatii krasnoarmeitsami detei v zalozhniki pri podavlenii vosstaniya krest'yan tambovskoi gubernii v 1921 in Vilensky, S. S., Kokurin, A. A., Atmashkina, A. G. and Novichenko, I. Yu. (eds) (2002), *Deti Gulaga. 1918–1956. Dokumenty*, Moscow, 18–23.

41 Goldman, *Women, the State and Revolution*, 65.

42 The Workers and Peasant Inspectorate (*Rabkrin)* was a body put in place in 1920 to oversee the efficiency of the administration.

43 'Iz doklada komissii VTsIK po uluchsheniyu zhizni detei v presidium VTsIK', in *Deti Gulaga*, 39.

44 See Smirnova, T. (2009) 'Children's Welfare in Soviet Russia: Society and the State, 1917–1930s', *The Soviet and Post-Soviet Review*, 36, 173. The *Zhenotdel* was the Women's Department of the Party Central Committee. It was abolished in 1930.

45 Kelly, *Children's World*, 196.

46 Ball, A. (1994) *And Now My Soul Is Hardened: Abandoned Children in Soviet Russia, 1918–1930*, Berkeley: University of California Press, 7. Smirnova, 'Children's Welfare', 172.

47 Frierson, C. and Vilensky, S. S. (2010) *Children of the Gulag*, New Heaven: Yale University Press, 7.

48 Frierson and Vilensky, *Children of the Gulag*, 46.

49 For Western relief operations, children and the famine see Mahood, L. and Satzewich, V. (2009) 'The Save the Children Fund and the Russian Famine of 1921–23: Claims and Counter Claims about Feeding "Bolshevik Children"', *Journal of Historical Sociology*, vol. 22, no. 1, 55–83.

50 'Iz doklada predsedatelyu VTsIk M.I. Kalininu ot zamestitelya predsedatelya TsIk Tatarskoi respubliky I upolnomecheniyu po uluchsheniyu zhizni detei tartrespubliki Iskhaka Kazakova' in *Deti Gulaga*, 47.

51 Goldman, *Women, the State and Revolution*, 73, f. 49.

52 Ball, *And Now My Soul Is Hardened*, 9–10.

53 Ball, *And Now My Soul Is Hardened*, 9.

54 Ball, *And Now My Soul Is Hardened*, 101.

55 See Tat'iana Smirnova (2010) 'Beloved Children of the Soviet Republic', *Russian Studies in History*, vol. 48, no. 4, 9–25 for the fate of these adopted peasant children.

56 The reception centres were officially called 'reception-distribution centres' – (*Primemniki-raspredetely*). They are referred to here reception centres for brevity.

57 Ball, *And Now My Soul Is Hardened*, 57.

58 Ball, *And Now My Soul Is Hardened*, 62.

59 Oushakine, S. (2004) 'The Flexible and the Pliant: Disturbed Organisms of Soviet Modernity', *Cultural Anthropology*, vol. 19, no. 3, 410.

60 Oushakine, 'The Flexible and the Pliant: Disturbed Organisms of Soviet Modernity', 410.

61 Oushakine, 'The Flexible and the Pliant: Disturbed Organisms of Soviet Modernity', 411.

62 Baron, 'Placing the Child', 19.

63 Konstantin Paustovsky, quoted in Ball, *And Now My Soul Is Hardened*, 73.

64 Goldman, *Women, the State and Revolution*, 93.

65 Ball, *And Now My Soul Is Hardened*, 156.

66 Chernyaeva, *Childcare Manuals*, 105.

67 Chernyaeva, *Childcare Manuals*, 105.

68 Goldman, *Women, the State and Revolution*, 110.

69 Nakachi, M. (2006) 'Population, Politics and Reproduction: Late Stalinism and Its Legacy', in J. Fürst (ed.), *Late Stalinist Russia: Society between Reconstruction and Reinvention*, Oxford: Routledge, 35.

70 Chernyaeva, *Childcare Manuals*, 107.

71 Partlett, W. (2004) 'Breaching Cultural Worlds with the Village School: Educational Visions, Local Initiative and Rural Experience at S.T. Shatskii's Kaluga School System, 1919–1932', *The Slavonic and East European Review*, vol. 82, no. 4, 876. Lisa Kirschenbaum ascribes a similar role to new Soviet preschool institutions.

72 '*Detskie sochineniia po razlichnoi teme*', quoted in Partlett, 'Breaching Cultural Worlds with the Village School', 862.

73 Partlett, 'Breaching Cultural Worlds with the Village School', 879.

74 Chernyaeva, *Childcare Manuals*, 130.

75 Ransel, *Village Mothers*, 53.

76 Ransel, *Village Mothers*, 62.

77 Ransel, *Village Mothers*, 213.

78 Ransel, *Village Mothers*, 54.

79 Decree on the Unified Labor School of the Russian Socialist Federated Soviet Republic. 16 October 1918. http://soviethistory.msu.edu/1917-2/rais ing-socialist-youth/raising-socialist-youth-texts/unified-labor-school/

80 See Partlett, W. (2004) 'Breaching Cultural Worlds with the Village School', 847–85.

81 Kirschenbaum, *Small Comrades*, 12.

82 Geiger, *The Family in Soviet Russia*, 274.

83 Geiger, *The Family in Soviet Russia*, 274.

84 Partlett, 'Breaching Cultural Worlds with the Village School', 854.

85 See Holmes, L. (1991) *The Kremlin and the Schoolhouse: Reforming Education in Soviet Russia, 1917–1931*, Bloomington: Indiana University Press for the rejection of radical pedagogy by Soviet society.

86 Partlett, 'Breaching Cultural Worlds with the Village School', 864.

87 Partlett, 'Breaching Cultural Worlds with the Village School', 866.

88 Kucherenko, O. (2011) *Little Soldiers: How Soviet Children Went to War*, Oxford: Oxford University Press, 34.

89 Kelly, *Children's World*, 550.

90 DeGraffenried, J. K. (2014) *Sacrificing Childhood: Children and the Soviet State in the Great Patriotic War*, Lawrence, University of Kansas Press, 79.

91 Lunacharsky, A. 'The State of Educational and Cultural Development Since the October Revolution', 15 October 1927 in Cummins, A. G. (ed.) (1991) *Documents of Soviet History. Volume 4 Stalin Grasps Power, 1926–28*, London: Academic International Press, 240–7.

92 Lunacharsky, *Documents of Soviet History*, 243.

93 Holmes, *The Kremlin and the School House*, 96.

94 Holmes, *The Kremlin and the School House*, 41.

95 Holmes, *The Kremlin and the School House*, 3.

96 Geiger, *The Family in Soviet Russia*, 39.

97 Ginsborg, *Family Politics*, 40.

98 http://soviethistory.msu.edu/1917-2/the-new-woman/the-new-woman-texts/code-of-laws-concerning-the-civil-registration-of-deaths-births-and-marriages/

99 Goldman, *Women, the State and Revolution*, 137–8.

100 Goldman, *Women, the State and Revolution*, 135.

101 Goldman, *Women, the State and Revolution*, 153.

102 Goldman, *Women, the State and Revolution*, 160–1.

103 See Cowley M. K. (2014) 'The Right of Inheritance and the Stalin Revolution', *Kritika*, vol. 15, no. 1, 103–23.

104 Goldman, *Women, the State and Revolution*, 106–8.

105 Ball, *And Now My Soul is Hardened*, 120. The Commissions would be abolished in 1935 when a more punitive approach was taken to juvenile delinquency.

106 Goldman, *Women, the State and Revolution*, 80.

107 Goldman, *Women, the State and Revolution*, 84.

108 Goldman, *Women, the State and Revolution*, 305.

109 Smirnova, 'Beloved Children', 17.

110 Smirnova, 'Beloved Children', 15.

111 Goldman, *Women, the State and Revolution*, 98.

112 The majority of the Code was extended to other Republics, with the exception of clauses relating to de facto marriage.

113 Cummins, *Documents of Soviet History*, 140.

114 Cummins, *Documents of Soviet History*, 131–57.

115 Green, R. (2016) 'Making Kin Out of Strangers: Soviet Adoption during and after the Second World War', in Baron, *Displaced Children*, 158.

116 Goldman, *Women, the State and Revolution*, 302.

117 Goldman, *Women, the State and Revolution*, 303.

118 Goldman, *Women, the State and Revolution*, 303.

119 On children's literature in this period, see Rothenstein, J. and Budashevskaya, O. (2013) *Inside the Rainbow: Russian Children's Literature 1920–1935: Beautiful Books, Terrible Times*, London: Redstone Press.

120 Balina, M. and Rudova, L. (eds) (2008) *Russian Children's Literature and Culture*, New York: Routledge, 11.

121 Kelly, *Children's World*, 455.

122 Kelly, *Children's World*, 475.

123 Kelly, *Children's World*, 480.

124 Baranova, A. R. (2007) '"Nyan'kat'sya budem?": memorial'noe obrazy sovetskogo detstva 1930–1950x godov', in A. Sal'nikova (ed.), *Rossiiskoe detstva v XX veke: Istoriya, teoriya, i praktika issledovaniya*, Kazan: Kazan State University, 209.

125 Harwin, *Children of the Russian State*, 10.

126 Franco, R. (2018) 'Stalin's Humanitarian Government: Class, Child Homelessness and State Security in a Historical Perspective (1930s–1940s)', *European Review of History*, vol. 25, no. 1, 121.

Chapter 5

1 Kelly, *Children's World*, 112; Fürst, J. (2008) 'Between Salvation and Liquidation: Homeless and Vagrant Children and the Reconstruction of Soviet Society', *The Slavonic and East European Review*, vol. 86. no. 2, April, 236.

2 Kucherenko, O. (2011) *Little Soldiers*, 7; Kirschenbaum, *Small Comrades*, 6.

3 DeGraffenried, J. *Sacrificing Childhood*, 3.

4 Kucherenko, *Little Soldiers*, 29.

5 Naftali, O. (2014) 'Chinese Childhood in Conflict: Children, Gender, and Violence in China of the "Cultural Revolution" Period (1966–1976)', *Oriens Extremis*, 99.

6 Ginsborg, P. *Family Politics: Domestic Life, Devastation and Survival, 1900–1950*, 416. Fragile and 'female-dominated' do not have to be linked; it was often women who held the family together. The role of the grandmother was particularly important.

7 Zhiromskaia, V. B. (2001) *Demograficheskaia istoriia Rossii v 1930 gg. Vzgliad v neizvestnoe*, Moscow, Rosspen, 45, 21, 33, in Frierson and Vilensky, *Children of the Gulag*, 143.

8 See Hoffmann, D. (2003) *Stalinist Values: The Cultural Norms of Soviet Modernity, 1917–1941*, Ithaca and London: Cornell University Press, for family policy during the Great Retreat.

9 Kelly, *Children's World*, 382.

10 Livschiz, A. (2006) 'Children's Lives after Zoia's Death: Order, Emotions and Heroism in Children's Lives and Literature in the Post-war Soviet Union', in J. Fürst (ed.), *Late Stalinist Russia: Society between Reconstruction and Reinvention*, Oxford: Routledge.

11 Raleigh, D. J. (2012) *Soviet Baby Boomers: An Oral History of Russia's Cold War Generation*, Oxford: Oxford University Press, 13, 16, 64–5.

12 Preface in Balina and Rudova *Russian Children's Literature and Culture*, xv. Julie DeGraffenreid lists as the 'state' producing this culture consisting of institutions such as *Narkompros* (The Ministry of Education), Young Pioneers, All-Union Radio, the Writers Union, as well as significant individuals in these institutions such as the writer Arkadii Gaidar. See DeGraffenried, *Sacrificing Childhood*, 3.

13 Kucherenko, *Little Soldiers*, 5.

14 Holmes, L. (1999) *Stalin's School: Moscow's Model School No. 25, 1931–37*, Pittsburgh: University of Pittsburgh Press, 295–6.

15 Creuzinger, C. (1996) *Childhood in Russia: Representation and Reality*, Lanham: University Press of America, 41–2. This nickname was derived from typical names for boys from intelligentsia families such as Igor, Georgii and Oleg.

16 Petrushevskaya, L. (2017) *The Girl from the Metropole Hotel*, New York: Penguin, 119.

17 *Pioner*, Molodaya Gvardiya, 20, 1929.

18 Kucherenko, *Little Soldiers*, 65. The Dneprostroi Dam was a hydroelectric power station in Ukraine, built during the first Five Year Plan; *Kolkhoz* is a collective farm and *Pyatiletka* is an abbreviation for Five Year Plan.

19 Channon, J. (2001) 'Technological and Scientific Utopias in Soviet Children's Literature, 1921–1932', *Journal of Popular Culture*, vol. 34, no. 4, Spring, 154.

20 https://www.lib.uchicago.edu/collex/exhibits/soviet-imaginary/individuals/samuil-marshak-and-mikhail-il/

21 Il'in was also the brother of the Soviet children's writer Samuil Marshak.

22 Kirschenbaum, *Small Comrades*, 134.

23 *Parents, Learn How to Bring Your Children Up* (1929), quoted in Kirschenbaum, *Small Comrades*, 142.

24 Goldman, *Women, the State and Revolution*, 310.

25 Kirschenbaum, *Small Comrades*, 139.

26 Goldman, *Women, the State and Revolution*, 318.

27 Geiger, *The Family in Soviet Russia*, 274.

28 See Bonner, *Mothers and Daughters* for a picture of an elite childhood in the 1930s. Her father was a senior figure in the Comintern. The state immediately removed all their benefits and luxuries when the family fell victim to the Terror in 1937.

29 See Baranova, N. (2004) 'Nyan'kat'sya budem?', in A. Salnikova (ed.), *Rossiiskoe detstvo v xx. Istoriya, teoriye, issledovanie*, Kazan, 34.

30 Geiger, *The Family in Soviet Russia*, 288.

31 Baranova, 'Nyan'kat'sya budem?', 35.

32 Dobrenko, 'The Entire Real World of Children', 228.

33 Kucherenko, *Little Soldiers*, 61.

34 *Pionerskaya Pravda*, March 1941.

35 See the collection *Deti o Staline* (1939) Moscow: Detizdat TsK VLKSM, which contained a series of images of Stalin with children from a range of Soviet publications.

36 'Iz vospominanii K.A. Strusevich', in *Deti Gulaga*, 102–3.

37 No. 130, Pis'mo Niny Shvetsovoi I.V. Stalinu' in *Deti Gulaga*, 224.

38 Krevsky, E. (2012) 'Arkadii Gaidar, the New Socialist Morality, and Stalinist Identity', *Canadian Slavonic Papers/Revue canadienne des slavistes*, vol. LIV, nos 1–2, 113–32.

39 Dobrenko, 'The Entire Real World of Children', 230.

40 The name was changed from *Detgiz* to *Detskaya literatura* in the 1960s.

41 Catriona Kelly, *Children's World*.

42 Channon, 'Technological and Scientific Utopias', 165.

43 Kucherenko, *Little Soldiers*, 33.

44 Kelly, *Children's World*, 456.

45 Krevsky, 'Arkadii Gaidar', 118.

46 *Pionerskaya Pravda*, 7 June 1928.

47 Kucherenko, *Little Soldiers*, 83.

48 Geiger, *The Family in Soviet Russia*, 295.

49 Holmes, *Model School*, 300.

50 Dobrenko,'The Entire Real World of Children', 225.

51 Quoted in Dobrenko, 'The Entire Real World of Children', 225–6; Krevsky, 'Arkady Gaidar', 122.

52 Geiger, *The Family in Soviet Russia*, 306.

53 Geiger, *The Family in Soviet Russia*, 292.

54 Geiger, *The Family in Soviet Russia*, 294.

55 Holmes, *Stalin's School*, 298.

56 Vilensky et al., *Deti Gulaga*, 272.

57 Geiger, *The Family in Soviet Russia*, 300.

58 Geiger, *The Family in Soviet Russia*, 300.

59 Geiger, *The Family in Soviet Russia*, 317.

60 For the post-Soviet history of the Pavel Morozov story, see Kelly, C. (2005) *Comrade Pavlik: The Rise and Fall of a Soviet Boy Hero*, London: Granta.

61 *Pionerskaya Pravda*, 21 December 1940.

62 Kelly, *Children's World*, 385.

63 Ransel, *Village Mothers*, 242.

64 Ransel, *Village Mothers*, 146.

65 Geiger, *The Family in Soviet Russia*, 277.

66 Frierson and Vilensky, *Children of the Gulag*, 88.

67 Frierson and Vilensky, *Children of the Gulag*, 113.

68 Frierson and Vilensky, *Children of the Gulag*, 85.

69 Frierson and Vilensky, *Children of the Gulag*, 94.

70 Vilensky et al., *Deti Gulaga*, 87.

71 Frierson and Vilensky, *Children of the Gulag*, 107.

72 Frierson and Vilensky, *Children of the Gulag*, 105.

73 Maksheev, V. N. (ed.) *Narymskaia khronika, 1930–1945: Tragediia spetspereselenstev. Dokumenty i vospominania*, Moscow: Russkii put', 43, quoted in Kazelson, M. and Baron, N. 'Memories of Displacement: Loss and Reclamation of Home/Land in the Narratives of Soviet Child Deportees of the 1930s', in Baron, ed., *Displaced Children*, 108.

74 'Pis'ma predsedatelyu VTsIK M.I.Kalininu', in Vilensky ed., *Deti Gulaga*, 77.

75 'Pis'ma predsedatelyu VTsIK M.I.Kalininu', in *Deti Gulaga*, 81.

76 Frierson and Vilensky, *Children of the Gulag*, 108.

77 Frierson and Vilensky, *Children of the Gulag*, 108.

78 'Predsedatelyu Detkomissii Pri VTsIK RFSRS tov. Semashko', in Vilensky, *Deti Gulaga*, 123.

79 Kelly, *Children's World*, 208.

80 Kazelson, 'Memories of Displacement', 115.

81 Frierson and Vilensky, *Children of the Gulag*, 114.

82 Franco, R. (2018) 'Stalin's Humanitarian Government', 127.

83 Kazelson and Baron, 'Memories of Displacement', 111.

84 Kazelson and Baron, 'Memories of Displacement', 111.

85 Partlett, 'Breaching Cultural Worlds', 881.

86 Holmes, L. E. (1993) 'Legitimizing the Soviet Regime: School No. 25, 1931–37', in B. Eklof, *School and Society in Tsarist Russia*, New York: St. Martin's Press, 184.

87 Kazelson and Baron, 'Memories of Displacement', 119.

88 MacKinnon, E. (2012) *The Forgotten Victims: Childhood and the Soviet Gulag, 1929–1953*, The Carl Beck Papers in Russian and East European Studies, 2203, 10.

89 MacKinnon, *The Forgotten Victims*, 10.

90 Frierson and Vilensky, *Children of the Gulag*, 163.

91 The state provided accommodation, usually via workplaces. Therefore, housing could be taken back when a person was arrested and lost their position.

92 'Operativnyi prikaz narodnogo komissara vnutrennykh del SSSR No. 00486 <Ob operatsii po repressirovaniyu zhen o detei izmennikov>, 15 August 1937', in *Deti Gulaga*, 234–8.

93 MacKinnon, *The Forgotten Victims*, 11.

94 Appendix III; Operation Order No. 00485, in Frierson, *Silence Was Our Salvation*, 253–5.

95 'O poryadke vydachi na opeku rodsvennikam detei, roditeli kotorykh repressirovany', *Deti Gulaga*, 275–6.

96 Frierson and Vilensky, *Children of the Gulag*, 155. This was a particularly daring response as Lenin and Krupskaya never had children of their own.

97 Bonner, *Mothers and Daughters*, 17.

98 This term apparently originated with the writer Ilya Ehrenburg. Bonner, *Mothers and Daughters*, 215.

99 This prestigious apartment block was built in 1931, and is also known as the 'House on the Embankment' after the 1976 novel by Yuri Trifonov which describes the fate of many of its inhabitants in the 1930s.

100 Shikheeva-Gaister, I. (2012) *Deti vragov naroda. Semeinaya khronika vremen kul'ta lichnosti 1925–1953*, Moscow: Vozvrashchenie, 14.

101 Shikhaeva-Gaister, *Deti vragov naroda, 59*.

102 MacKinnon, *The Forgotten Victims*, 6.

103 Frierson, *Silence Was Our Salvation*, 244. Note how the achieved status of Pioneer membership reads like an invocation.

104 Frierson and Vilensky, *Children of the Gulag*, 169.

105 'Iz pisem detei repressirovannykh v memorial', *Deti Gulaga*, 242.

106 Franco, 'Stalin's Humanitarian Government,' 128.

107 Smirnova, T. M. (2012) 'Detskie doma i trudkolonii: zhizn' <<gosudarstvennyikh detei>> v sovetskoi rossii v 1920-1930 gg.', *Vestnik Rossiiskogo Universiteta druzhby narodov*, 27.

108 Goldman, *Women, the State and Revolution*, 318–9.

109 Goldman, *Women, the State and Revolution*, 323.

110 Berman, N. (1937) 'Juvenile Delinquency, the Family and the Court in Soviet Russia', *American Journal of Sociology,* vol. 42, no. 5, 682–92

111 Geiger, *The Family in Soviet Russia*, 96.

112 Goldman, *Women, the State and Revolution*, 332.

113 Krinko, E. and Yurchuk, I. (2010) ' "Za nashi shchastlivoe detstvo": voprosy ugolovnoi otvetstvennosti nesovershennoletnykh v sovetskom zakonodatelnoste 1920-1940-x gg.', *European Researcher*, no. 2, 140; 'Rabota s nesovershennoletnimi I beznadzornymi', *Deti Gulaga*, 331–2.

114 Franco, 'Stalin's Humanitarian Government', 133.

115 Franco, 'Stalin's Humanitarian Government', 132.

116 Franco, 'Stalin's Humanitarian Government', 126.

117 Franco, 'Stalin's Humanitarian Government', 134.

118 Geiger, *The Family in Soviet Russia*, 156.

119 Ewing, T. E. (2002) *The Teachers of Stalinism: Politics, Practices and Power in the Soviet Schools of the 1930s*, New York: Peter Lang, 57.

120 Holmes, *The Kremlin and the Schoolhouse*, 133.

121 Ewing, *The Teachers of Stalinism*, 62.

122 Ransel, *Village Mothers*, 72.

123 Holmes, L. (1997) 'Part of History: The Oral Record and Moscow's Model School No. 25, 1931–1937', *Slavic Review*, vol. 56, no. 2, 279–306.

124 Holmes, *Model School*, 280.

125 Livschiz, 'Children's Lives after Zoia's Death', 203.

126 *Pionerskaya Pravda*, 4 January 1941.

127 *Pionerskaya Pravda*, 29 January 1941.

128 Ewing, T. E. (2010) *Separate Schools: Gender, Policy and Practice in Postwar Soviet Education*, Dekalb: Northern Illinois Press, 129.

129 Fradkin, F. A. 'Soviet Experimentalism Routed: S.T. Shatsky's Last Years', in Eklof (ed.), *School and Society in Tsarist and Soviet Russia*, 155.

130 Partlett, 'Breaching Cultural Worlds', 872.

131 Ewing, *The Teachers of Stalinism*, 197.

132 Ewing, *The Teachers of Stalinism*, 222.

133 Ewing, *The Teachers of Stalinism*, 208.

134 Quoted in Ewing, *The Teachers of Stalinism*, 217.

135 Ewing, *Separate Schools*, 57–8.

136 Ewing, *Separate Schools*, 21.

137 Peacock, M. (2014) *Innocent Weapons: The Soviet and American Politics of Childhood in the Cold War*, Chapel Hill: University of North Carolina Press, 39.

138 Naftali, 'Chinese Childhood in Conflict', 99.

139 Ewing, *Separate Schools*, 42.

140 Ewing, *Separate Schools*, 34.

141 Kirschenbaum, *Small Comrades*, 143.

142 Gouzenko, S. (1961) *Before Igor: Memories of a Soviet Youth*, London: Cassell, 210.

143 Ewing, *Separate Schools*, 63–4.

144 Ewing, *Separate Schools*, 107–8. Natasha Rostova and Dolly Oblonskaya are female characters from Tolstoy's *War and Peace* and *Anna Karenina* respectively.

145 Ewing, *Separate Schools*, 127.

146 Ewing, *Separate Schools*, 127.

147 Petrushevskaya, *The Girl from the Metropole Hotel*, 124.

148 Kucherenko, *Little Soldiers*, 9.

149 Kucherenko, *Little Soldiers*, 89.

150 Kucherenko, *Little Soldiers*, 92.

151 Kucherenko, *Little Soldiers*, 90.

152 Kucherenko, *Little Soldiers*, 90.

153 *Pionerskaya Pravda*, 26 November 1940.

154 *Pionerskaya Pravda*, 12 November 1940. Kliment Voroshilov was Commissar for Defence between 1935 and 1940.

155 DeGraffenried, *Sacrificing Childhood*, 120–1.

156 *Pionerskaya Pravda*, 8 March 1940.

157 See *Deti voennoi poroi* (1984) Moscow and Aleksievich, S. (2004) *Poslednie svideteli: Sto nedetskykh kolybelnikh* for life writings on experiencing the war as a child.

158 DeGraffenried, *Sacrificing Childhood*, 10.

159 Franco, 'Stalin's Humanitarian Government', 135.

160 DeGraffenried, *Sacrificing Childhood*, 38, 141.

161 See White, E. (2008) 'The Evacuation of Children from Leningrad during World War II', in M. Parsons (ed.), *Children: The Invisible Victims of War. An Interdisciplinary Study*, Peterborough: DSM.

162 *RGASPI*, f.17, op. 126, d. 19, l 20.

163 *Deti Leningrada*, 29.

164 Kozhina, E. (2001) *Through the Burning Steppe: A Memoir of Wartime Russia, 1942–1943*, New York: Riverhead Books.

165 DeGraffenried, *Sacrificing Childhood*, 29. See Dunstan, J. (1997) *Soviet Schooling in the Second World War*, Basingstoke: Macmillan for a full account of the impact of the war on education.

166 Kucherenko, *Little Soldiers*, 2–3.

167 Kucherenko, *Little Soldiers*, 198.

168 Gaidar, *Sovietskaia Ukraina*, 9 August 1941, quoted in Kucherenko, *Little Soldiers*, 140.

169 Kucherenko, *Little Soldiers*, 149.

170 Kucherenko, *Little Soldiers*, 153.

171 Kucherenko, *Little Soldiers*, 162.

172 *TsGASPb*, f 7384, op 17, d 1514, l 36.

173 Kucherenko, *Little Soldiers*, 178–80.

174 Kucherenko, *Little Soldiers*, 229–30.

175 DeGraffenried, *Sacrificing Childhood*, 145.

176 Borossa, J. and Gulina, M. (2005) 'Child Survivors of the Siege of Leningrad: Notes from a Study on War Trauma and Its Long Term Effects on Individuals', *Children in War: The International Journal of Evacuee and War Child Studies*, vol. 1, no. 3, 51–2.

177 Zima, V. F. (2000) *Mentalitet narodov Rossii v voine 1941–1945 godov*, Moscow, 49.

178 DeGraffenried, *Sacrificing Childhood*, 43.

179 GMISPb (Gosudarstvennyi Muzei Istorii Sankta-Peterburga), fdf kp. 426566.

180 DeGraffenried, *Sacrificing Childhood*, 43.

181 Fürst, 'Between Salvation and Liquidation', 252.

182 Fürst, 'Between Salvation and Liquidation', 245.

183 DeGraffenried, *Sacrificing Childhood*, 44.

184 DeGraffenried, *Sacrificing Childhood*, 87.

185 DeGraffenried, *Sacrificing Childhood*, 78.

186 DeGraffenried, *Sacrificing Childhood*, 81.

187 DeGraffenried, *Sacrificing Childhood*, 49.

188 DeGraffenried, *Sacrificing Childhood*, 50–1.

189 DeGraffenried, *Sacrificing Childhood*, 53.

190 DeGraffenried, *Sacrificing Childhood*, 57.

191 DeGraffenried, *Sacrificing Childhood*, 58.

192 Petrushevskaya, *The Girl from the Metropol Hotel*, 22.

193 DeGraffenried, *Sacrificing Childhood*, 62.

194 DeGraffenried, *Sacrificing Childhood*, 111.

195 Balina, M. (2018) 'Writing Usable Futures: Narratives of War Childhood', *Filoteknos*, vol. 8, 39–40.

196 Voronina, O. (2018) 'Sons and Daughters of the Regiment: The Representation of the WWII Child Hero in the Soviet Media and Children's Literature of the 1940s', *Filoteknos*, vol. 8, 17–18.

197 Petrushevskaya, *The Girl from the Metropol Hotel*, 16.

198 DeGraffenried, *Sacrificing Childhood*, 92.

199 Quoted in DeGraffenried, *Sacrificing Childhood*, 33. From the Siege of Leningrad, 1944, Boris Skoromovsky, E.G. Morris, New York, 56.

200 Quoted in Voronina, 'Sons and Daughters of the Regiment', 15.

201 Inber, V. 149, quoted in DeGraffenried, *Sacrificing Childhood*, 35.

202 Nakachi, M. (2006) 'Population, Politics and Reproduction', 47.

203 Nakachi, 'Population, Politics and Reproduction,' 36.

204 Geiger, *The Family in Soviet Russia*, 259.

205 Nakachi, 'Population, Politics and Reproduction', 37.

206 See Rachel Faircloth Green, 'Making Kin Out of Strangers', 164. See also Fürst, 'Soviet Homeless and Vagrant Children' for wartime and post-war adoptions.

207 Green, 'Making Kin Out of Strangers', 171.

208 TsGASPb, f 7384, op 17, d 1514, l 36.

209 DeGraffenried, *Sacrificing Childhood*, 35.

210 Nakachi, 'Population, Politics and Reproduction', 23.

211 Miller, L. (2000) *Dim and Distant Days*, Moscow: Glas New Russian Writing, 87–8.

212 DeGraffenried, *Sacrificing Childhood*, 67.

213 DeGraffenried, *Sacrificing Childhood*, 26.

214 Voronina, 'Sons and Daughters of the Regiment', 31.

215 Livschiz, 'Children's Lives after Zoya's Death', 192–208.

216 Livschiz, 'Children's Lives after Zoya's Death', 204.

217 Petrushevskaya, *Girl from the Metropol Hotel*, 92.

218 *RGASPI*, f 17, op 126, d 19, ll 8-9.

219 *TsGASPb*, f. 7384, op 17, d 1514, 1 54.

220 Vakser, A. (2005). *Leningrad Poslevoennyi: 1945–1982*, St Petersburg: Ostrov, 90.

221 See Kozhina, E. *From the Burning Steppe*, and German, M. (2000), *Slozhnoe proshedshee*, St Petersburg: Isskustvo.

222 Fürst, 'Between Salvation and Liquidation', 233.

223 *Leningradskaya Pravda*, 9 August 1945, 1.

224 *Leningradskaya Pravda*, 12 January 1945, 3.

225 See White, E. (2011) 'The Return of Evacuated Children to Leningrad, 1944–6', in J. Reinisch and E. White (eds), *The Disentanglement of Populations: Migration, Expulsion and Displacement in Post-War Europe, 1944–9*, Basingstoke: Palgrave, 251–70.

226 Peacock, *Innocent Weapons*, 35.

227 Peacock, *Innocent Weapons*, 21.

228 Gradovskaya, Yu. (2007) 'Sovetskii detskii sad i 'upravlenie' detstvom v 1970–1980-x godax: pedagogicheskoe znachenie i normativy zaboty', in A. Salnikova, *Rossisskoe Detstvo*, 320.

229 Kirschenbaum, *Small Comrades*, 159.

230 Ewing, *The Teachers of Stalinism*, 60.

231 Frierson, *Silence Was Salvation*, 3.

232 Frierson and Vilensky, *Children of the Gulag*.

233 Frierson and Vilensky, *Children of the Gulag*, 139.

234 Franco, 'Stalin's Humanitarian Government', 123.

235 Chernyaeva, *Childcare Manuals*, 199.

236 Dobrenko, 'The Entire Real World of Children', 228.

Chapter 6

1 Time, Events, Place, M, 1958, in Geiger, *The Family in Soviet Russia*, 279.

2 Muckle, J. (1987) 'The New Soviet Child: Moral Education in Soviet Schools', in G. Avis (ed.), *The Making of the Soviet Citizen: Character Formation and Civic Training in Soviet Education*, London: Croom Helm Backhouse, 4.

3 Bykov, D. (ed.) (2016) *Shkola zhizhni. Chestnaya kniga: lyubov'-druz'ya-uchitelya -zhest'*, Moscow: AST, 120.

4 Bykov, *Shkola Zhizni*, 33.

5 Raleigh, *Soviet Baby Boomers*, 3.

6 Filtzer, D. (1993) *The Khrushchev Era: De-Stalinisation and the Limits of Reform in the USSR, 1953–1964*, Basingstoke: Macmillan, 72.

7 Field, D. (2007) *Private Life and Communist Morality in Khrushchev's Russia*, New York: Peter Lang.

8 Reid, S. (2014) 'Khrushchev in Wonderland: The Pioneer Palace in Moscow's Lenin Hills, 1962', in A. Müller and S. Pietsch (eds), *Walls That Teach*, Amsterdam: Japsam, 127–56.

9 Schmidt, V. and Shchurko, T. (2014) 'Children's Rights in Post-Soviet Countries: The Case of Russia and Belarus', *International Social Work*, vol. 57, no. 5, 450.

10 Makarevich, G. and Bezrogov, V. 'Soviet Childhood Evolution in the 1940s Primers', *Romanian Journal of Population Studies*, vol. viii, no. 2, 51.

11 Kelly, C. (2008) 'Defending Children's Rights, "In Defense of Peace": Children and Soviet Cultural Diplomacy', *Kritika: Explorations in Russian and Eurasian History*, vol. 9, no. 4, 731.

12 See Creuziger, C. for an ethnographical study of Soviet kindergartens and orphanages in the 1980s.

13 Geiger, *The Family in Soviet Russia*, 187.

14 Holt, A. (1980) 'Domestic Labour and Soviet Society', in J. Brine, M. Perrie and A. Sutton (eds), *Home, School and Leisure in the Soviet Union*, London: Allen & Unwin, 47

15 Chernyaeva, *Childcare Manuals*, 228.

16 Raleigh, *Soviet Baby Boomers*, 46.

17 Geiger, *The Family in Soviet Russia*, 192; Kelly, *Children's World*, 409; Gradovskaya, Yu. 'Sovetskii detskii sad i 'upravlenie' detstvom v 1970-1980-x godax', 316.

18 Harwin, *Children of the Russian State*, 38.

19 Harwin, *Children of the Russian State*, 39.

20 Silova, I. and Palanjian, G. (2018) 'Soviet Empire, Childhood and Education', *Revista Española de Educacíon Comparada*, vol. 6, no. 31, 152.

21 Hans, *The Russian Tradition in Education*, 162.

22 Lovell, S. (2010) *In the Shadow of War: Russia and the USSR, 1941 to the Present*, Malden: Wiley, 117.

23 Dunstan, J. (1980) 'Soviet Boarding Education: Its Rise and Progress', in Brine et al. (ed.), *Home, School and Leisure*, 119.

24 Dunstan, 'Soviet Boarding Education: Its Rise and Progress', 116.

25 Dunstan, 'Soviet Boarding Education: Its Rise and Progress', 122, 132.

26 B. Kerblay (1983), Modern Soviet Society, London: Methuen., 151.

27 Lovell, *In the Shadow of War*, 119.

28 See Raleigh, *Soviet Baby Boomers*.

29 Lovell, *In the Shadow of War*, 120.

30 Tudge, J. (1991) 'Education of Young Children in the Soviet Union: Current Practice in Historical Perspective', *The Elementary School Journal*, vol. 92, no. 1, 122.

31 Bykov, *Shkola Zhizni*, 96.

32 Nataliya Sokolovskaya, 'Voina i mir na zvezde KETs', in Bykov, *Shkola Zhizni*, 30.

33 Bykov, *Shkola Zhizni*, 33.

34 Koutaissoff, E. 'Secondary Education for All in a Forward-Looking Society', in *Home, School and Leisure*, 74.

35 Koutaissoff, 'Secondary Education for All in a Forward-Looking Society', 76.

36 Bronfenbrenner, U. (1970) *Two Worlds of Childhood: US and USSR*, New York: Russell Sage Foundation, 21.

37 Bykov, *Shkola Zhizni*, 140.

38 Bykov, *Shkola Zhizni* 148.

39 Silova and Palanjian, 'Soviet Empire, Childhood and Education',

40 Boldyrev, N. I. (ed.), *Programma vospitatelnoi raboty shkoly*, Moscow, 1960, in Bronfenbrenner, *Two Worlds of Childhood*, 30.

41 Boldyrev, *Programma vospitatelnoi raboty shkoly* in Bronfenbrenner, *Two Worlds of Childhood*, 36.

42 Boldyrev, *Programma vospitatelnoi raboty shkoly*, Moscow, 1960, in Bronfenbrenner, *Two Worlds of Childhood*, 30.

43 Ewing, *The Teachers of Stalinism*, 192.

44 L. Trunova, 'Devyatka', in Bykov, *Shkola Zhizni*, 23. There are issues with the memory of the Soviet Union being reworked in light of post-Soviet disillusionment, particularly for an older generation.

45 Morrison, J. 'Recent Developments in Political Education in the Soviet Union', in G. Avis (ed.), *The Making of the Soviet Citizen: Character Formation and Civic Training in Soviet Education*, London: Croom Helm, 33–4.

46 Muckle, 'The New Soviet Child', 1–22.

47 Reid, 'Khrushchev in Wonderland', 1.

48 Reid, 'Khrushchev in Wonderland', 1.

49 Kelly, *Children's World*, 558.

50 Reid, 'Khrushchev in Wonderland', 3.

51 For a dystopian fictional version of the Pioneer camp and its cosmonautic focus, see Russian novelist Victor Pelevin's *Omon Ra*.

52 See Rajagopalan, S. (2019) 'Remix Vidoes and the Mnemonic Imagination: Emotional Memories of Late Soviet Childhood', *International Journal of Cultural Studies*, vol. 22, no. 1, 9–36.

53 Silova and Palanjian, 'Soviet Empire', 153.

54 Morison, J. (1983) 'The Political Content of Education in the USSR' in J.J. Tomiak (ed), *Soviet Education in the 1980s*, New York: St Martin's Press.

55 *Pionerskaya Pravda*, 11 April 1970.

56 Lovell, *In the Shadow of War*, 130.

57 Bykov, *Shkola Zhizni*, 235.

58 Levina, M. (2017) 'Under Lenin's Watchful Eye: Growing Up in the Soviet Union', *Surveillance and Society*, vol. 15, no. 3/4, 532.

59 Bronfenbrenner, *Two Worlds of Childhood*, 39–48.

60 Quoted in Geiger, *The Family in Soviet Russia*, 113.

61 Geiger, *The Family in Soviet Russia*, 208.

62 Raleigh, *Baby Boomers*, 36.

63 Koenker, D. (2009) 'Whose Right to Rest? Contesting the Family Vacation in the Postwar Soviet Union', *Comparative Studies in Society and History*, vol. 51, no. 2, 412.

64 Koenker, 'Whose Right to Rest?', 401–25.

65 Koenker, 'Whose Right to Rest?', 423.

66 Kerblay, *Modern Soviet Society*, 35, 122.

67 Kerblay, *Modern Soviet Society*, 127.

68 Lovell, *Shadow of War*, 151.

69 Bykov, *Shkola zhizni*, 279.

70 Kerblay, *Modern Soviet Society*, 115.

71 http://soviethistory.msu.edu/1961-2/moral-code-of-the-builder-of-commu nism/moral-code-of-the-builder-of-communism-texts/moral-code-of-the-bu ilder-of-communism/.

72 Dobrenko, E. (2005) ' "The Entire Real World of Children": The School Tale and "Our Happy Childhood"', *Slavic and East European Journal*, vol. 49, no. 2, 240.

73 Bardiak, A. (1961) 'Samyi blizkii, rodnoi chelovek', Sem'ya i shkola, no. 3, 7, quoted in Field, *Private Life and Communist Morality* 84.

74 Field, *Private Life and Communist Morality*, 88.

75 Kletenik, L. (1955) ' "Trudnyie' deti i trudnyie roditeli," Rabotnitsa, no. 1, in Field, *Private Life and Communist Morality*, 89.

76 Field, *Private Life and Communist Morality*, 90.

77 Drake, M. 'Soviet Child Care: It's Organisation at Local Level', in Brine et al., *Home, School, Leisure*, 157.

78 Field, *Private Life and Communist Morality*, 90.

79 Field, *Private Life and Communist Morality*, 92.

80 Field, *Private Life and Communist Morality*, 31.

81 Harwin, *Children of the Russian State*, 45.

82 Nakachi, 'Population, Politics and Reproduction', 68.

83 Tarusina, N. and Isaeva, E. (2017) 'Russian Family Law Legislation: Revolu- tion, Counter-Revolution, Evolution', *BRICS LAW JOURNAL*, vol. IV, no. 5, 73.

84 Gradovskaya, Yu. (2010) 'Educating Parents: Public Preschools and Parenting in Soviet Pedagogical Publications, 1945–1989', *Journal of Family History*, vol. 35, no. 3, 271–85.

85 Harwin, *Children of the State*, 35.

86 Harwin, *Children of the State*, 36–8.

87 Gradovskaya, 'Educating Parents', 280. By 1989, a mother was entitled to 18 months of partially paid maternity leave and additional unpaid leave until a child was three, with the right to return to work and an unbroken work record.

88 Harwin, *Children of the Russian State*, 68.

89 Harwin, *Children of the Russian State*, 78.

90 Peacock, *Innocent Weapons*, 97.

91 *Pionerskaya Pravda, multiple editions.*

92 Peacock, *Innocent Weapons*, 46.

93 Kelly, *Children's World*, 738.

94 Peacock, *Innocent Weapons*, 204.

95 Raleigh, *Soviet Baby Boomers*, 151.

96 http://soviethistory.msu.edu/1968-2/third-world-friendships/third-world-friendships-music/cuba-my-love-1962/

97 Peacock, *Innocent Weapons*, 203.

98 Peacock, *Innocent Weapons*, 203.

99 'Radiosbornik: Sto voprosov i otvetov o Sovetskom Soyuz', 16 March 1961, GARF f. 6903, op. 23, d. 43, l. 19, in Peacock, *Innocent Weapons*, 105.

100 Raleigh, *Soviet Baby Boomers*, 150.

101 Rosslyn, W. 'Peace Education in the Soviet Union', in Avis, *The Making of the Soviet Citizen*, 177.

102 Rosslyn, 'Peace Education', 176.

103 Rosslyn, 'Peace Education', 162.

104 Kelly, 'Defending Children's Rights', 733–4.

105 Sokolovskaya, 'Voina i mir na zvezde KETs', 35.

106 Levina, 'Under Lenin's Watchful Eye', 530, 534.

107 Levina, 'Under Lenin's Watchful Eye', 530.

108 Silova and Palanjian, 'Soviet Empire, Childhood and Education', 156.

109 Raleigh, *Soviet Baby Boomers*, 108.

110 *Kniga vozhatogo* (Molodaya Gvardiya, Moscow, 1982), quoted in Dunstan, J., 'Atheistic Education in the USSR' in Avis, *The Making of the Soviet Citizen*, 63.

111 Prokhorov, A. (2007) 'The Adolescent and the Child in the Cinema of the Thaw', *Studies in Russian and Soviet Cinema*, vol. 1, no. 2, 115–29.

112 Prokhorov, 'The Adolescent and the Child in the Cinema of the Thaw', 117.

113 Balina, 'Writing Usable Futures', 16.

114 Reid, 'Khrushchev in Wonderland', 29.

115 Raleigh, *Soviet Baby Boomers*, 133.

116 Kelly, *Children's World*, 478.

117 Beumers, B. in Balina, *Russian Children's Literature and Culture*, 154.

118 Geiger, *The Family in Soviet Russia*, 40

119 Clark, K. (1981) *The Soviet Novel. History as Ritual*, Chicago, University of Chicago Press.

120 Geiger, *The Family in Soviet Russia*, 324.

121 Geiger, *The Family in Soviet Russia*, 311.

122 Ransel, *Village Mothers*, 230.

123 Harwin, *Children of the Russian State*, 39.

124 Riordan, J. 138, 149.

125 See Yurchak, S. (2005) *Everything Was Forever, Until It Was No More. The Last Soviet Generation*, Princeton: Princeton University Press.

126 Bykov, *Shkola zhizni*, 6.

127 Raleigh, *Soviet Baby Boomers*, 16, 166.

128 Raleigh, *Soviet Baby Boomers*, 163, 166.

Chapter 7

1 'Vladimir Putin on Raising Russia's Birth Rate' (2006) *Population and Development Review*, vol. 32, no. 2, June, 385.

2 UNICEF, 82, https://www.unicef.org/about/annualreport/files/Russian_Federation_COAR_2010.pdf.

3 Kulmala, M., Rasell, M. and Chernova, Zh. (2017) 'Overhauling Russia's Child Welfare System: Institutional and Ideational Factors behind the Paradigm Shift', *Journal of Social Policy Studies*, vol. 15, no. 3, 353–65, 362–3.

4 Kaganov, V. Sh. (2016) 'Realizatsiya Natsional'noi strategii v interesakh detstva; itogi 2015 goda', *Psychological Science and Education*, vol. 21, no. 1, 16.

5 Kaganov, 'Realizatsiya', 18.

6 Kaganov, 'Realizatsiya', 19.

7 Kaganov, 'Realizatsiya', 15–29, 18.

8 Kaganov, 'Realizatsiya', 19.

9 https://rg.ru/2015/06/08/vospitanie-dok.html

10 Memory Watch is a campaign to remember the fallen of the Great Patriotic War, started in 1988, which became a movement for searching for, recovering and burying the dead of the war as well as the organization of various other memorial events and meetings throughout the year. The Immortal Regiment marches across the Russian Federation, and in places with Russian populations there are participatory spectacles of personal and familial mourning which have taken place on Victory Day since 2012. Marchers hold portraits of family members who participated in the war. This evolved as a grassroots event but the Russian state has increasingly co-opted it.

11 https://www.economist.com/europe/2018/05/26/vladimir-putins-latest-pet-project-a-school-for-clever-students

12 United Nations, Convention on the Rights of the Child, 25 February 2014, CRC/C/RUS/CO/7.

13 Laruelle, M. (2015) 'Patriotic Youth Clubs in Russia: Professional Niches, Cultural Capital and Narratives of Social Engagement', *Europe-Asia Studies*, vol. 67, no. 1, 8–27.

14 UNICEF, 70.

15 Kumala et al., 'Overhauling Russia's Child Welfare System', 353.

16 Kumala et al., 'Overhauling Russia's Child Welfare System', 355.

17 Kumala et al., 'Overhauling Russia's Child Welfare System', 362.

18 Kumala et al., 'Overhauling Russia's Child Welfare System', 359.

19 Kumala, et al., 'Overhauling Russia's Child Welfare System', 359.

20 Schmidt and Shchurko, 'Children's Rights in Post-Soviet Countries', 447–58, 447.

21 United Nations, Convention on the Rights of the Child, 25 February 2014, CRC/C/RUS/CO/7.

22 Martin, L. M. (2008) 'The Universal Language Is Not Violence – Its Love: The Pavlis Murder and Why Russia Changed the Family Code and Policy on Foreign Adoptions', *Penn State International Law Review*, vol. 26, no. 3, 710–11.

23 Martin, 'The Universal Language Is Not Violence', 709–33, 710–1.

24 The Federal Law also places sanctions on certain American citizens. It is widely viewed as a form of political revenge for the Magnitsky Act which was signed by President Obama in December 2012. This placed sanctions on Russian officials suspected in the murder of Sergei Magnitsky, an accountant who had made allegations of corruption by the Russian state.

25 'Abandoned by the State'. https://www.hrw.org/report/2014/09/15/abandon ed-state/violence-neglect-and-isolation-children-disabilities-russian.

26 For the Parents' Movement in the Russian Federation, see Höjdestrand, T. (2016) 'Nationalism and Civicness in Contemporary Russia: Grassroots Mobilization in Defense of Traditional Family Values', Working paper, forthcoming in Korolczuk, E. and Fábián, K. (eds), *Rebellious Parents: Parents Movements in Russia and Central and Eastern Europe*, Indiana University Press; and Höjdestrand, T. (2016) 'Social Welfare or Moral Warfare? Popular Resistance against Children's Rights and Juvenile Justice in Contemporary Russia', *International Journal of Children's Rights*, vol. 24, no. 4, 826–50.

27 Höjdestrand, 'Social Welfare or Moral Warfare?', 17–18.

28 Schmidt and Shchurko, 'Children's Rights in Post-Soviet Countries: The Case of Russia and Belarus', 52.

29 Höjdestrand, T. (2016) 'Social Welfare or Moral Warfare?', 24.

30 Tarusina, N. and Isaeva, E. (2017), 'Russian Family Law Legislation: Revolution, Counter-Revolution, Evolution', *BRICS Law Journal*, vol. IV, no. 5, 85.

31 United Nations, Convention on the Rights of the Child, 25 February 2014, CRC/C/RUS/C0/4-5.

32 UNICEF, 54.

33 https://www.licensingmagazine.com/2018/07/25/major-italian-theme-park-to-open-massive-new-masha-and-the-bear-area/?lang=en.

34 http://www.digitaljournal.com/entertainment/entertainment/op-ed-russian-car toon-masha-and-the-bear-soft-russian-propaganda/article/537170.

35 Antoniazzi, A. (2016) 'Masha and the Bear: A New Educational Paradigm,' *Journal of Theories and Research in Education*, vol. 11, no. 3, 70.

Chapter 8

1 Silova and Palandjian, 'Soviet Empire, Children and Education', 149.

2 Kirschenbaum, *Small Comrades*, 13.

3 Holmes, *Stalin's School*, 280.

4 Chernyaeva, 'Childcare Manuals', 156.

5 See Zenzinov, V. (1931) *Deserted: The Story of the Children Abandoned in Soviet Russia*, London: H. Joseph.

6 Kelly, *Children's World*, 2–3.

7 Gorshkov, *Russia's Factory Children*; Kelly, *Children's World*.

8 DeGraffenreid, *Sacrificing Childhood*; Reid, 'Khrushchev in Wonderland', 127–56.

9 Kirschenbaum, *Small Comrades*, 5.

10 Makarevich, and Bezrogov, 'Soviet Childhood Evolution in the 1940s Primers', 37–53.

11 See Lewin, M. (1994) *The Making of the Soviet System*, New York: The New Press.

12 Silova and Palanjian, 'Soviet Empire, Childhood and Education', 150–1.

13 Andreev, 'On the Modernization of Education', 11.

14 Alston, *Education and the State*, 93.

15 Speech by Dr. Lawrence Derthick to the National Press Club on 13 June 1958, reproduced in the *Congressional Record*, 13 July 1958, 11075, in Peacock, *Innocent Weapons*, 61.

16 Ewing, *The Teachers of Stalinism*, 152.

17 Ginsborg, *Family Politics*, 66.

18 Field, *Private Life and Communist Morality*, 80.

19 James, A. Jenks, C. and Prout, A. (2007) *Theorizing Childhood*, London: Polity, 8–10.

20 James, Jenks and Prout, *Theorizing Childhood*, 10.

21 James, Jenks and Prout, *Theorizing Childhood*, 38.

22 See Baron, 'Placing the Child', 1–39.

23 Naftali, 'Chinese Childhood in Conflict', 53.

24 James, et al., *Theorizing Childhood*, 69.

25 In reality of course, Pavel Morozov was a child from a poor village murdered by family members, along with his younger brother.

26 Fedyukin, 'School Buildings', 212.

27 Kirschenbaum, *Small Comrades*, 153.

28 Quoted in Kirschenbaum, *Small Comrades*, 153–4.

29 Kelly, *Children's World*, 521.

30 Hans, *The Russian Tradition*, 152–3.

31 Hans, *The Russian Tradition*, 152–3.

32 Ransel, *Village Mothers*, 3.

33 Frierson and Vilensky, *Children of the Gulag,* 5.

34 Frierson and Vilensky, *Children of the Gulag*, 15.

35 Frierson and Vilensky, *Children of the Gulag*, 15.

36 James, et al., *Theorising Childhood*, 138.

37 Miller, *Dim and Distant Days*, 30.

38 Levina, 'Under Lenin's Watchful Eye', 530.

39 Gouzenko, *Before Igor*, 75–6.

40 See for example, the report on discussions at the 2018 conference meeting, Children and Youth as Subjects, Objects, and Agents. Approaches to Research in a Global Context. http://www.shcy.org/features/commentaries/children-and-youth-as-subjects-objects-and-agents/.

41 Frierson and Vilensky, *Children of the Gulag*, 7.

42 Fass, 'Is There a Story in the History of Childhood?', 11.

Bibliography

Alston, P. L. (1969) *Education and the State in Tsarist Russia*, Stanford: Stanford University Press.

Andreev, A. L. (2013) 'On the Modernization of Education in Russia: A Historical Sociological Analysis', *Russian Social Science Review*, vol. 54, no. 5, 4–21.

Ariès, P. (1965) *Centuries of Childhood: A Family History of Social Life*, London: Random House.

Avis, G. (ed.) (1987) *The Making of the Soviet Citizen: Character Formation and Civic Training in Soviet Education*, London: Routledge.

Balina, M. and Rudova, L. (eds) (2008) *Russian Children's Literature and Culture*, New York: Routledge.

Balina, M. (2018) 'Writing Usable Futures: Narratives of War Childhood', *Filoteknos*, vol. 8, 26–41.

Ball, A. (1994) *And Now My Soul Is Hardened: Abandoned Children in Soviet Russia, 1918–1930*, Berkeley: University of California Press.

Baranov, A., Namazova-Baranova, L. and Albitsky, V. (2015) 'Paediatrics in Russia: Past, Present and Future', *Archives of Diseases in Childhood*, vol. 102, no. 8, 774–8.

Baranova, A. R. (2007) '"Nyan'kat'sya budem?": memorial'noe obrazy sovetskogo detstva 1930–1950x godov' in A. Sal'nikova (ed.), *Rossiiskoe detstva v XX veke: Istoriya, teoriya, i praktika issledovaniya*, Kazan: Kazan State University, 209–25.

Baron, N. (ed.) (2016) *Displaced Children in Russia and Eastern Europe, 1915– 1953. Ideologies, Identities, Experiences*, Leiden: Brill.

Berman, N. (1937) 'Juvenile Delinquency, the Family and the Court in Soviet Russia', *American Journal of Sociology*, vol. 42, no. 5, 682–92.

Blakesley, R. (2014) 'Ladies-in-Waiting in Waiting: Picturing Adolescence in Dmitry Levitsky's Smolny Portraits, 1772–76', *Art History*, vol. 37, February, 10–37.

Bonner, E. (1992) *Mothers and Daughters*, New York: Alfred A. Knopf.

Borossa, J. and Gulina, M. (2005) 'Child Survivors of the Siege of Leningrad: Notes from a Study on War Trauma and Its Long Term Effects on Individuals', *Children in War. The International Journal of Evacuee and War Child Studies*, vol. 1, no. 3, 51–2.

Brine, J., Perrie, M. and Sutton, A. (eds) (1980) *Home, School and Leisure in the Soviet Union*, London: George Allen & Unwin.

Bronfenbrenner, U. (1970) *Two Worlds of Childhood: US and USSR*, New York: Russell Sage Foundation.

Bushkovitch, P. (2001) *Peter the Great*, Lanham: Rowman and Littlefield.

Butler, W. (2015) *Russian Family Law*, London: Wildy, Simmonds and Hill Publishing.

Byford, A. (2013) 'Parent Diaries and the Child Study Movement in Late Imperial and Early Soviet Russia', *Russian Review*, vol. 72, no. 2, 212–41.

Byford, A. (2016) 'V.M. Bekhterev in Russian Child Science, 1900s–1920s: "Objective Psychology/Reflexology" as a Scientific Movement', *Journal of the History of the Behavioural Sciences*, vol. 52, no. 2, 99–123.

Byford, A. (2017) 'The Imperfect Child in Early Twentieth Century Russia', *History of Education*, vol. 46, no. 5, 595–617.

Bykov, D. (ed.) (2016) *Shkola zhizhni. Chestnaya kniga: lyubov – druz'ya-uchitelya-zhest'*, Moscow: AST.

Channon, J. (2001) 'Technological and Scientific Utopias in Soviet Children's Literature, 1921–1932', *Journal of Popular Culture*, vol. 34, no. 4, Spring, 153–69.

Chernyaeva, N. (2009) 'Childcare Manuals and Construction of Motherhood in Russia, 1890–1990', PhD (Doctor of Philosophy) thesis, University of Iowa. https://ir.uiowa.edu/etd/344/

Choe, H. (2014) 'Marx on the Family and Class Consciousness', *Rethinking Marxism*, 04/2014, vol. 26, no. 2, 262–77.

Cotta Ramusino, P. (2005) 'How to Behave at Home and in Society: Karion Istomin's *Domostroj* and Its Possible Sources', *Studi Slavistici* II, 53–65.

Cowley. M. K. (2014) 'The Right of Inheritance and the Stalin Revolution', *Kritika*, vol. 15, no. 1, 103–23.

Cracraft, J. (1973) 'Feofan Prokopovich', in J. Garrard (ed.), *Russia in the Eighteenth Century*, Oxford: Clarendon, 75–105.

Creuzinger, C. (1996) *Childhood in Russia. Representation and Reality*, Lanham: University Press of America.

Cummins, A. G. (ed.) (1991) *Documents of Soviet History.* Volume 4 *Stalin Grasps Power, 1926–28*, London: Academic International Press.

Cunningham, H. (2006) *The Invention of Childhood*, London: BBC Books.

Czap, P. Jr. (1978) 'Marriage and Peasant Joint Family', in D. L. Ransel (ed.), *The Family in Imperial Russia. New Lines of Historical Research*, Urbana: University of Illinois Press, 103–23.

DeGraffenried, J. K. (2014) *Sacrificing Childhood: Childhood and the Soviet State in the Great Patriotic War*, Kansas: Kansas University Press.

De Madariaga, I. (1979) 'The Foundation of the Russian Educational System by Catherine II', *The Slavonic and East European Review*, vol. 57, no. 3, 369–95.

Deti o Staline (1939) Moscow: Detizdat TsK VLKSM

Dobrenko, E. (2005) '"The Entire Real World of Children"': The School Tale and "Our Happy Childhood"', *Slavic and East European Journal*, vol. 49, no. 2, 225–48.

Dukes, P. (1982) *The Making of Russian Absolutism, 1613–1801*, Harlow: Longman.

Dunn, P. (2006) '"That Enemy Is the Baby": Childhood in Imperial Russia', in L. deMause (ed.), *The History of Childhood*, Oxford: Rowman and Littlefield, 383–405.

Dunstan, J. (1987) 'Atheistic Education in the USSR' in G. Avis (ed.), *The Making of the Soviet Citizen: Character Formation and Civic Training in Soviet Education*, London: Routledge.

Dunstan, J. (1997) *Soviet Schooling in the Second World War*, Basingstoke: Macmillan

Eklof, B. (1986) *Russian Peasant Schools: Officialdom, Village Culture and Popular Pedagogy, 1861–1914*, Berkeley and Los Angeles: University of California Press.

Eklof, B. (ed.) (1993) *School and Society in Tsarist and Soviet Russia*, New York: St. Martin's Press.

Engel, B. A. (1978) 'Mothers and Daughters', in D. Ransel (ed.), *The Family in Imperial Russia. New Lines of Historical Research*, Urbana: University of Illinois Press, 44–59.

Ewing, T. E. (2002) *The Teachers of Stalinism: Policy, Practice and Power in Soviet Schools of the 1930s*, New York: Peter Lang.

Ewing, T. E. (2010) *Separate Schools: Gender, Policy, and Practice in Postwar Soviet Education*, DeKalb: Northern Illinois Press.

Ewing, T. E. (2012) '"Life Is a Succession of Disappointments": A Soviet Girl Contends with the Stalinist Dictatorship', in J. Helgren and C. A. Vasconcellos (eds), *Girlhood: A Global History*, New Brunswick: Rutgers University Press.

Fass, P. S. (ed.) (2013) *The Routledge History of Childhood in the Western World*, Oxford: Routledge.

Fedyukin, I. (2016) 'Nobility and Schooling in Russia, 1700s-1760s: Choices in a Social Context', *Journal of Social History*, vol. 49, no. 3, 558–84.

Fedyukin, I. (2018a) 'Shaping Up the Stubborn: School Building and "Discipline" in Early Modern Russia', *The Russian Review*, vol. 77, 200–18.

Fedyukin, I. (2018b) 'The "German" Reign of Empress Anna: Russia's Disciplinary Moment?', *Kritika: Explorations in Russian and Eurasian History*, vol. 19, no. 2, Spring, 363–84.

Fen, E. (1970) *A Girl Grew Up in Russia*, London: Andre Deutsch.

Field, D. A. (2007) *Private Life and Communist Morality in Khrushchev's Russia*, New York: Peter Lang.

Figes, O., (2007) *The Whisperers: Private Life in Stalin's Russia*, London: Penguin.

Filtzer, D. (1993) *The Khrushchev Era: De-stalinisation and the Limits of Reform in the USSR, 1953–1964*, London: Macmillan.

Fradkin, F. A. (1993) 'Soviet Experimentalism Routed: S.T. Shatsky's Last Years', in B. Eklof (ed.), *School and Society in Tsarist and Soviet Russia*, New York: St. Martin's Press.

Franco, R. (2018) 'Stalin's Humanitarian Government: Class, Child Homelessness and State Security in a Historical Perspective (1930s–1940s)', *European Review of History: Revue européenne d'histoire*, vol. 25, no. 1, 121–46.

Fraser, E. (2010) *The House by the Dvina: A Russian Childhood*, Reading: Cox and Wyman.

Frierson, C. A. (2015) *Silence Was Salvation: Child Survivors of Stalin's Terror and World War II in the Soviet Union*, New Haven: Yale University Press.

Frierson, C. A. and Vilensky, S. S. (2010) *Children of the Gulag*, New Haven: Yale University Press.

Fürst, J., (ed.) (2006) *Late Stalinist Russia. Society between Reconstruction and Reinvention*, Oxford: Routledge.

Fürst, J. (2008) 'Between Salvation and Liquidation: Homeless and Vagrant Children and the Reconstruction of Soviet Society', *The Slavonic and East European Review*, vol. 86, no. 2, April, 232–58.

Geiger, H. K. (1968) *The Family in Soviet Russia*, Harvard: Harvard University Press.

Ginsborg, P. (2014) *Family Politics. Domestic Life, Devastation and Survival 1900–1950*, Yale: Yale University Press.

Glagoleva, O. E. (2005) 'The Illegitimate Children of the Russian Nobility in Law and Practice, 1700–1860', *Kritika: Explorations in Russian and Eurasian History*, vol. 6, no. 3, Summer, 461–99.

Goldman, W. (2008) *Women, the State and Revolution: Soviet Family Policy and Social Life, 1917–1936*, Cambridge: Cambridge University Press.

Gorshkov, B. (2009) *Russia's Factory Children: State, Society and Law, 1800–1917*, Pittsburgh: University of Pittsburgh Press.

Gouzenko, S. (1961) *Before Igor: Memories of a Soviet Youth*, London: Cassell.

Gradovskaya, Yu. (2005) 'Sovetskii detskii sad i 'upravlenie' detstvom v 1970–1980-x godax: pedagogicheskoe znachenie i normativy zaboty', in Alla Salnikova (ed.), *Rossiiskoe detstvà v XX veke: Istoriya, teoriya, i praktika issledovaniya*, Kazan: Kazan State University.

Grant, S. (2012) 'The Russian Gentry Family: A Contrarian View', *Jahrbücher für Geschichte Osteuropas*, Neue Folge, Bd. 60, H. 1, 1–33.

Green, R. (2016) 'Making Kin Out of Strangers: Soviet Adoption during and after the Second World War', in N. Baron (ed.), *Displaced Children in Russia and Eastern Europe, 1915–1953*, Leiden: Brill, 155–86.

Gromova, O. (2014) *Sakharnyi rebyonok*, Moscow: KompassGid.

Hajtó, V. (2016) *Milk Sauce and Paprika: Migration, Childhood and Memories of the Interwar Belgian-Hungarian Child Relief Project*, Leuven: Leuven University Press.

Hans, N. (1963) *The Russian Tradition in Education*, London: Routledge & Kegan Paul.

Hartley, J. (1989) 'The Boards of Social Welfare and the Financing of Catherine II's State Schools', *The Slavonic and East European Review*, vol. 67, 211–27.

Harwin, J. (1996) *Children of the Russian State: 1917–95*, Aldershot: Ashgate.

Hellman, B. (2013) *Fairy Tales and True Stories: The History of Russian Literature for Children and Young People*, Leiden: Brill.

Heywood, C. (2001) A *History of Childhood: Children and Childhood in the West from Medieval to Modern Times*, Cambridge: Polity.

Hoffmann, D. (2003) *Stalinist Values: The Cultural Norms of Soviet Modernity, 1917–1941*, Ithaca and London: Cornell University Press.

Holmes, L. E. (1991) *The Kremlin and the Schoolhouse: Reforming Education in Soviet Russia, 1917–1931*, Bloomington: Indiana University Press.

Holmes, L. E. (1993) 'Legitimizing the Soviet Regime: School No. 25, 1931–37', in B. Eklof (ed.), *School and Society in Tsarist Russia*, New York: St. Martin's Press.

Holmes, L. (1997) 'Part of History: The Oral Record and Moscow's Model School No. 25, 1931–1937', *Slavic Review*, vol. 56, no. 2, 279–306.

Holmes, L. (1999) *Stalin's School: Moscow's Model School No. 25, 1931–1937*, Pittsburgh: University of Pittsburgh Press.

Jablonka, I. (2015) 'Social Welfare in the Western World and the Rights of Childhood', in P. S. Fass (ed.), *The Routledge History of Childhood in the Western World*, New York: Routledge, 380–99.

James, A., Jenks C. and Prout, A. (2007) *Theorizing Childhood*, London: Polity.

Kazelson, M. and Baron, N. (2016) 'Memories of Displacement: Loss and Reclamation of Home/Land in the Narratives of Soviet Child Deportees of the

1930s', in N. Baron (ed.), *Displaced Children in Russia and Eastern Europe, 1915–1953. Ideologies, Identities, Experiences*, Leiden: Brill, 97–130.

Kelly, C. (2001) *Refining Russia: Advice Literature, Polite Culture and Gender from Catherine to Yeltsin*, Oxford: Oxford University Press.

Kelly, C. (2006) *Comrade Pavlik: The Rise and Fall of a Soviet Boy Hero*, London: Granta.

Kelly, C. (2007) *Children's World: Growing Up in Russia, 1890–1991*, Yale: Yale University Press.

Kelly, C. (2008) 'Defending Children's Rights, "In Defense of Peace": Children and Soviet Cultural Diplomacy', *Kritika: Explorations in Russian and Eurasian History*, vol. 9, no. 4, 711–46.

Kerblay, B. (1983) *Modern Soviet Society*, London: Methuen.

Khromov, O. R. (2015) 'The Primer of Karion Istomin with Handwritten Additions by Diomid Yakovlev syn Serkov as a Monument of XV11-Century Russian Book Culture', *Russian Education and Society*, vol. 57, no. 12, 1019–31.

Kirschenbaum, L. (2001) *Small Comrades: Revolutionising Childhood in Soviet Russia*, New York: Routledge.

Koenker, D. P. (2009) 'Whose Right to Rest? Contesting the Family Vacation in the Postwar Soviet Union', *Comparative Studies in Society and History*, vol. 51, no. 2, 401–25.

Kopelev, L. (1980) *The Education of a True Believer*, London: Harper Collins.

Kosheleva, O. (2015) 'What Should One Teach? A New Approach to Russian Childhood Education as Reflected in Manuscripts from the Second Half of the Seventeenth Century', in M. Di Salvo, D. H. Kaiser and V. A. Kivelson (eds), *Word and Image in Russian History: Essays in Honor of Gary Marker*, Boston: Academic Studies Press.

Krevsky, E. (2012) 'Arkadii Gaidar, the New Socialist Morality, and Stalinist Identity', *Canadian Slavonic Papers/Revue canadienne des slavistes*, vol. LIV, nos 1–2, 113–32.

Krinko, E. and Yurchuk, I. (2010) "Za nashi shchastlivoe detstvo': voprosy ugolovnoi otvetstvennosti nesovershennoletnykh v sovetskom zakonodatelnoste 1920–1940-x gg.', *European Researcher*, no. 2, 140.

Kucherenko, O. (2011) *Little Soldiers: How Soviet Children Went to War*, Oxford: Oxford University Press.

Kucherenko, O. (2015) *Soviet Street Children and the Second World War: Welfare and Social Control under Stalin*, London: Bloomsbury Academic Press.

Kuxhausen, A. (2013) *From the Womb to the Body Politic: Raising the Nation in Enlightenment Russia*, Madison: University of Wisconsin Press.

Levina, M. (2017) 'Under Lenin's Watchful Eye: Growing Up in the Soviet Union', *Surveillance and Society*, vol. 15, no. 3/4, 529–34.

Lindenmeyr, A. (1996) *Poverty Is Not a Vice: Charity, Society, and the State in Imperial Russia*, Princeton: Princeton University Press.

Listovki grazhdanskoi voini v SSSR, 1918–1922-g (1942) OGIZ: Gospolizdat'.

Livschiz, A. (2006) 'Children's Lives after Zoia's Death. Order, Emotions and Heroism in Children's Lives and Literature in the Post-war Soviet Union', in J. Fürst (ed.), *Late Stalinist Russia: Society between Reconstruction and Reinvention*, Oxford: Routledge.

MacKinnon, E. (2012) *The Forgotten Victims: Childhood and the Soviet Gulag, 1929–1953*, The Carl Beck Papers in Russian and East European Studies, Pittsburgh: Pittsburgh University Press.

Mahood, L. and Satzewich, V. (2009) 'The Save the Children Fund and the Russian Famine of 1921–23: Claims and Counter Claims about Feeding "Bolshevik Children"', *Journal of Historical Sociology*, vol. 22, no. 1, 55–83.

Makarevich, G. and Bezrogov, V. 'Soviet Childhood Evolution in the 1940s Primers', *Romanian Journal of Population Studies*, vol. Viii, no. 2, 37–53.

Marshall, D. (1999) 'The Construction of Children as an Object of International Relations: The Declaration of Children's Rights and the Child Welfare Committee of League of Nations, 1900–1924', *The International Journal of Children's Rights*, vol. 7, no. 2, 103–48.

Marx, K. and Engels, F. (2012) *The Communist Manifesto: A Modern Edition*, London: Verso.

Matveenko, V. E., Nazartseva, E. A. and Zharkova, E. Kh. (2018) 'State Policy of Russia in the Field of Science and Education (the End of 17th–Early 18th Centuries)', *Journal of History, Culture and Art Research*, vol. 7, no. 1, 90–102.

Miller, L. (2000) *Dim and Distant Days*, Moscow: Glas New Russian Writing.

Mintz, S. (2012) 'Why the History of Childhood Matters', *Journal for the History of Childhood and Youth*, vol. 5, no. 1, Winter, 15–28.

Mironov, B. N. (2016) 'Long Term Trends in the Development of Family Structure in Christian Russia from the Sixteenth to the Twentieth Centuries: An Analytic Overview of Historiography', *Journal of Family History*, vol. 41, no. 4, 355–77.

Nabokov, V. (2000) *Speak, Memory: An Autobiography Revisited*, London: Penguin.

Naftali, O. (2014) 'Chinese Childhood in Conflict: Children, Gender, and Violence in China of the "Cultural Revolution" Period (1966–1976)', *Oriens Extremis*, 53, 85–110.

Nakachi, M. (2006a) 'N.S. Khrushchev and the 1944 Soviet Family Law: Politics, Reproduction, and Language', *East European Politics and Societies*, vol. 20, no. 1, 40–68.

Nakachi, M. (2006b) 'Population, Politics and Reproduction: Late Stalinism and Its Legacy', in J. Fürst (ed.), *Late Stalinist Russia: Society between Reconstruction and Reinvention*, Oxford: Routledge.

Nikitenko, A. (2001) *Up from Serfdom: My Childhood and Youth in Russia, 1804–1924*, New Haven: Yale University Press.

Obolensky, D. (1999) *Bread of Exile: A Russian Family*, London: Harvill Press.

Okenfuss, M. (1973) 'The Jesuit Origins of Petrine Education', in J. G. Garrard (ed.), *The Eighteenth Century in Russia*, Oxford: Clarendon Press, 106–30.

Okenfuss, M. (1980) *The Discovery of Childhood in Russia: The Evidence of the Slavic Primer*, Newtonville, MA: Oriental Research Partners.

Oushakine, S. (2004) 'The Flexible and the Pliant: Disturbed Organisms of Soviet Modernity', *Cultural Anthropology*, vol. 19, no. 3, 392–428.

Pankier Weld, S. (2018) 'Paradoxes of the Russian Empress Catherine the Great's Writings for Children', *International Research in Children's Literature*, vol. II, no. 2., 147–59

Partlett, W. (2004) 'Breaching Cultural Worlds with the Village School: Educational Visions, Local Initiative and Rural Experience at S.T. Shatskii's Kaluga School

System, 1919–1932', *The Slavonic and East European Review*, vol. 82, no. 4, 876.

Peacock, M. (2014) *Innocent Weapons: The Soviet and American Politics of Childhood in the Cold War*, Chapel Hill: University of North Carolina Press.

Petrushevskaya, L. I. (ed.) (1997) *Deti russkoi emigratsii: Kniga, kotoruyu mechtali no ne smogli izdat' izgnanniki*, Moscow: Terra.

Petrushevskaya, L. (2017) *The Girl from the Metropol Hotel: Growing Up in Communist Russia*, New York: Penguin.

Philipponnat O. and Lienhardt, P. (2011) *The Life of Irène Némirovsky*, London: Vintage.

Pickering Antonova, K. (2017) *An Ordinary Marriage: The World of a Gentry Family in Provincial Russia*, Oxford: Oxford University Press.

Pollock, L. (1990) *A Lasting Relationship: Parents and Children Over Three Centuries*, University Press of New England.

Raeff, M. (1962) 'Home, School, and Service in the Life of the 18th-Century Russian Nobleman', *The Slavonic and East European Review*, vol. 40, no. 95, 295–307.

Raeff, M. (1973) 'The Enlightenment in Russia', in J. G. Garrard (ed.), *The Eighteenth Century in Russia*, Oxford: Clarendon Press, 25–47.

Rajagopolan, S. (2019) 'Remix Ideas and the Mnemonic Imagination. Emotional Memories of Late Soviet Childhood', *International Journal of Cultural Studies*, vol. 22, no. 1, 9–36.

Randolph, J. (2007) *The House in the Garden: The Bakunin Family and the Romance of Russian Idealism*, Ithaca and London: Cornell University Press.

Ransel, D. (ed.) (1978) *The Family in Imperial Russia: New Lines of Historical Research*, Urbana: University of Illinois Press.

Ransel, D. (1980) 'Ivan Betskoi and the Institutionalization of the Enlightenment in Russia', *Canadian-American Slavic Studies*, vol. 14, no. 3, 327–38.

Ransel, D. (1988) *Mothers of Misery: Child Abandonment in Russia*, Princeton: Princeton University Press.

Ransel, D. (2000) *Village Mothers: Three Generations of Change in Russia and Tataria*, Bloomington: Indiana University Press.

Riasanovsky, N. (2005) *Russian Identities: A Historical Survey*, Oxford: Oxford University Press.

Riordan, J. (1987) 'The Role of Youth Organisations in Communist Upbringing in the Soviet School', in G. Avis (ed.), *The Making of the Soviet Citizen*, London: Croom Helm.

Rogers, R. (2005) 'Porous Wall and Prying Eyes: Control, Discipline, and Morality in Boarding Schools for Girls in Mid-Nineteenth Century France', in *Secret Gardens, Satanic Mills: Placing Girls in European History*, Bloomington: Indiana University Press, 113–30.

Rose, N. (1991) *Governing the Soul: The Shaping of the Private Self*, London: Routledge.

Rothenstein, J. and Budashevskaya, O. (2013) *Inside the Rainbow: Russian Children's Literature 1920–1935: Beautiful Books, Terrible Times*, London: Redstone Press.

Salnikova, A. (ed.) (2007) *Rossiiskoe detstva v XX veke: Istoriya, teoriya, i praktika issledovaniya*, Kazan: Kazan State University.

Saunders, D. (1992) *Russia in the Age of Reaction and Reform 1801–1881*,
    Harlow: Longman.
Shikheeva-Gaister, I. (2012) *Deti vragov naroda. Semeinaya khronika vremen
    kul'ta lichnosti 1925–1953*, Moscow: Vozvrashchenie.
Silova, I. and Palanjian, G. (2018) 'Soviet Empire, Childhood and Education',
    Revista Española de Educacíon Comparada, vol. 6, no. 31, 147–71.
Smirnova, T. (2009) 'Children's Welfare in Soviet Russia: Society and the State,
    1917–1930s', *The Soviet and Post-Soviet Review*, vol. 36, 169–81.
Smirnova, T. (2010) "Beloved Children of the Soviet Republic", *Russian Studies in
    History*, vol. 48, no. 4, 9–25.
Smirnova, T. M. (2012) 'Detskie doma i trudkolonii: zhizn' <<gosudarstvennyikh
    detei>> v sovetskoi rossii v 1920–1930 gg.' *Vestnik Rossiiskogo Universiteta
    druzhby narodov*, 16–37.
Stearns, P. (2011) *Childhood in World History*, Oxford: Routledge.
Timberlake, C. (1993) 'N. A. Korf (1834–83): Designer of the Russian Elementary
    School Classroom', in B. Eklof (ed.), *School and Society in Tsarist and Soviet
    Russia*, New York: St. Martin's Press, 12–35.
Tovrov, J. (1978) 'Mother-Child Relations among the Russian Nobility', in D. L.
    Ransel (ed.), *The Family in Imperial Russia: New Lines of Historical Research*,
    Urbana: University of Illinois Press, 15–43.
Tudge, J. (1991) 'Education of Young Children in the Soviet Union: Current
    Practice in Historical Perspective', *The Elementary School Journal*, vol. 92,
    no. 1, 122.
Veremenko, V. A. (2015) *Deti v dvoryanskikh sem'yakh Rossii (vtoraya polovina
    XIX- nachalo XXv.)*, St Petersburg: Leningradskii gosudarstvennyi universitet.
Vilensky, S. S., Kokurin, A. A., Atmashkina, A. G. and Novichenko I. Yu. (eds)
    (2002) *Deti Gulaga. 1918–1956. Dokumenty*, Moscow: Mezhdunarodnaya
    fond 'Demokratiya'
Wachtel, A. (1990) *The Battle for Childhood: Creation of a Russian Myth*,
    Stanford: Stanford University Press.
Wagner, W. (1995) 'Family Law, the Rule of Law, and Liberalism in Late Imperial
    Russia', *Jahr-bücher für Geschichte Osteuropas*, vol. XLIII, no. 4, 519–35.
Waldron, P. (1997) *The End of Imperial Russia, 1855–1917*, London: Palgrave.
Winkler, M. (2017) 'Children, Childhood and Stalinism', *Kritika: Explorations in
    Russian and Eurasian History*, vol. 18, no. 3, Summer, 628–37.
Zelizer, V. (1985) *Pricing the Priceless Child: The Changing Social Value of
    Children*, Princeton: Princeton University Press.
Zenzinov, V. (ed.) (1925) *Deti emigratsii. Sbornik statei*, Prague: Pedagogicheskoe
    buiro po delam srednei I nizhshei shkoly zagranitsei.
Zenzinov, V. (1931) *Deserted: The Story of the Children Abandoned in Soviet
    Russia*, London: H. Joseph.

Index

Note: Page numbers followed by "n" refer to notes.